For the Love of

Seafood

For the Love of Seafood

100 Flawless, Flavorful Recipes
That Anyone Can Cook

KARISTA BENNETT

Countryman Press

An Imprint of W. W. Norton & Company
Celebrating a Century of Independent Publishing

Printed in the United States of America

For information about permission to reproduce selections from this book, write to
Permissions, Countryman Press, 500 Fifth Avenue, New York, NY 10110

For information about special discounts for bulk purchases, please contact
W. W. Norton Special Sales at specialsales@wwnorton.com or 800-233-4830

Manufacturing by Versa Press
Book design by Allison Chi
Production manager: Devon Zahn

Countryman Press
www.countrymanpress.com

An imprint of W. W. Norton & Company, Inc.
500 Fifth Avenue, New York, NY 10110

www.wwnorton.com

978-1-68268-731-4

10 9 8 7 6 5 4 3 2 1

for my sister, Kristin, and
my brother, Cameron

Contents

11 Introduction
13 How to Use This Book
14 Seafood 101

CHAPTER 1.

40 Easy Like a Weeknight

42 Wild Albacore Tuna Salsa
44 Smoked Salmon Lox with Crème Fraîche on Mini Corncakes
47 Lemon Herb Ricotta Toasts with Anchovies
48 Open-Face Bay Shrimp Salad Melts on Thick Toast
51 Bay Shrimp and Pepper Jack–Stuffed Roasted Mini Peppers
52 Vintage Macaroni and Shrimp Salad
55 Wild Albacore Tuna Cakes with Chipotle Lime Dipping Sauce
57 Salmon en Papillote with Easy Lemon Aioli (Salmon Baked in Parchment)
61 Weeknight Lemon-Baked Cod with Pesto Yogurt Dressing
63 Roasted Five-Spice White Fish Tacos with Apple Cabbage Slaw
66 Baked Spicy Dijon and Parmesan-Crusted Salmon
68 Spicy Orange Marmalade–Roasted Salmon
71 Citrus-Roasted Cod with Honey-Tarragon Brown Butter
73 Roasted Teriyaki Sole with Shelled Edamame and Cilantro-Lime Rice
76 Mediterranean Roasted Fish Fillets with Parmesan Polenta
79 Roasted Furikake Salmon
83 Za'atar-Spiced Fish with Orange Cumin Vinaigrette and Fresh Greens
85 Chile-Spiced Rockfish with Summer Peach and Jalapeño Quinoa Salad
88 Hoisin Five-Spice Sauce Baked Fish with Ramen Noodles and Broccolini
90 Basic Pan-Cooked Salmon with Lemon Dill Crème Fraîche and Persian Cucumber
93 Simple Fish Meunière
95 Pan-Cooked White Fish with Papaya Red Pepper Salsa
99 Pan-Seared White Fish with Sauce Verte
101 Grilled Salmon Caesar Salad with Parmesan Garlic Bread Crumbs
104 Pan-Cooked Fish with Summer Blackberry Orange Relish
106 Easy Whipped Pimiento Sauce with Pan-Cooked Fish
109 Easy Curry Poached Fish with Mango Ginger Pearled Couscous
111 Simple Brazilian Fish Stew (Moqueca)
115 Basque-Style Tuna and Potato Stew (Marmitako)
117 Basic Pan-Cooked Sea Scallops with Miso Ginger Butter
120 Salmon Fried Rice
122 Pan-Cooked Shrimp with Lemon, Garlic, and Fresh Herbs
124 Classic White Wine–Steamed Clams with Garlic and Herbs

CHAPTER 2.

126 Show Off Those Skills

128 Classic Crab Cakes with Tangy Dipping Sauce
130 Imperial-Style Crab Dip
132 Crab Louis–Style Salad
135 Crab and Boursin Cheese Quiche
137 New England–Style Clam Chowder
140 Spanish-Style Steamed Clams
143 Sake-Steamed Mussels with Lemongrass and Lime
145 Southern-Style Shrimp and Cheesy Grits
148 English Prawn Cocktail
150 Shrimp Enchilada Soup with Lime Crema
153 Grilled Shrimp Tacos
156 Shrimp, Black Bean, and Corn Chilaquiles
158 My Favorite Shellfish Boil
161 Spicy Salmon Poke Bowl
164 Salmon Lox and Three-Cheese Puff Pastry Pinwheels
166 Pasta with Brown Butter, Peas, Mint, and Salmon
169 Roasted Salmon with Savory Strawberry Sauce
172 Grilled Salmon with Pistachio Lemon Pesto
175 Grilled Fish Steaks with Blueberry Ginger Butter
178 Seared Ahi Tuna Wonton Tacos with Mango Pico de Gallo
181 Grilled Swordfish with Elote-Style Corn and Roasted Poblanos
184 Spaghetti with Anchovies and Olives
187 Basic White Fish Ceviche
188 Easy Acqua Pazza (Fish in Crazy Water)
191 Spiced Butter Fish
193 Fish Taco Buddha Bowls with Creamy Blender Chimichurri
196 Crispy White Fish Burgers with Smoked Provolone and Special Sauce
199 Salt and Vinegar Potato Chip–Crusted Fish Fingers with Dipping Sauces
202 Panko Panfried Fish with Japanese-Style Tartar Sauce and Kimchi Slaw
205 Simple Oven-Roasted Whole Fish
208 Moroccan-Style Roasted Fish
210 Fish Amandine
213 Orange, Fennel, and Avocado Salsa with Pan-Cooked Fish
216 Pan-Cooked Fish with Herbed Gremolata and White Beans
219 Butter-Poached Halibut with Roasted Cherry Tomatoes, Leeks, and Potatoes

CHAPTER 3.

222 A Little Fancy

224 Homemade Seafood Stock
225 Coconut Shrimp with Sweet and Spicy Apricot Glaze
229 Butter Lettuce with Grilled Shrimp, Avocado, Bacon, and Creamy Herb Dressing
231 Shrimp Panzanella Salad with Basil Vinaigrette
235 Shrimp Po'boy with Spicy Cajun Dressing
237 Shrimp and Sausage Jambalaya
240 Shrimp Étouffée

243 Panko-Fried Oysters with Remoulade Sauce
247 Baked Oysters Mornay
249 Date Night Linguine with Pink Clam Sauce
253 Pan-Seared Scallops with Tomato Ginger Jam
255 Crab and Spinach–Stuffed Shells with White Cheddar Béchamel
258 Pappardelle Alfredo with Crab
260 Broiled Lobster Tails with Cilantro-Lime Butter
262 Classic Lobster Rolls
265 Summer Seafood Board with Dipping Sauces
268 Seafood Risotto
271 Flatbread with Anchovies, Smoked Mozzarella, Olives, and Arugula
275 Avocado, Tomato, and Sardines Toast with Pickled Onions and Herb Dressing
276 Asian Salmon Sliders with Quick-Pickled Cucumbers and Cilantro-Lime Aioli
279 Salmon, Leek, and Potato Potpie
282 Spicy Ahi Tuna Sushi Stacks
285 Bacon-Wrapped Stuffed Trout with Lemon White Wine Pan Sauce
287 West African–Inspired Fish Stew
291 Bourride (French-Style Fish Stew with Aioli)
293 Irish-Style Fish Chowder
296 Salsa Verde Fish Enchiladas
299 Cornmeal-Crusted Fish Tacos with Mandarin-Radish Slaw
303 Curried Fish Cakes with Lime and Mint Yogurt Sauce
305 Sablefish with Creamy Piquillo Pepper Sauce and Lemon Cream
309 Pan-Cooked Fish with Honey-Poached Kumquats, Fennel, and Olives
311 Halibut and Leek au Gratin

315 Resources
317 Acknowledgments
318 Index

Introduction

I HAVE A CONFESSION to make: I didn't always like seafood. As a child, my preferred seafood of choice was a popular chain restaurant "fish and chips" with a healthy dose of malt vinegar and tartar sauce. As a teenager, my friends and I used our community "Friday Night Catfish Fry" as a convenient hangout where inevitably I filled my plate with mostly hush puppies and coleslaw. And although I am certain there were assorted seafood offerings at our community potlucks and socials, my unadventurous palate always led me straight to the potato salad.

It wasn't that I found seafood completely objectionable, but more that the flavor and texture didn't excite my taste buds. This could be due to all those bland and mushy fish sticks I ate as a child or one too many stinky tuna salad sandwiches from the school cafeteria.

When I reached adulthood, seafood was still not my first choice for dinner. It wasn't until my seafood-loving husband asked me to try the most amazing pan-cooked fillet of red snapper, which forever altered my idea of seafood.

It was my husband's birthday and, because fish is his entrée of choice, he opted for a small seafood bistro in town. My face told him I was delighted, but my food-loving heart died a little inside. However, as we walked into the restaurant, I saw that the tables were covered in soft, white tablecloths and candlelight flooded the cozy dining room. It was warm and inviting, and as we were seated, I felt more reassured that I just might enjoy my dinner that evening.

When our entrées arrived, I could see that the fish had been carefully, and what felt almost reverently, prepared. It was tender on the inside yet perfectly crisp in the faintest golden-brown crust. It was topped with succulent jumbo lump crabmeat and drizzled with a luscious lemon beurre blanc sauce. From the first bite, I was utterly smitten.

My curiosity flourished from that point, and several years later, I gratefully found myself in a seafood class at culinary school. This was the course that changed the way I approach seafood. During that class I realized seafood is like a blank canvas. It can be paired with a vast array of ingredients and incorporated into recipes as simple or as complex as I choose. My love of seafood may have begun with that gorgeous pan-cooked snapper, but understanding how to use the salty, sometimes briny, and buttery essence of seafood with complementary ingredients delighted my flavor-loving palate.

Over the last 20 years, I've had the opportunity to practice, develop, and prepare a multitude of seafood recipes for clients of my private chef business, readers, my home cook students, and my family and friends. I've been lucky enough to have lived in a handful of culturally and geographically diverse locations within the United States, including the Gulf Coast, the East Coast, and the Pacific Coast, which is now home. Each location is unique in cuisine and local ingredients, and all contributed to my culinary journey and love of flavor.

In *For the Love of Seafood*, you will find 100 enchanting seafood recipes that anyone can cook. I know that sounds like a tall order; however, the book is broken down into three chapters, starting with simple and moving into modestly easy and eventually kind of fancy dishes. There's really something here for everyone. In each chapter, I give detailed instructions on cooking methods that are best for a particular seafood, along with seasonal ingredient pairings, recommendations, and substitutions so that every seafood recipe is achievable and satisfying.

Although seafood is a staple in my own home kitchen, my love and respect for the sea and local fisheries and fishing families continues to be at the center of my seafood purchases. In the chapters to follow, I share my experience, knowledge, and resources to inform, inspire, and build confidence in purchasing and preparing seafood.

From the very beginning, I wanted to make this book a culinary adventure in flavor-filled seafood. Recipes that anyone can cook but can also wow the taste buds as intensely as mine were when I tasted that brilliant red snapper so many years ago.

My hope is that this is the beginning of your love affair with our precious fruits from the sea.

With love and peace from my table to yours,

Karista

How to Use This Book

I BEGIN THIS BOOK with a section called "Seafood 101." This section addresses some of those nagging seafood questions, such as "What do I look for when buying seafood?" and "How do I know it was sustainably sourced?" as well as "What kind of fish are considered mild, flaky white fish?" and "What ingredients pair best with seafood?"

"Seafood 101" is a little bit like cooking class and a basic seafood primer, all in one. It is meant to be your go-to guide whenever you have questions about a cooking method, ingredient pairing, flavor and texture profiles of fish, fish purchases, equipment, and more.

Then, the three recipe chapters are arranged according to skill level, "Easy Like a Weeknight" is the first, filled with recipes perfect for beginner home cooks, cooks new to seafood or cooks looking for a quick seafood meal.

This first chapter is arranged by cooking technique and begins with the simplest of seafood recipes. And although the recipes are easy, they do not fall short in flavor. As you move through this chapter, the recipes build in cooking techniques from baking, then steaming, to roasting. Toward the middle of the chapter, we tackle pan cooking and then poaching. At the end of this chapter, we cover the basics of cooking shellfish.

The second recipe chapter, "Show Off Those Skills," adds a few more cooking techniques, new ingredient pairings, and a little more prep time, and introduces new types of seafood to use. This chapter is arranged according to type of seafood. It begins with shellfish, then moves into salmon, ahi tuna, swordfish, and anchovies. The last half of this chapter's recipes are prepared with various types of white fish.

The third recipe chapter is titled "A Little Fancy." This chapter is also organized according to type of seafood, beginning with shellfish. From there, recipes move to anchovies, salmon, trout, then mixed seafood, and end with white fish. This last chapter is filled with my version of some traditional favorites—recipes that require more time in the kitchen, contain a wider variety of ingredients, and are a bit more special. These are the dishes I prepare for family dinners, date nights, holidays, and celebrations.

I end this book with a list of resources that will help you source ingredients, online sustainable seafood resources, community-supported fisheries, and additional sources of seafood information.

And now, let's get cooking!

Seafood 101

SEAFOOD *SHOULD* BE one of the easiest proteins to prepare, and it has plenty of upsides. It cooks quickly, easily absorbs seasoning, pairs well with a broad variety of ingredients, can be economical, and is also a healthy ingredient option. Seafood is often less expensive than meat and it's high in protein and essential nutrients, such as heart-healthy omega-3 fatty acids and vitamin D.

However, sometimes buying and preparing seafood can feel like one big mystery. Does the seafood need to be purchased fresh or frozen? How do I know my seafood is sustainable and what does that even mean? What kind of seafood is best on the grill or roasted in the oven? What kind of pan is best for pan cooking seafood?

In this section, I address many of these questions surrounding seafood and the questions I hear most often from home cooks. The advice and recommendations I give here have culminated from 20 years of culinary experience and working with some of the most talented chefs and culinarians in the business. Although there are specific guidelines for food safety that should always be followed, methods of preparation, ingredient pairings, and the like have always varied from chef to chef and home cook to home cook.

I encourage you to make the recipes that appeal to your tastes, and then to use them as a guideline for your own version. Enjoy the process, experiment, play with your food, and most of all, savor the flavor.

Purchasing Seafood

Know Your Options

COMMUNITY-SUPPORTED FISHERIES (CSF) are much like community-supported agriculture (CSA), where seafood is sold directly to the consumer from the fishery. We call this "boat to table" seafood and it's one of my favorite options for purchasing seafood.

ONLINE FISH MARKETS have popped up over the last several years and they are also an excellent choice for purchasing seafood. With such markets as Salmon Sisters, Sitka Salmon Shares, Vital Choice, Sea to Table, Taylor Shellfish Farms, and so on, the list seems endless these days, with so many quality businesses to choose from. Each online fish market sources a variety of seafood along with a variety of purchasing options. The hard part is deciding which one is right for you!

FARMERS' MARKETS are now more than just produce, food artisans, and art. I regularly find meat, egg, and poultry stands at my local market, and over the past few years, we've had several fresh-off-the-boat seafood stands. If you live near coastal regions or large freshwater regions, be sure to check your local farmers' markets for a seafood stand. This is a great way to support local seafood in your region.

LOCAL SEAFOOD MARKETS are another excellent choice for purchasing seafood. These specialized markets are a great place to find not only the most common seafood, but also a selection of special seafood, such as an array of local or regional oysters, crawfish, smoked fish, and hard-to-find pantry staples for seafood preparation.

LOCAL CO-OP MARKETS typically source produce, meat, poultry, and fish locally and regionally. The fish will most likely be quality fresh frozen, which is great! I've given thawing instructions later in this section.

LOCAL GROCERY STORES always have a selection of seafood that range from small to extensive. This is another good option, especially if you're in a location that is farther

from a coast. However, with more fisheries vacuum sealing and blast freezing seafood, quality seafood is becoming more readily available.

Regardless of where you purchase your seafood, be sure to find out which is a "best choice" or "good alternative" by accessing seafood watch websites. I've listed several in the Resources (page 315).

Sustainability

Today's consumers have a lot of options for purchasing seafood. But two questions that seem to loom over consumers are *How do I know which seafood is sustainable?* and *What does "sustainable" really mean?* The short answer is that sustainable seafood is caught or farmed in a way that ensures long-term health of a species, the oceans, and fishing-dependent communities.

This is an important subject, and one that has been and continues to be discussed and debated at length. We touch on the subject here, but for more detailed information on sustainable seafood, I've listed books and websites related to this subject in the Resources (page 315).

The easiest way to find out if you are purchasing sustainable seafood is to access the information on one of several seafood websites, such as Monterey Bay Aquarium's Seafood Watch. I've also listed several additional websites that I use in the Resources (page 315).

These online seafood guides also address sustainability regarding aquaculture. Aquaculture is the process of raising fish in freshwater or saltwater–controlled environments. It has gained popularity with many good results, and some not so good results.

I haven't always been a fan of farmed fish; however, after doing my own research and reading several books on the subject written by well-known authors, I realize there is a place for aquaculture in our society if it's ethically and responsibly managed.

Fresh or Frozen? Which Is Best?

There was a time when, if asked this question, I would have told you fresh is best. And although a fresh piece of fish cooked hours after being plucked from the sea is divine, it isn't always an option. According to Mike Baran, CSF manager with Port Orford Sustainable Seafood, "It's important to understand how fish get from the ocean to the consumer." Today, many fishing boats/fisheries, such as Port Orford Sustainable Seafood, process, vacuum seal, and blast freeze seafood within hours of being caught. This preserves flavor, texture, and even nutrients in the seafood.

Whether your seafood is purchased from a community-supported fishery, an online seafood market, local seafood market, or at the docks on the coast, know that if the seafood has been properly frozen and sealed, it will taste just as delicious as if it were fresh.

If purchasing frozen fish from a big box store or market, be sure to look for products labeled "FAS" or "frozen at sea," which indicates the fish will have been caught, processed, and frozen on the same boat. Another label to look for is "IQF" or "individually quick frozen." This method means the fish is flash frozen within hours of being caught. This is also a good alternative but be sure to inspect the product for freezer burn or ice crystals prior to purchasing.

If you find fish at your local grocery store with the label "previously frozen," the fish could have been frozen at sea and then thawed prior to arriving at the market. Be sure to ask your fishmonger how long the fish has been thawed and whether it was thawed at the market. You want to consume thawed fish as soon as possible, for the best taste and texture.

Seafood isn't terribly forgiving, so if it's not truly fresh or properly thawed, it makes for a disappointing seafood meal. Taking the time to learn how the seafood was frozen or thawed will make all the difference with recipe success.

Frequently Asked Questions

Q ***How should my seafood look and smell?***

A As with all seafood, it should smell like the sea, briny, salty, fresh, and mild. Some fish have a stronger smell than others but should never be stinky.

- ✦ **WHOLE FISH** should have clear eyes that are bright and bulging, except for walleye, which have naturally cloudy eyes. The skin should be glossy and feel firm, as if the fish just came out of the water.
- ✦ **FISH FILLETS/CUTLETS/STEAKS** should look moist, glossy, and firm with no discoloration. They should not be sitting in any liquid or have dry edges.
- ✦ **SHELLFISH** should smell like the sea—briny and salty—and not be sitting in liquid. Clams and mussels should be closed with no broken shells. Unless the shrimp are fresh off the boat, I usually purchase my shrimp frozen. I provide thawing instructions later in this section.

Q ***What does it mean when a recipe refers to "mild-flavored white fish"?***

A "White fish" covers many species of fish. However, most white fish readily available to consumers are mild to lightly sweet in flavor and therefore work with a large variety of ingredients. There will be subtle flavor and texture differences among white fish, but for the most part, they can be used for many of the same recipes.

White fish can span in texture from delicate and flaky, such as Dover sole, or medium firm and slightly flaky, such as cod. So, before preparing your recipe, check to see what the recommended cooking method is. This might determine which mild-flavored white fish you choose to use. For instance, because Dover sole is such a delicate and flaky, mild-flavored white fish, I typically pan cook it, unless it's stuffed and then it bakes well in the oven. However, cod, also a mild-flavored white fish, can hold up to baking, roasting, poaching, and pan cooking due to its medium-firm, flaky texture.

Most of the recipes in this book will have a fish recommendation and substitutions. As you practice cooking fish, you'll eventually learn the nuances in texture for each fish and how to use them in recipes.

Q ***What are fish steaks?***

A Most fish we see in markets are fish fillets. They are cut from the head to the tail in one long piece. However, fish steaks are cut horizontally from the whole fish and typically contain bones. Some fish steaks have a bit of a horseshoe or U shape; and

others, such as swordfish, look meaty like a steak. Fish steaks make a great option for grilling.

Q ***What is cheek meat?***

A Some call this the oyster of the fish. The cheek meat is found just below the eye and is tender and luscious. Most often I find halibut cheeks; however, I've also gotten lingcod cheeks in my CSF box, and they are equally delicious. If you find them, buy a few and pan cook them in butter on the stovetop.

Q ***Skin on or skin off?***

A It's all up to you, unless the recipe calls for skin on or skin off. Personally, I like to pan cook or grill salmon with the skin on. But I don't care for halibut with the skin on. It's a personal preference and most often doesn't interfere in the cooking process.

Q ***What is seasoning to taste?***

A This term is used in every recipe. It really does mean season the recipe to your taste. If you taste a stew, soup, or sauce and it doesn't taste seasoned enough, or maybe it's bland, add a little more salt. Taste it again, and if it still doesn't taste right, salt it a little bit more. As well, sometimes as stews, soups, and sauces rest, the flavor increases.

Some chefs recommend salting or "seasoning" as you go. And although there are some recipes where I recommend this, in many I do not. The reason is that if I'm using a broth or stock or anchovies or some other ingredient that can be salty in flavor, I hold off on seasoning until the end. And once you've oversalted, there is no going back. I know this from experience.

Another tip, if you're making a stew or soup, or a sauce, such as a tomato sauce or cream sauce: After you've seasoned several times, if it still doesn't wow your taste buds, stir in 1 teaspoon of white wine vinegar. Then, taste again. More than likely, this will do the trick. The vinegar brightens and balances and brings all those delicious flavors together.

Q ***What kind of salt should I use?***

A This is a personal preference; however, I use kosher salt most often while cooking and a coarse or blended sea salt as a finishing salt.

Kosher salt has flat, coarse grains that are easy to pinch with fingers and allow more control for seasoning while cooking. It has a clean taste that enhances the flavor of food, contains no iodine or preservatives, and is minimally processed. I find that I use less salt when I use kosher salt.

There are a lot of options for salt, so I've listed several salt and spice companies that I use in the Resources (page 315).

Q ***What is a fishmonger?***

A According to *Collins Dictionary*, a fishmonger is a shopkeeper who sells fish and the fishmonger's is a shop where fish is sold. Most fishmongers are highly knowledgeable about fish and always willing to source what you need. When purchasing fish, don't forget to ask them to remove the skin from the fish. It's so much easier having the fishmonger do this rather than trying to do it when you get home.

Q ***What is the difference between shrimp and prawns?***

A At a glance, these two species of crustaceans look and taste quite similar and can be found in both saltwater and freshwater. However, there are a few differences between them.

Prawns are the decapod suborder of Dendrobranchiata and have a few physiological differences from shrimp, including being larger in size. Shrimp are the decapod suborder Pleocyemata and tend to be smaller in size.

As far as taste, they are similar, but shrimp and prawn flavor profiles can vary due to diet, habitat, and region. According to the website Chefs Resources, most chefs agree that "like lobster, cold water shrimp and prawns tend to be sweeter, more tender and succulent. And as a general rule, wild shrimp/prawns tend to have a richer flavor than farmed shrimp/prawns when compared to the same species."

I use both sustainably caught wild and sustainably farmed shrimp depending on what I'm cooking and what is available at my local market or in season. I prefer a mild-flavored shrimp, but I encourage you to cook with both to find out which you like best.

For more information on which shrimp are a "best or good choice," refer to the seafood watch websites listed in the Resources (page 315).

Q ***What is shrimp sizing?***

A Shrimp sizes can be confusing, especially when they are categorized by such labels as "large," "extra-large," or "jumbo." Basically, shrimp are sold by count per pound.

For instance, U16/20 (U = under) means there are under 16 to 20 shrimp in a pound. U21/25 means there are under 21 to 25 shrimp in a pound. The larger the shrimp, the fewer shrimp in a pound.

I typically use 16/20- or 13/15-count shrimp for grilling and 16/20- or 21/30-count shrimp for such recipes as soups, stews, tacos, or jambalaya.

Q ***What are bay shrimp?***

A Bay shrimp are also called salad shrimp, pink shrimp, or Oregon shrimp. These small shrimp are found in coastal areas around North America and are typically sold cooked.

They are easily found in most markets, and when fresh, taste clean, slightly sweet, and a tiny bit salty. Many markets stock them flash frozen and then thaw and package them by weight. This is perfectly fine; however, be sure to give the package a sniff. If they smell fishy, they've probably been sitting in the cooler for too long. Bay shrimp shouldn't smell like anything other than the ocean.

Q ***What type of wine should I pair with seafood?***

A I live in a region with over 900 wineries and 1,200 vineyards so, as you can imagine, we take our wine seriously here. That said, I believe wine pairing is a personal preference. There are no hard-and-fast rules about wine pairing, other than that seafood pairs best with white wine. I have several favorite kinds of wine that I use in, and pair with, my seafood recipes. Feel free to use my guidelines or select the wine that makes your taste buds happiest.

- Most seafood pairs best with a dry or semidry white wine, rosé, and sparkling wine.
- Salmon, steelhead trout, and tomato-based seafood recipes pair nicely with a light-bodied pinot noir.
- Spicy recipes, such as fish curry, pair well with a sweeter white wine; for instance, a medium-dry Riesling or fruit-forward Chardonnay.
- The wine you choose also depends on the ingredients in the recipe. If the fish is the main ingredient, pair the wine according to the seafood.
- Most flaky, mild white fish pair well with sauvignon blanc, pinot grigio, pinot gris, dry pinot blanc, dry Riesling, dry chardonnay, and other similar dry-profile wine.
- Medium- or heavier-textured fish pair well with such wine as an oaked chardonnay or medium-bodied Viognier.
- If the seafood is taking a backseat to other ingredients, such as a tomato sauce or curry, then I pair according to both the seafood and the ingredients. These more robust recipes pair well with a light-bodied pinot noir, semidry Riesling, off-dry rosé, Cava, or Prosecco.
- I like to pair shellfish recipes with a medium-bodied chardonnay or semidry Riesling; and for panfried or fried fish, I adore a brut Cava or Prosecco.
- When cooking a seafood recipe with wine, I always use a light-bodied, dry white wine such as a French, California, or Pacific Northwest sauvignon blanc, dry unoaked chardonnay, pinot grigio, or dry Riesling.

Whatever wine you choose, make it something you love. Wine is a delicious complement to food and can enhance the flavor as well as the moment.

Seafood Chart

Although many sustainable seafood options are available to consumers, in the following chart, I've chosen to highlight seafood that is most commonly purchased by home cooks.

I've included the basic taste and texture, popular methods of cooking, and popular ingredient pairings of each seafood. Now, this doesn't mean you have to strictly follow this guide. This is just to give you, the home cook, an idea of what ingredients are most often paired with a particular seafood and how it's typically cooked.

Feel free to use your palate as a guide and pair whatever ingredients you love with your seafood. The lovely quality about seafood is that it's like a blank canvas, and it is up to you, the cook, to make it delicious.

FINFISH	TASTE/TEXTURE	POPULAR METHODS OF COOKING	POPULAR INGREDIENT/FLAVOR PAIRINGS
Acadian redfish	Mild flavor/medium flaky texture	Bake, deep-fry, grill, pan cook, poach, steam, roast	Aromatics, Cajun, citrus, Creole, creamy sauces, herbs, Mediterranean, sauces, spices
Anchovies	Distinct flavor/soft oily texture	Use in or as flavoring for dressings, sauces, soups, stews, crostini	Citrus, dairy, Mediterranean, pasta, pizza, tomato sauces
Arctic char	Pink flesh, sweet but rich flavor/semi-firm texture	Bake, grill, pan cook, poach, roast	Aromatics, Asian, citrus, herbs, mushrooms, spices, tomatoes
Atlantic cod	Delicate, slightly sweet white fish/firm, flaky texture	Bake, deep-fry, poach, salted	Aromatics, citrus, creamy sauces, herbs, Mexican, spices, tomatoes
Atlantic Spanish mackerel	Full flavor, sweet and rich/medium-firm texture	Bake, broil, grill, pan cook, roast, steam	Acidic sauces, aromatics, citrus, Mediterranean, sweet peppers, tomatoes
Barramundi, aka giant perch	Sweet, mild, and buttery white fish/firm, moist texture	Bake, broil, pan cook, roast	Aromatics, Asian, citrus, herbs, Mexican
Black sea bass	Mild white fish, delicate flavor/lean but tender texture	Bake, broil, pan cook, steam, roast	Aromatics, Asian, citrus, herbs, light sauces, Mediterranean, spices
Bluefish	Full flavored, some call it robust/buttery white flaky texture	Bake, broil, grill, pan cook, roast	Aromatics, citrus, herbs, spices, tomatoes, tropical fruit and flavors
Branzino, aka European sea bass	Mild, sweet flavor white fish/flaky, delicate texture	Bake, pan cook, pan sear, steam, roast	Aromatics, citrus, herbs, Mediterranean, sauces, spices
Catfish	Mild to slightly flavorful white fish/medium-firm texture	Deep-fry, pan cook	Bread crumb or cornmeal-coated, citrus, herbs, pickles, sauces, spices

FINFISH	TASTE/TEXTURE	POPULAR METHODS OF COOKING	POPULAR INGREDIENT/FLAVOR PAIRINGS
Cobia	White fish, mild in flavor/firm and flaky in texture	Grill, fry, pan cook, steam	Aromatics, Cajun, Caribbean, citrus, herbs, Mediterranean, Mexican, salsas, sauces, tropical fruit
Flounder	Mild white fish/soft, moist texture	Bake, pan cook, panfry, poach, steam, roast	Aromatics, Asian, berries, citrus, creamy sauces, herbs, Mediterranean, peaches, salsas, spices, tropical fruit
Grouper	Distinctive flavor, mild white fish/lean firm texture	Fry, pan cook, poach, steam	African, Aromatics, citrus, creamy sauces, herbs, Mediterranean, soups, stews, tomatoes
Haddock	Mild white fish/firm flaky texture	Bake, deep-fry, grill, pan cook, steam	Aromatics, chowders, citrus, creamy sauces, herbs, mushrooms, soups, stews, tomatoes
Hake	Mild white fish/flaky, delicate texture	Bake, pan cook, panfry, poach, steam, roast	African, Aromatics, Asian, citrus, herbs, Mediterranean, sauces, soups, stews
Halibut	Mild white fish/firm but tender texture	Grill, pan cook, panfry, poach, steam, roast	Apricots, aromatics, Asian, berries, citrus, curries, herbs, Mediterranean, Mexican, peaches, sauces, soups, spices, tropical fruits
Lingcod	Mild white fish with distinct flavor/ medium firm texture	Broil, deep-fry, pan cook, steam, roast	Aromatics, Asian, berries, citrus, creamy sauces, curries, herbs, Mediterranean, Mexican, salsas, spices, tropical fruit

FINFISH	TASTE/TEXTURE	POPULAR METHODS OF COOKING	POPULAR INGREDIENT/FLAVOR PAIRINGS
Mahi-mahi, aka dorado	Mild flavor/firm texture	Grill, pan cook, panfry, poach, roast	Aromatics, Asian, barbecue, Caribbean, citrus, coconut, Hawaiian, herbs, Mexican, spices, tropical fruit
Monkfish	Mild flavor/firm, moist texture	Bake, grill, pan cook, poach, steam, roast	Aromatics, citrus, creamy sauces, herbs, Mediterranean, spices
Opah	Pinkish flesh, sweet and distinctive flavor/firm, fatty texture	Grill, pan cook, panfry	Aromatics, Asian, citrus, Hawaiian, herbs, spices, tropical fruit
Perch	Delicate flavor white fish/moderately firm	Bake, pan cook, panfry, steam, roast	Aromatics, Cajun, Caribbean, citrus, Creole, herbs, sauces, spices
Petrale sole	Mild white fish/flaky texture	Pan cook, panfry, steam, roast	Aromatics, citrus, creamy sauces, herbs, Mediterranean, mushrooms, soups, stews
Pollack	Mild white fish/sturdy flaky texture	Deep-fry, pan cook, panfry, poach, roast	Aromatics, citrus, cornmeal-crusted, creamy sauces, herbs, Mediterranean, peppers, spices
Pompano	Mild sweet flavor/firm but flaky	Bake, grill, pan cook, roast	African, aromatics, Asian, Caribbean, citrus, herbs, Latin American, sauces, spices
Red drum, aka Drum	Mild sweet flavor/firm with large flaky texture	Bake, grill, pan cook, panfry, steam, roast	Aromatics, Asian, Cajun, Caribbean, citrus, Creole, herbs, sauces, spices
Rockfish	Mild white fish with delicate, sweet flavor/lean, medium-firm texture	Deep fry, grill, pan cook, panfry, poach, stream, roast	African, aromatics, Asian, berries, citrus, creamy sauces, curries, herbs, Mediterranean, Mexican, peppers, sauces, spices

FINFISH	TASTE/TEXTURE	POPULAR METHODS OF COOKING	POPULAR INGREDIENT/FLAVOR PAIRINGS
Sablefish, aka black cod or butterfish	Rich, slightly sweet in flavor/flaky white fish	Grill, pan cook, panfry, poach, steam roast	Aromatics, Asian, citrus, creamy sauces, herbs, Mediterranean, spices
Salmon	Light orange or pink flesh, distinctive, rich flavor/flaky texture with higher fat content	Grill, bake, pan cook, poach, steam, roast	Aromatics, Asian, berries, citrus, creamy sauces, cucumber, herbs, Latin American, Mediterranean, Mexican, salsas, spices, tropical fruit
Sardines, canned	Distinctive in flavor/ meaty or firm in texture	Canned, grill, fry	Crostini, pasta, pizza, salads, straight out of the can
Snapper	Mild white fish/firm, moist, slightly oily texture	Bake, grill, pan cook, panfry, poach, steam, roast	African, aromatics, Asian, citrus, creamy sauces, cucumber, herbs, Latin American, Mediterranean, Mexican, salsas, spices
Sole, e.g. Dover, English	Delicate, mild sweet taste/firm, flaky white fish	Bake, pan cook, poach, steam	Aromatics, citrus, creamy sauces, herbs, Mediterranean, mushrooms, spices
Squid/calamari	Mild sweet taste/firm and meaty texture	Grill, panfry, poach, steam	Aromatics, Asian, chiles, citrus, herbs, Mediterranean, Mexican, peppers, spices
Striped bass	Mild, slightly sweet in flavor/large flaky texture	Bake, grill, fry, pan cook, roast	Aromatics, citrus, herbs, sauces, spices
Swordfish	Mild flavor/firm meaty texture	Grill, pan cook	Aromatics, Asian, Caribbean, citrus, coconut, herbs, Latin American, Mexican, sauces, spices, tropical fruit
Tilapia	Mild flavor/tender but firm flaky white fish	Bake, deep-fry, pan cook, steam, roast	African, aromatics, Asian, citrus, cornmeal-crusted, curries, herbs, spices

FINFISH	TASTE/TEXTURE	POPULAR METHODS OF COOKING	POPULAR INGREDIENT/FLAVOR PAIRINGS
Tilefish	Mild flavor/firm, flaky texture	Grill, fry, pan cook, poach, roast	Aromatics, Caribbean, citrus, Latin American, Mexican, sauces, spices, tropical fruit
Trout	Mild in flavor/delicate texture	Grill, pan cook, panfry, steam, roast	Aromatics, brown butter, citrus, creamy sauces, herbs, spices
Tuna (ahi)	Mild flavor/tender oily texture	Grill, pan sear, sushi	Aromatics, Asian, citrus, coconut, herbs, Mexican, sauces, sesame, spices, tropical fruit
Tuna (fresh albacore)	Mild to medium flavor/firm with large flakes	Grill, pan cook, poach	Aromatics, Asian, berries, citrus, curries, herbs, Mexican, sauces, soups, stews, tropical fruit
Wahoo, aka ono	Mild flavor/firm, lean texture	Grill, pan cook	Aromatics, Asian, citrus, Hawaiian, herbs, sauces, spices, tropical fruit

SHELLFISH	TASTE/TEXTURE	COMMON METHODS OF COOKING	COMMON INGREDIENT/FLAVOR PAIRINGS
Clams	Distinctive, slightly salty/firm in texture	Steam / meat used in various recipes	Aromatics, Asian, citrus, chowders, herbs, Mediterranean, soups, stews, spices
Crab	Slightly sweet, sometimes rich flavor/soft, meaty texture	Boil, grill / use meat in various recipes	Aromatics, butter, citrus, herbs, spices
Crawfish, aka crayfish	Distinctive flavor, slightly sweet/soft, meaty texture	Boil / meat used in soups, stews, and other recipes	Aromatics, Cajun, citrus, Creole, herbs, spices
Lobster	Sweet rich flavor/soft meaty texture	Boil, broil, grill, poach / meat used in recipes	Aromatics, butter, citrus, creamy sauces, herbs, spices

SHELLFISH	TASTE/TEXTURE	COMMON METHODS OF COOKING	COMMON INGREDIENT/FLAVOR PAIRINGS
Mussels	Distinct mild flavor with faint sweetness/ soft, meaty texture	Steam / meat can be used in recipes	Aromatics, Asian, citrus, Mediterranean, herbs, spices
Oysters	Sweet, salty, briny, or buttery in flavor/ plump, creamy and springy	Broil, grill, raw / or use meat in recipes	Acidic flavors, aromatics, citrus, creamy sauces, cucumber, spinach
Shrimp/prawns	Slightly sweet, briny, mild/meaty, snappy texture	Grill, pan cook, poach, steam	Aromatics, citrus, herbs, sauces, spices; is suited to most types of ethnic cuisine

Basic Prep Tips for Recipe Success

How to Thaw Fish

- Overnight thawing: Place the sealed frozen fish on a plate in the refrigerator for 8 to 24 hours, until thawed. Once thawed, remove from the sealed packaging, dry with a paper towel, and cook.
- For a quick thaw, place the sealed fish in a bowl or baking dish filled with cold water, changing the water every 10 minutes or so. It should thaw in 30 to 45 minutes, depending on thickness. Remove it from the package, dry with a paper towel, and cook.
- Never refreeze thawed fish, as this will cause loss of flavor and texture.

How to Thaw Shrimp/Prawns

- Overnight thawing: Remove the shrimp from the package and place them on a clean kitchen towel– or paper towel–lined bowl and let them thaw in the refrigerator overnight. Once thawed, rinse with cold water and remove the shells, if needed.
- Quick thaw: Remove the shrimp from the bag and place them in a colander. Run cold water over the shrimp, tossing them so all the shrimp have been showered with water. Then, let them sit in the colander for about 5 minutes. Repeat the process two or three more times until the shrimp begin to thaw. The shrimp should be thawed in 20 to 30 minutes. I find that "almost thawed" shrimp are easier to peel and devein.

- Store thawed shrimp in the refrigerator for no more than 1 to 2 days.
- If the shrimp were thawed in the refrigerator, you can refreeze them. Otherwise, I'd recommend cooking them.

How to Thaw Scallops

- Overnight thaw: Remove the scallops from their packaging and place them on a clean kitchen towel– or paper towel–lined plate or bowl. Cover the bowl lightly and place them in the refrigerator overnight or up to 8 hours. You can refreeze any scallops that you don't need. I think this is the best option for thawing scallops.
- Quick thaw: Place the scallops in a large, resealable plastic bag and seal tightly. Place the bag in a bowl of cold water and submerge. Place a plate or bowl on the bag if it won't stay under the water. Let the bag sit in the water, changing the water if it gets too cold, for 30 to 45 minutes. Move the bag around the water every 5 minutes or so.
- Another quick thaw: This is an option that I do as a last resort. Scallops are notorious for soaking up liquid, so if you use this method, be sure to pat the scallops completely dry before cooking. Place the scallops in a colander and run cold water over them, tossing so all the scallops have been showered with water. Then, let them sit in the colander for about 5 minutes. Repeat the process two or three more times until the scallops begin to thaw, 20 to 30 minutes total.

How to Thaw Lobster Tails

- Overnight thaw: Remove the lobster tails from their packaging and place them on a paper towel–lined plate to chill in the refrigerator overnight or up to 24 hours. This is an important step and will help prevent the uncooked lobster meat from sticking to the shell. This method is recommended when preparing the Broiled Lobster Tails recipe (page 260).
- Quick thaw: Place the lobster tails in a large, resealable plastic bag and seal tightly. Use the same "quick thaw" method as for scallops. However, this method will take up to 60 minutes for lobster.

Prepare Your Fish for Cooking

- Remove seafood from the refrigerator 15 minutes prior to cooking. This will allow your fish to come to room temperature and cook more evenly and efficiently.

- ✦ Gently dry the fish with a paper towel before cooking. This is extremely important for recipe success. Extra moisture on fish or shellfish will steam the fish rather than crisp it, or will make the finished dish weepy.
- ✦ Remove the pin bones, which run along the spine of the fish. Now, back in culinary school, we ran the back of a knife down the spine of the fillet to expose the bones and then, holding the flesh with our fingers, pulled out the bones. Several years ago, a cooking student of mine showed me a better way, and I've used this method ever since. Take a large mixing bowl, turn it upside down, and lay the fillet, flesh side up, over the bottom of the bowl. This will expose all those tiny little pin bones. Using fish tweezers, pull them out. I dip my tweezers in a small bowl of water to get the bones off my tweezers.
- ✦ If you're faced with a large fillet, cut it into manageable pieces. Often I purchase a 1½-pound fish fillet and divide it up in four to six pieces. This not only makes it easier to cook the fish, but the fish will cook more evenly and will brown nicely.
- ✦ If you are roasting individual fish fillets and one end of a fillet is thinner than the other end, simply tuck the thin end under a bit to even out the thickness of the fillet. I find that this is most common with salmon. I've given an example of this in the first chapter, "Easy Like a Weeknight."
- ✦ For seafood dinner success, be sure to prepare the side dishes first. As with many seafood recipes, fish cooks quickly and is best served as soon as it's finished cooking. It doesn't sit well while the sides are being prepared.
- ✦ Mise en place: a French term that basically means have all your ingredients ready and in place before you begin to cook. This will help the home cook assemble a meal more easily and efficiently.

How to Devein Shrimp/Prawns

- ✦ Most shrimp are sold without the heads. But should you purchase shrimp with heads, just give the heads a little twist and they will pull right off.
- ✦ To devein shrimp with tail on, pull off the legs, grab the shell from underneath (where the legs were) and pull it off, leaving the tail section on. Lay the shrimp on a cutting board and use a paring knife to slice down the back of the shrimp to reveal the vein. Remove the vein, gently rinse the shrimp, and place in a bowl of ice.
- ✦ To devein shrimp with tail off, use same method but gently pull from the tail end to remove. Place the shrimp in a bowl of ice until ready to cook.

A Few Basic Methods for Preparing Fish

Some basic cooking methods used in preparing seafood are either dry methods, such as roasting, grilling, or pan cooking. Some are moist methods, such as poaching, steaming, or simmering. The method of course is determined by the ingredients in the recipe but also by the type of seafood used.

The following are my favorite methods for preparing seafood along with a definition and/or brief description of each method.

As a rule, fish will cook through in about 10 minutes for every inch of thickness. Some fish, such as salmon, I cook for about 8 minutes for every inch of thickness to achieve a medium-rare result. USDA recommends a safe internal temperature of 145°F, or until the fish is opaque and flakes easily.

As with most everything in life, the more you practice, the easier it gets. This is true for cooking. The more you cook seafood, becoming familiar with the subtle nuances of fish and shellfish and the ingredients that complement these unique flavors, the more confident you'll be.

BAKING: There are few things to remember when using the dry method of baking seafood. I like to cover a baked fish with a sauce, glaze, citrus slices, olive oil, and spices or parchment. There are times when all that is needed is oil and seasoning, depending on the type of fish being baked. The key is to preheat the oven, remove the fish from the refrigerator 15 minutes prior to cooking, and cook the fish for 10 minutes for every inch of thickness.

Baking is basically roasting, but it uses a lower oven temperature. Baking is convenient and allows the home cook to put the fish recipe in the oven and let it cook while side dishes or condiments are assembled. It's one of the easiest methods for cooking seafood, especially if you're new to seafood or need a quick meal.

BROILING: This is another dry method of cooking. It uses the oven's upper heating element at high heat, around 500°F. I find this method is best for finishing dishes to give them some color or for cooking shellfish, such as the Broiled Lobster Tails (page 260). This method requires the home cook's full attention. If left too long, the top of the fish will burn.

DEEP-FRYING: Also a dry method of cooking used for starch- or other ingredient–coated fish that is submerged in fat and fried to a deep golden brown. The oil or fat should always be between 350° and 375°F while frying. If it dips below this, you could end up with soggy fish; too high and it'll burn. I recommend a deep-fry or candy thermometer when deep-frying or using an electric deep fryer.

GRILLING: I reserve this method of dry cooking for fish steaks, salmon, tuna, swordfish, shrimp skewers, lobster, and scallops. This doesn't mean you can't grill other types of seafood, but these are the easiest to master.

Grilling requires clean grates that have been oiled. Some experts recommend lighting your grill to high heat and allowing the heat to cook off any remaining food stuck on the grates. Then, with a wire grill brush, scrape the charred remains off the grate. Turn the heat down or off and, using a basting brush, brush a little vegetable oil onto the grates. Gently wipe off any excess with a wadded-up paper towel, using tongs.

To grill fish, preheat a grill to 400° to 425°F. Brush the fish with oil and season with your preferred seasoning. Place the fish, flesh side down, diagonally on the oiled grill. Close the lid and let the fish cook for 5 to 7 minutes, depending on thickness. Using tongs, try to ease the fish up off the grill and flip. If it doesn't flip easily, it isn't ready. Let it sit about 30 seconds longer. Once the fish is flipped, let it finish cooking, about another 3 to 4 minutes, or as needed.

PAN COOKING: This is the method of cooking I use most for fish. Pan cooking is a dry method of cooking on the stovetop in a heavy-bottomed skillet or sauté pan. It's also referred to as sautéing and panfrying. Pan cooking is incredibly easy and requires just a few steps.

Dry the fish with a paper towel, brush with a little high-heat oil, and then season. Add the recipe's recommended amount of oil or ghee to a skillet or sauté pan over medium-high heat. (Note: It is recommended that nonstick pans be heated over no greater than medium heat.)

Once the oil is hot and shimmering, add the fish to the skillet and let it cook. It should begin to look golden brown around the edges after 4 to 5 minutes. With a fish spatula or tongs, gently lift the fish, and if it doesn't lift, leave it for another minute. Once the fish lifts easily off the pan, flip it to the other side, flipping away from you so you don't get splattered with hot oil. Cook just until the fish is golden on the bottom, another 3 to 4 minutes, until the fish slightly flakes with a fork and is opaque. Most fish will cook through in 8 to 10 minutes for every inch of thickness.

PAN SEARING: Some experts also call this method pan roasting. This is a dry method whereby a piece of fish is seared on one side on the stovetop in an ovenproof skillet and then finished in the oven. This is another excellent method for thicker pieces of fish like halibut, or fish with a higher fat content, such as salmon.

As always, dry the fish with a paper towel, brush with oil, and then season with salt and pepper or your preferred seasoning. Preheat the oven to the recommended temperature (usually 400°F). Heat an ovenproof skillet over medium-high heat on the stovetop and add the recipe's recommended amount of oil or ghee. When the oil is hot and shimmering, add the fish, flesh side down. Cook for 3 to 4 minutes, until the bottom has formed a nice golden-brown crust. Flip the fish over and pop that skillet into the oven. Let it cook for another 5 to 10 minutes, depending on thickness. The fish will be done when it slightly flakes with a fork and is opaque.

POACHING: When fish or shellfish are poached properly, the result is a tender and lush texture. This moist heat method of cooking can be done two ways, either deep poaching or shallow poaching. Deep poaching is the method I use most and the method I've used in this book. Deep poaching submerges seafood in a lightly simmering liquid (between 160° and 185°F) that gently cooks. The key to poaching is to never boil the seafood. It's always barely at a simmer. The poaching liquid can be flavored with herbs, aromatics, spices, wine, vegetables, and more. Poaching works well with most seafood; however, I find that firm flesh fish or shellfish are best suited to this method of cooking.

STEAMING: The moist heat method of steaming is also incredibly easy for both fish and shellfish. In this book, I've given recipes for clams and mussels steamed in wine or sake along with herbs and aromatics. Another recipe is salmon steamed in parchment or what is called en papillote, whereby the salmon is layered with citrus, aromatics, fresh herbs, and olive oil, then wrapped in parchment and cooked in the oven. The result is a tender, flaky fish infused with all the gorgeous flavors. It's one of my go-to weeknight meals, but it's delicious enough to be served to dinner guests. This method of cooking is excellent for most any type of fish. This steaming method can also be done on a grill, but using foil packets instead of parchment.

ROASTING: This method of dry heat is just like baking but at a higher temperature. I typically roast fish at 400° to 425°F, and just like baking it, I brush the fish with oil and seasoning or layer it with citrus, sauce, or parchment over the top before baking. This is another quick and easy way to cook fish.

Basic Cooking Terms and Definitions

BASTE: To moisten food while its cooking.

CHOP: To cut into pieces approximately the same size.

DEGLAZE: To loosen the brown bits (called fond) off the bottom of a pan by adding liquid to the hot pan.

DICE: To cut ingredients into more uniform cubes. You can dice ingredients into various sizes:

- ✦ Small dice is approximately ¼-inch squares (about the size of the tip of the pinkie finger);
- ✦ Medium dice is approximately ½-inch squares;
- ✦ Large dice is approximately ¾-inch squares.

EMULSIFY: To slowly combine a fat (such as butter or oil) with another liquid (such as vinegar, lime juice, or water) to create a creamy, silky texture.

FOND: A French term that describes all the delicious brown bits that stick to the bottom of a pan.

GARNISH: To add finishing touches, such as chopped fresh herbs, to your prepared dish.

MINCE: To cut ingredients into very fine pieces smaller than a dice or a chop; this is often used for garlic and ginger.

MIREPOIX: The aromatics that are added to the fat at the beginning of a recipe; typically onion, carrot, and celery but can include garlic and other aromatics. This term is also referred to as *sofrito* in Latin American cooking and *soffritto* in Italian cooking, or as the Holy Trinity in Cajun and Creole cuisine.

MISE EN PLACE: A French term for having all the ingredients prepped and kitchen tools and equipment set out and ready before you begin to cook a meal.

PUREE: To mash, strain, or chop an ingredient and turning it into a smooth paste.

REDUCE: To thicken a liquid by simmering it slowly.

ZEST: To gently scrape or shred pieces of the outer rind of citrus.

Basic Ingredients That Complement Seafood

All types of ingredients across many ethnic cuisines complement seafood. However, the following are a few of my favorite seafood ingredient pairings that I find close to home.

Aromatics

These are the ingredients that enhance and deepen the flavor of a recipe. They are typically the first ingredients added to the fat, such as:

carrots
celery
chiles
fennel bulb
garlic
ginger
leeks
onions
peppers
shallots

Herbs

Most fresh herbs complement seafood; however, these are a few of my favorites:

basil
chives
cilantro
curly parsley
dill
flat-leaf, aka Italian, parsley
lemon thyme
lemongrass
mint
oregano
rosemary
savory
tarragon
thyme

Spices

Each type of cuisine has its own list of traditional spices, and they usually complement seafood beautifully. These happen to be the spices I reach for most often:

- bay leaves
- cayenne pepper
- chili powder
- Chinese five-spice powder
- coriander
- cumin
- curry powder
- fennel seeds
- ginger
- mustard
- paprika
- pepper
- red pepper flakes
- saffron
- salt (kosher/sea)
- seafood seasoning blends
- smoked paprika
- turmeric
- za'atar

Vegetables

Most vegetables complement seafood, but these are a few that I like to use most often:

- artichokes
- arugula
- asparagus
- avocados
- broccolini
- cauliflower
- chile peppers
- corn
- cucumbers
- fennel bulb
- green beans
- green onions
- leeks
- legumes
- mushrooms
- mustard greens
- napa cabbage
- onions
- peas
- poblano peppers
- potatoes
- salad greens
- spinach
- sweet peppers
- sweet potatoes
- Swiss chard
- tomatoes
- zucchini

Fruit

Without a doubt, citrus pairs perfectly with all seafood, as does tropical fruit. But berries and stone fruit can also be a lovely pairing with seafood:

- apricots
- blackberries
- blueberries
- dried cherries
- grapefruit
- grapes
- kiwis
- lemons
- limes
- mangoes
- nectarines
- oranges
- papayas
- peaches
- pineapple
- star fruit
- strawberries

Dairy

There are a few die-hard "no dairy with seafood" critics out there but I'm not one of them. The dairy used typically depends on the type of seafood, aromatics, and herbs in the recipe. These are a few that I use in my recipes:

- butter
- cream cheese
- goat cheese
- Gruyère
- heavy cream
- Parmesan
- Swiss
- white Cheddar

Basic Pantry Items to Keep in Stock

This is a list of my favorite pantry staples for cooking seafood as well as ingredients that can help a home cook whip up a last-minute seafood meal with complementary side dishes.

- anchovies
- avocado oil
- balsamic vinegar (golden and traditional, good quality)
- Better Than Bouillon brand Fish Base
- Better Than Bouillon brand Lobster Base
- black beans
- cannellini beans
- capers
- clarified butter (ghee)
- coconut milk
- coconut oil
- couscous
- Dijon mustard
- extra-virgin olive oil
- farro
- harissa paste or sauce
- hoisin sauce
- linguine
- mandarin orange segments (canned)
- miso (white)
- olives
- orange marmalade
- orzo
- panko bread crumbs
- pearled barley
- quinoa
- rice
- risotto
- seafood stock
- seasoned rice wine vinegar
- spaghetti
- tamari
- Thai sweet chili sauce
- tomato paste
- tomatoes (canned)
- tuna

Helpful Cookware and Utensils for Preparing Fish

You don't need a new set of pans or kitchen utensils to prepare a delicious seafood meal. What you already have is probably sufficient. However, there are a few pieces of equipment that make cooking seafood easier.

Fish spatula (if I were to splurge on one new kitchen utensil for seafood, it would be a fish spatula; these spatulas are thin, flexible, and slide flawlessly under a piece of fish)

10- or 12-inch skillet of carbon steel, stainless steel, cast iron, ceramic coated, nonstick, or whatever is comfortable for you to cook with

Cast-iron grill pan (optional, but always good to have)

Oven-safe skillet for pan searing and finishing in the oven

A good-quality knife to make prep work easy

Splatter screen for pan cooking

Whisk

Tongs

Parchment paper

Cutting boards

Baking sheets

Baking dishes

Fish tweezers (find them in most kitchen stores and online)

Dutch oven or large pot for soups and stews

CHAPTER ONE

Easy Like a Weeknight

Whether you're new to cooking seafood, or you simply want to get dinner on the table without too much fuss, this chapter is for you. In the pages that follow, we dive into the basics of seafood and several easy cooking methods for preparing seafood.

The recipes in this chapter are organized by simplicity of preparation and cooking method. We begin with several appetizers that are quickly assembled with canned or pouched seafood and only require a little oven or stovetop time. They're a great introduction to seafood flavors without much fuss.

From there, I introduce several easy-to-prepare baked white fish and salmon recipes. Further into the chapter, we use the roasting method along with pan cooking, pan searing, and poaching.

I've also included two fish stews that are simply perfect for a warm meal on a cool evening. I end the chapter with basic recipes for cooking shrimp, scallops, and clams.

The recipes created for this chapter include fresh ingredients along with some pantry staples. They also highlight some of the most common seafood found in local markets, and pair the seafood with seasonal ingredients. I often list fish substitutions, just in case a particular seafood isn't in season or isn't found in your area.

As always, approach these delicious recipes with ease and preparation. If you've got everything in its place, or what we call mise en place, your cooking experience will be much more enjoyable and less stressful. And it's okay if you don't get something right the first time; just try it again. I promise, over time, cooking skills are honed, and eventually, cooking seafood will become second nature.

If you're unsure about a technique, a seafood substitution, or an ingredient pairing, or you are looking for a resource, be sure to refer to the "Seafood 101" section (page 14) or the Resources (page 315). This will help you build your knowledge and your confidence in the kitchen.

Although I refer to this chapter as "entry-level" recipes, I often make them in my home kitchen. Summer doesn't pass without serving the Pan-Cooked Fish with Summer Blackberry Orange Relish (page 104), and a weekend snack staple is my Wild Albacore Tuna Salsa (page 42). With short or moderately short ingredient lists, these are the recipes that make it easy for the home cook to step into the world of seafood.

Wild Albacore Tuna Salsa

SERVES 2 OR 3

Wild albacore tuna gives the home cook a lot of simple and delicious recipe options. It's a pantry staple in my house, not only for tuna salad sandwiches but for this fun and easy appetizer.

Many years ago, my brother Cameron came back from South America and made this salsa for me. During his travels, he was served an albacore tuna dish that included red onion, cilantro, and a little lime juice along with patacones as "chips." Patacones are fried plantains and make the most wonderful accompaniment to this salsa.

I adore this salsa, and over the years, I added diced jalapeño and a drizzle of my best olive oil. Sometimes, I make patacones, but most of the time, I serve this with blue or yellow corn chips. It makes a tasty little starter, weekend nibble, or late-night snack.

10 ounces canned wild albacore tuna (about 2 cans), drained

⅓ cup chopped fresh cilantro

⅓ cup small-diced red onion

Juice of 1 lime

1 small jalapeño pepper, seeded and diced (optional)

Drizzle of extra-virgin olive oil

Salt and freshly ground black pepper

Mix the ingredients together in a medium bowl, seasoning with salt and pepper to taste, and serve with blue or yellow corn chips. You can keep any leftovers in the refrigerator for up to 3 days. But I bet there won't be any leftovers.

Note

I have also been known to use the leftovers from this recipe for a super flavorful tuna melt using slices of buttermilk or whole-grain bread along with Cheddar or Monterey Jack.

Smoked Salmon Lox with Crème Fraîche on Mini Corncakes

MAKES 12 TO 14 CAKES

I remember the day I tasted salmon for the first time. I wasn't immediately enamored, but with several years, and a move to the Pacific Northwest, I grew to love it. Smoked salmon, or salmon lox, is easy to find in most markets, and it's a perfect ingredient for nights when you don't have time to cook the salmon yourself, or if you're just starting out with seafood—perfect for a simple starter like this one.

Fresh dill is a natural pairing with salmon, and crème fraîche has a slight tang that complements the fish. Cornmeal cakes had to be involved because I grew up eating them. And, well, the subtle sweetness of the corn complements all the ingredients.

I adore salmon lox in this dish, but if you have smoked salmon fillets or pieces, that'll work just fine. Salmon lox are cured rather than smoked. They are thinly sliced and buttery in texture. They are also easily folded, making them a lovely option for this recipe. However, if you prefer the slight smoky flavor of smoked salmon, feel free to use that.

1 cup yellow cornmeal
½ cup all-purpose flour
1 teaspoon baking powder
½ teaspoon salt
1 tablespoon sugar
2 tablespoons oil
1 large egg, whisked
⅔ to ¾ cup buttermilk
½ cup crème fraîche
4 to 6 ounces smoked salmon or salmon lox
2 tablespoons fresh dill

1 Mix together the cornmeal, flour, baking powder, salt, and sugar in a medium bowl.

2 Whisk together the oil, egg, and ⅔ cup of the buttermilk in a separate bowl. Combine the wet ingredients with the dry ingredients just until smooth and it feels like pancake batter. Add additional buttermilk, if needed. Don't overwhisk.

3 Heat a stovetop griddle or non-stick skillet over medium to medium-low heat. Once the pan is hot, ladle a few tablespoon-sized dollops of batter onto the skillet, 2 to 3 inches in diameter. You want them to be bite-size.

4 Once the edges turn golden brown and the center is bubbly, flip the corncakes, and cook the other side. Transfer them to a platter and let cool.

5 To serve, place the corncakes on a platter and dollop with crème fraîche. Top each corncake with a piece of smoked salmon and fresh dill. Serve immediately.

Note

The cornmeal cakes can be prepared a day in advance and stored in a covered container until ready to serve.

Note

Most anchovies are filleted, cured, and then preserved in oil. They are easily found in local markets, and many specialty markets carry fancy whole anchovy varieties.

Lemon Herb Ricotta Toasts with Anchovies

SERVES 6 TO 8 AS AN APPETIZER

At home, I refer to this dish as Bruno's crostini. It was inspired by my visit to Tuscany many years ago while sharing a meal with colleagues at a party hosted by Tuscan grape grower Bruno Rosetti and his family.

We had been seated around a long table filled with an assortment of beautiful food and several plates of crostini, dining al fresco under the autumn Tuscan sun. As conversation flowed, along with several bottles of Chianti, I asked Signor Rosetti, "What is your favorite crostini"? He replied, "Simply ricotta on crostini with an anchovy." Then, he proceeded to give me one of his million-dollar smiles, which, of course, melted my heart.

When I returned home, this was one of the first recipes I made. Of course, over the years, I tweaked it a little—the chef in me couldn't resist. And now, every time I serve these toasts, I tell the story of Signor Rosetti.

1 cup whole-milk ricotta

1 tablespoon finely chopped fresh herbs, such as parsley, basil, and chives, plus more for garnish (optional)

Zest of 1 lemon

1 garlic clove, minced

1 baguette, sliced into ½-inch rounds (crostini)

2 to 3 tablespoons extra-virgin olive oil

One to two 2-ounce cans whole flat anchovies in oil

1. Preheat the oven to 400°F.
2. Drain the ricotta: Place a layer of cheesecloth in a mesh colander. Place the ricotta in the lined colander and then set it over a plate or bowl. Let it drain for about an hour or even overnight. Then, mix together the ricotta, herbs, lemon zest, and garlic.
3. Next, brush the baguette slices with a little olive oil on one side and place them oil side up on a baking sheet.
4. Place the baking sheet in the oven and toast the baguette slices until soft and slightly golden, 5 to 8 minutes.
5. Remove the baking sheet from the oven and let the baguette slices cool.
6. To serve, place a dollop of ricotta on a crostini and then top with one anchovy. Garnish with additional fresh herbs, if desired. Serve immediately.

Open-Face Bay Shrimp Salad Melts on Thick Toast

MAKES 4 TOASTS

Years ago, while working as a private chef, I developed this recipe for one of my clients. My client adored bay shrimp and wanted me to include it in a few salads. After some recipe testing, this delicious shrimp salad was created. Eventually, I used the leftovers to make this drool-worthy shrimp salad melt on thick toast.

It's important to dry with a paper towel or squeeze the excess liquid out of the shrimp so the salad won't omit a lot of liquid when heated. I've chosen to use Texas Toast for this recipe, but if you can't find it, any thick-sliced toast will work.

1 pound small bay shrimp, squeezed of excess liquid

⅓ cup mayonnaise

One 4-ounce jar pimientos, well drained

1 teaspoon lemon zest

½ cup thinly sliced green onion

1 tablespoon chili sauce or cocktail sauce

Salt and freshly ground black pepper

1 cup shredded Cheddar, plus a little reserved for topping

4 slices Texas toast or thick-sliced toast

2 tablespoons unsalted butter

Chopped fresh chives for garnish

1. Preheat the oven to 400°F.
2. Combine the shrimp, mayonnaise, pimientos, lemon zest, green onion, and chili sauce in a large bowl and gently mix.
3. Season to taste with salt and black pepper.
4. Gently fold in the Cheddar.
5. Lightly toast the bread slices in a toaster or in the oven and then spread with butter.
6. Place the toast on a baking sheet and top each slice of toast with about ¼ cup or more of the shrimp salad. Sprinkle shredded Cheddar and chives on top.
7. Put the baking sheet into the oven and bake for about 5 minutes, or until the cheese is melted.
8. Remove the baking sheet from the oven and serve.

Note

Be sure to purchase the freshest cooked bay shrimp possible (it should not have a fishy smell) and pat it dry before using. For more information about bay shrimp, refer to page 21.

Bay Shrimp and Pepper Jack–Stuffed Roasted Mini Peppers

MAKES 16 TO 20 PEPPER HALVES

The day after Christmas, our family and a few friends gather in one beautiful, mountain location for several days of winter activities, board games, loads of laughter, conversation, and, of course, food. Almost everyone ends up in the kitchen at some point, making a dish or two. One of my "holiday sons," Erik, made a pepper Jack and bay shrimp–stuffed jalapeño popper one year. And every year after, they've become a tradition.

After the holidays, I often make these enchanting appetizers at home but with a few tweaks. Mini peppers replace the jalapenos, the bacon is omitted, and then I garnish with some garlic-Parmesan bread crumbs.

8 to 10 mini peppers, halved
6 ounces bay shrimp, patted dry and lightly chopped
4 ounces cream cheese, at room temperature
4 ounces or ½ cup packed shredded pepper Jack
1 garlic clove, finely minced
½ teaspoon salt
¼ teaspoon freshly ground black pepper
2 tablespoons seasoned bread crumbs
2 tablespoons grated Parmesan
1 tablespoon extra-virgin olive oil
Chopped fresh chives for garnish (optional)

1 Preheat the oven to 400°F.

2 Place the halved mini peppers on a baking sheet. Roast for 8 to 10 minutes, until slightly soft. Remove from the oven and let cool. Leave the oven on.

3 Mix together the bay shrimp, cream cheese, pepper Jack, garlic, salt, and black pepper in a medium to large bowl until nicely combined.

4 Then, fill each pepper half with a dollop of the shrimp mixture, patting them down into the pepper half, if needed.

5 Mix together the bread crumbs, Parmesan, and olive oil in a small bowl. Sprinkle this mixture over each mini pepper.

6 Place the peppers back in the oven for another 5 to 8 minutes, until the crumbs are golden and the peppers are warmed through the center.

7 Remove from the oven and serve slightly warm or room temperature. Garnish with chopped chives, if desired. These are also delicious served chilled.

Vintage Macaroni and Shrimp Salad

SERVES 6 TO 8

Back in my private chef days, I had a particular client who requested I make a macaroni and shrimp salad. He had definite ideas about how it should look and what it should taste like. Well, after many attempts at several different versions, I finally perfected this recipe. To my client's absolute delight, of course. It thrilled my chef heart that this simple macaroni and shrimp salad made him so happy.

I've modified the recipe just a bit over the years, substituting cavatappi pasta for macaroni. Mostly because I love cavatappi and it stands up well to the bay shrimp (often referred to as salad shrimp) and cubed Cheddar. I added green onion for additional flavor, which I think works really well here. It also gives the salad some additional color.

This salad is best served the same day it's prepared, but it can be tossed together a few hours before serving.

12 ounces dried cavatappi pasta

½ cup sliced green onion

½ cup diced sweet onion

¾ cup diced celery

¾ cup sweet pickle relish

6 ounces diced or small-cubed Cheddar

1½ cups mayonnaise

Salt and freshly ground black pepper

12 ounces bay shrimp, patted dry with a paper towel, or squeezed to eliminate excess liquid

1 tablespoon chopped fresh parsley (optional)

1. Prepare the cavatappi according to the package directions and let cool completely.
2. Transfer the pasta to a large bowl and then toss with the green onion, sweet onion, celery, pickle relish, Cheddar, and mayonnaise. Season to taste with salt and pepper.
3. Next, gently fold in the bay shrimp and parsley (if using). Adjust the seasoning as needed.
4. Refrigerate for about 30 minutes before serving.

Note

Be sure to purchase the freshest cooked bay shrimp possible (it should not have a fishy smell) and pat it dry before using. For more information about bay shrimp, refer to page 21.

Wild Albacore Tuna Cakes with Chipotle Lime Dipping Sauce

MAKES TEN TO TWELVE 3-INCH CAKES

Canned albacore tuna is extremely versatile. It can be used so many different ways, from salads to sandwiches or like this tuna cake recipe.

This comes together easily, requires a quick pan cook, and can be served as a last-minute appetizer, easy lunch, or light dinner. However, making any kind of fish cake requires just the right amount of wet-to-dry ingredients so that the cakes can be formed into patties and stick together. If you feel the mixture is too dry, add a bit more mayonnaise. If it feels too wet, add a bit more bread crumbs.

Don't skip rolling the formed patties in bread crumbs or refrigerating them for at least 10 minutes prior to pan cooking. These steps will help keep the cakes from breaking while cooking. And be sure to use a fish spatula, as it makes flipping the cakes much easier. If, for some reason, a tuna cake breaks, just squish it back together and keep cooking. It might not look perfect, but it'll taste delicious.

For information on purchasing wild albacore tuna, refer to the seafood watch websites in the Resources (page 315).

FIND YOUR FISH: For a delicious variation, I've also prepared this recipe with canned wild salmon.

TUNA CAKES

10 ounces wild albacore tuna (about 2 cans), drained

½ teaspoon salt

½ teaspoon chili powder, Tajín seasoning, or chili-lime seasoning, or more to taste (I adore Chile con Limon from Spiceology)

¼ teaspoon freshly ground black pepper

½ cup thinly sliced green onion

¼ cup chopped fresh cilantro

¼ cup panko bread crumbs, plus about ½ cup for dipping cakes

¼ cup mayonnaise

⅓ cup shredded Cheddar

1 large egg, whisked

Juice of ½ lime

High-heat oil for frying

DIPPING SAUCE

¼ cup mayonnaise

¼ cup sour cream

2 teaspoons freshly squeezed lime juice

1 chipotle pepper in adobo (½ chipotle for less heat)

½ teaspoon sugar

CONTINUES ➡

1 Mix together the tuna, salt, chili powder, black pepper, green onion, cilantro, ¼ cup of the bread crumbs, mayonnaise, Cheddar, egg, and lime juice in a large bowl until nicely incorporated.

2 Form 10 cakes, each about 3 inches wide and 1½ inches thick. Spread the remaining ½ cup of bread crumbs on a plate. Gently toss the cakes in the bread crumbs and place them on a baking sheet. Refrigerate for about 10 minutes.

3 Heat a large skillet over medium to medium-low heat and add enough high-heat oil to cover the surface of the skillet. This is important so the tuna cakes don't stick to the pan.

4 When the oil is hot, place three or four cakes in the skillet and brown on each side, 1 to 2 minutes per side. Watch the heat, as the oil gets hot quickly and can burn the tuna cakes. When the cakes are done, transfer to a paper towel–lined plate.

5 Make the dipping sauce: Place the mayonnaise, sour cream, lime juice, chipotle pepper, and sugar in a food processor. Process until completely combined. If the sauce is too spicy, add additional sour cream or mayonnaise.

6 Serve the tuna cakes warm with the dipping sauce.

Note

All chili powder blends taste different and can vary from one another in their level of heat. So, be sure to taste your chili powder before you use it.

Salmon en Papillote with Easy Lemon Aioli
(SALMON BAKED IN PARCHMENT)

SERVES 4

"En papillote" (in paper) is a simple cooking technique that steam-cooks ingredients in parchment packets in the oven. This method of cooking is ideal for fish or shellfish, and it's one of the first methods of cooking that I learned.

I used to make salmon en papillote for my great aunt and uncle when they visited my home many years ago. It was one of my aunt's favorite seafood recipes. I served this with a Parmesan orzo, pearled couscous, or wild rice, Caesar salad, and of course a warm crusty baguette, from which my aunt always requested the end piece.

It's been 20 years since I first served this enchanting seafood dish, and my family still enjoys it at least once or twice a month. The only change I've made over the years is to add an easy lemon aioli to drizzle over the top, just for something special.

I've included two aioli recipes. One is homemade, and the other uses prepared mayonnaise. Both are delicious, but if you're in a hurry or you're not quite sure you're ready to tackle making an aioli, the shortcut version will do just fine. I use both!

The instructions might look long, but I assure you, it's the easiest recipe to assemble. I've given step-by-step instructions and photos on how to fold the parchment packets for steam-cooking success.

CONTINUES ➡

FIND YOUR FISH: Although I typically make this recipe with salmon, I've also prepared it with halibut, swordfish, lingcod, and sablefish. I think most any white fish, such as flounder, haddock, bass, snapper, or cod, will work—whatever fresh fish you can find in your local market. This is definitely a recipe when "fresh" is best, but if the fish has been "flash frozen" and thawed properly, the texture should turn out lovely using this method. Refer to page 28 for more information on flash-frozen seafood and thawing options.

SALMON EN PAPILLOTE

Four 13 x 15-inch rectangles parchment paper (not waxed paper)

2 lemons, sliced (you'll want 2 to 3 slices of lemon per piece of salmon)

1½ pounds salmon fillets, cut into 4 pieces and removed from the refrigerator at least 15 minutes prior to cooking

2 tablespoons extra-virgin olive oil

Salt and freshly ground black pepper

1 to 2 shallots, peeled and sliced

4 sprigs each parsley, thyme, and chives (add more if you like!)

EASY HOMEMADE AIOLI

1 large egg yolk

1 teaspoon Dijon or stone-ground mustard

1 tablespoon freshly squeezed lemon juice, plus more to taste

1 garlic clove, minced

½ cup extra-virgin olive oil

1 teaspoon chopped fresh dill

SHORTCUT AIOLI

½ cup mayonnaise

2 tablespoons fresh lemon juice

1 garlic clove, minced

1 teaspoon Dijon mustard

1 teaspoon chopped fresh dill

1 Preheat the oven to 375°F.

2 Take one parchment rectangle and fold it in half (6½ by 15 inches when folded). Unfold it and position one long (15-inch) side nearest you.

3 Place two or three lemon slices in the center of the bottom half of the parchment (below the fold). Next, place a piece of salmon on the lemon slices. Brush the salmon with olive oil and sprinkle with salt and pepper.

4 Then, layer the salmon with a quarter of the shallot slices, one sprig each of the parsley, thyme, and chives.

5 Next, you want to fold the parchment packet securely—refer to the photos of this. To start, fold the top half of the parchment over the fish.

6 Beginning at one corner, fold and make a sharp crease. Then, starting at about the center of the first fold, make a second fold. Do the same thing all the way around the parchment until the packet edges are securely folded.

7 Brush the top of the parchment with a little olive oil and then place it on a baking sheet. Prepare the remaining three packets as instructed and place them on the baking sheet.

8 Put the baking sheet in the oven and bake for 15 to 20 minutes, depending on the thickness of your fish. I usually bake it for 12 to 15 minutes, and then I remove the baking pan from the oven and let the packets rest on the pan for about 5 minutes before serving. Fish will cook a little bit more as it rests.

9 While the fish cooks, prepare the aioli: To make the homemade aioli, place the egg yolk in a medium to large bowl. Next, whisk in the Dijon, lemon juice, and garlic. Then, while whisking, slowly drizzle in the olive oil until the mixture has thickened and is creamy. Stir in the dill and season to taste with salt and pepper. If making the shortcut version, mix together the mayonnaise, lemon juice, garlic, mustard, and dill in a medium bowl.

10 To serve, place each fish packet on an individual plate and cut open the top of each packet with scissors. Remove the cooked herbs, if desired, and serve with the aioli on the side. Sometimes, I serve the packets unopened and let my dinner guests break open the packets of steaming fish.

Weeknight Lemon-Baked Cod with Pesto Yogurt Dressing

SERVES 4 TO 6

This dish is a great starter recipe for any home cook who has little experience cooking seafood, or a home cook who wants to prepare a healthy, delicious meal with minimal time in the kitchen. Baking seafood is simple if you follow a few easy steps.

There are several ways to bake fish in the oven. When baking leaner types of fish, I either cover the fish with citrus slices and fresh herbs, plus a dash of olive oil or white wine, or I cover lightly with a piece of parchment paper. This is so the fish stays moist while baking.

For this recipe, I've chosen to cover the fish pieces with lemon slices, and I've added a drizzle of olive oil for additional moisture. When the fish is done, I simply plate and serve it topped with this easy pesto yogurt dressing.

FIND YOUR FISH: Every good seafood meal begins with fish that looks firm and glossy and that smells like the ocean. Be sure to review my tips on purchasing seafood on page 14. For this recipe, I typically use Pacific cod, but you can also prepare this recipe with most any flaky, mild white fish, such as sole, haddock, pollack, grouper, snapper, or flounder. If you're using fish with the skin on, place the fish skin side down in the baking dish.

4 ounces good-quality prepared pesto

4 ounces plain Greek yogurt

1½ to 2 pounds cod or mild, flaky white fish, cut into 4 to 6 pieces, removed from the refrigerator at least 15 minutes prior to cooking and checked for bones (refer to the section on deboning and fish tweezers in the "Seafood 101" section, page 14)

1 to 2 tablespoons extra-virgin olive oil

Salt and freshly ground black pepper

1 large lemon, sliced

Squeeze of lemon juice

Chopped fresh basil or parsley for garnish

CONTINUES ➡

1 Preheat the oven to 375°F.

2 Mix together the pesto and yogurt in a medium bowl.

3 Dry the fish with a paper towel, removing as much liquid as possible, and then brush your fish with a little oil and season with salt and pepper.

4 Place the fish in a glass or ceramic baking dish, always skin side down. So that your fish cooks evenly, make sure all the pieces of fish are the same thickness. If not, tuck thinner portions of each piece under to create an even thickness. (Refer to the baking and roasting fish instructions in the "Seafood 101" section, page 14).

5 Place a lemon slice or two on each piece of fish and give the fish another drizzle of olive oil.

6 Bake for about 10 minutes for every inch of thickness. Whole fillets might require a longer baking time, but fillet pieces can often bake more quickly. For this recipe, my cod pieces were done in 10 minutes, but they were just a bit less than 1 inch thick and cut into individual pieces. The fish is done when it's opaque and flakes slightly with a fork. The internal temperature should be 140° to 145°F.

7 Remove the fish from the oven and then transfer to a platter or plates.

8 Remove the lemon slices, if desired, and squeeze a bit of fresh lemon juice over each piece of fish. Top with the pesto yogurt, garnish with basil or parsley, and serve immediately.

Side Dish Suggestions

herb and garlic roasted new potatoes ✦ pearled couscous, rice, farro, or orzo ✦ mixed green salad ✦ steamed vegetables

Roasted Five-Spice White Fish Tacos with Apple Cabbage Slaw

SERVES 4

This is one of at least 10 seafood taco recipes I make at home on a regular basis. I adore Chinese five-spice powder paired with white fish, and the sweetness of shredded apple in the cabbage slaw brings together all the delicious flavors.

And because I believe every taco must have a sauce, I've added one here as well. It's an easy sauce to whip together and makes the perfect creamy, slightly sweet condiment for the white fish. If sriracha isn't your hot sauce of choice, you can replace it with sambal oelek or gochujang.

Roasting the fish makes this dish easy for a weeknight meal. Be sure to remove your fish from the refrigerator at least 15 minutes prior to cooking. This will increase the temperature of the fish so that it cooks more evenly in the oven.

I recommend either warming your tortillas in the oven on a baking sheet, steaming them in a stovetop steamer, or frying them. Because I usually fry the tortillas for this recipe, I have included instructions for frying.

1 to 1½ pounds mild white fish (such as: rockfish, halibut, flounder, cod, haddock, or petrale sole), removed from the refrigerator at least 15 minutes prior to cooking

4 tablespoons extra-virgin olive oil

1 teaspoon salt

2 to 3 teaspoons Chinese five-spice powder (found in most markets or online)

3 cups shredded cabbage (or prepackaged coleslaw; just don't use the dressing)

1 apple, cored and julienned or grated

½ cup packed fresh cilantro (about 1 small bunch)

2 tablespoons seasoned rice wine vinegar

½ cup mayonnaise

1 tablespoon honey

Juice of 1 large lime

1 to 2 teaspoons sriracha or your favorite hot sauce

Corn tortillas, warmed in the oven, steamed, or fried (see sidebar)

1 tablespoon sesame seeds (optional)

Sliced green onions for garnish

Lime wedges

CONTINUES ➡

1 Preheat the oven to 400°F.

2 Place the fish in a baking dish and brush it with 1 to 2 tablespoons of the olive oil. Mix together the salt and five-spice powder and then season the fish.

3 Place the baking dish in the oven and bake for 10 to 12 minutes, until the fish is cooked through. I used a 1-pound halibut fillet for this photo, and it took about 14 minutes to cook through. Whole fish fillets often require a little longer cook time than do individual portions of fish fillets. (Rule of thumb: Fish will cook through in 8 to 10 minutes for every inch of thickness, so time the fish accordingly.)

4 While the fish cooks, prepare the slaw: Place the cabbage, apple, and cilantro in a bowl and toss.

5 Whisk together the rice vinegar and remaining 2 tablespoons of olive oil in a small bowl.

6 Mix together the mayonnaise, honey, lime juice and sriracha in a separate small bowl to make a crema. Set aside.

7 When the fish is done, remove it from the oven. Let it cool for about 5 minutes. Meanwhile, toss the rice vinegar dressing with the cabbage slaw.

8 Flake the fish for the tacos and then assemble. Be sure to watch for bones! I like to add the fish at the bottom of the tortilla, drizzle with some crema, and then top with the dressed apple cabbage slaw and sesame seeds (if using).

9 Garnish with sliced green onions and squeeze of lime juice and eat!

To fry the tortillas: Line a plate or platter with paper towels and place it on the counter to one side. Add enough high-heat oil to a skillet to cover its surface. Place the skillet over medium heat. You may have to adjust the heat consistently while frying the tortillas.

When the oil is hot and slightly smoking, add one tortilla, using tongs. Let it brown just a bit and then flip to the other side to brown just a bit. Don't walk away! Stay at the pan while frying, adjusting the heat lower or higher as needed. Transfer the tortilla to the paper towel–lined plate and fold it in half like a taco. Do this with as many tortillas as you like.

Note

You can also serve this as a taco bowl without the tortillas.

Baked Spicy Dijon and Parmesan-Crusted Salmon

SERVES 4

Salmon is consistently on my dinner menu and for good reason. It's flavorful and one of the easiest finfish to prepare due to its higher content of fat than most other finfish.

Salmon adapts well to most methods of cooking, and it holds up to a variety of seasonal ingredients and flavor profiles, making it a well-suited option for every level of home cook. This recipe is one of my family's favorite weeknight meals and it pairs well with most seasonal vegetables and salads.

For more detailed information about sourcing sustainably caught or farmed salmon, refer to the seafood watch websites in the Resources (page 315).

1½ pounds salmon, cut into 4 pieces, removed from the refrigerator at least 15 minutes prior to cooking

2 tablespoons extra-virgin olive oil, divided

Salt and freshly ground black pepper

¼ cup Dijon mustard

¼ cup mayonnaise

1 garlic clove, minced

¼ cup panko bread crumbs

¼ cup grated Parmesan

1. Preheat the oven to 375°F.
2. Place the four salmon pieces on a parchment-lined or foil-lined baking sheet. If your salmon has skin, place it skin side down.
3. Salmon fillets are usually thick at one end and a bit thinner at the opposite end. To help the salmon cook evenly, tuck the thin piece under. It's like tucking a tail under the fillet. This will usually make all the salmon fillets look equal in size and it makes a nice presentation when cooked.
4. Brush the salmon with 1 tablespoon of olive oil and season with salt and pepper.
5. Mix together the Dijon, mayonnaise, and garlic in a small bowl.
6. Then, in another small bowl, mix together the panko bread crumbs, Parmesan, and the remaining tablespoon of olive oil.
7. Spread 2 tablespoons of the Dijon mixture over the top of each fillet.
8. Next, sprinkle the Parmesan bread crumbs over each fillet, pressing down a little to secure them.

9 Place the baking sheet in the oven and bake for 10 to 12 minutes, until the salmon is done. Most fish cook through in 8 to 10 minutes per inch of thickness. So, if your salmon is 1 inch or thicker, it might need 10 to 15 minutes of cook time. Salmon is done when it is light pink, opaque, and reaches 145°F internal temperature.

10 Once the salmon is done, remove it from the oven and let it rest for a few minutes prior to serving. Salmon will continue to cook for the next 5 minutes.

Side Dish Suggestions

roasted, steamed, or grilled seasonal vegetables ✦ green salad ✦ herb and lemon roasted potatoes ✦ braised fennel ✦ spinach gratin ✦ rice, couscous, or pasta salad

Spicy Orange Marmalade–Roasted Salmon

SERVES 3 TO 4

The sweet, tart orange flavor of marmalade stands up well to the bold flavor of salmon and creates one of my favorite sweet and savory seafood recipes.

For extra umami, I add a mild harissa sauce to the marmalade, which gives this recipe a ton of sweet and spicy flavor.

1 to 1½ pounds whole salmon fillet or cut into 3 or 4 pieces of equal size, removed from the refrigerator 15 minutes prior to cooking

1 tablespoon extra-virgin olive oil

Salt and freshly ground black pepper

½ cup orange marmalade

¼ cup harissa sauce (I use a mild harissa sauce), or 1 teaspoon harissa paste, or to taste

2 tablespoons white wine

Chopped fresh green onions for garnish (optional)

1 Preheat the oven to 425°F.

2 Place the salmon in a baking dish or on a baking sheet and brush with the olive oil, and then sprinkle it with a bit of salt and pepper.

3 Mix together the orange marmalade, harissa, and white wine in a small bowl.

4 Pour three-quarters of the marmalade mixture over the top of the fish. Reserve the remainder of the sauce for serving.

5 Place the fish in the oven and bake for 8 to 10 minutes for thin fillets, or 10 minutes for every inch of thickness. Note: If my salmon fillet is somewhat thick, I sometimes end up roasting it for about 15 minutes. I do find that whole fillets, versus individual portion sizes, require a bit longer cook time. The salmon should be a little pink inside. It'll continue to cook once you remove it from the oven.

6 Let the salmon cool for about 5 minutes, garnish with sliced green onions, if desired, and then serve with the remaining sauce.

Side Dish Suggestions

pearled couscous, rice, quinoa, or farro ✦ roasted or stir-fried vegetables and rice ✦ a salad of mixed greens

Note

If you cannot find harissa sauce or paste in your local market, it can easily be found online. However, if you decide to make this without the harissa, add one minced garlic clove and a teaspoon of grated fresh ginger. This will give it flavor and heat and pair deliciously with the marmalade and wine.

Citrus-Roasted Cod with Honey-Tarragon Brown Butter

SERVES 3 TO 4

Fish is well suited to most methods of cooking, especially baking. However, baking fish has the potential to dry it out, and we want to maintain that perfect, buttery texture. Here are a few things home cooks can do to keep their baked seafood dishes juicy and delicious.

First, be sure to brush the fish with oil and season to taste. If you're baking a thicker piece of lean, flaky white fish, such as cod or halibut, a great way to achieve extra flavor and moisture is to add a bit of liquid (about ¼ cup), such as wine or seafood stock, to the baking dish.

For this recipe, I also layer citrus slices on top of the fish. The citrus juices provide extra moisture and additional flavor, and it makes a pretty presentation. Once the fish is done, it's finished with a silky honey tarragon brown butter.

The bonus to all these steps for maintaining texture is that they are simple yet pack tons of flavor, making this a lovely weeknight meal or Sunday dinner.

1 to 1½ pounds cod (1 skinless fillet, such as true cod, Pacific cod, lingcod, black cod, or pollack; check seafoodwatch.org for the best choices), removed from the refrigerator 15 minutes prior to cooking

1 to 2 tablespoons extra-virgin olive oil

Salt and freshly ground black pepper

1 large lemon, sliced

1 medium navel orange, sliced

1 to 2 blood oranges, sliced

¼ cup white wine

8 tablespoons (1 stick) unsalted butter

1 tablespoon minced fresh tarragon (if you don't care for tarragon, replace with fresh basil)

Squeeze of lemon juice

1 tablespoon honey

1 garlic clove, minced

1 Preheat the oven to 400°F.

2 Place the cod fillet in an oval or rectangular baking dish and drizzle with the olive oil. Season with salt and pepper.

3 Place the lemon and orange slices over the fish, alternating among the citrus. Then, drizzle with the white wine.

CONTINUES ➡

4 Transfer the baking dish to the oven and bake for 12 to 15 minutes, depending on the thickness of your fish fillet. Most fish will cook through in 10 minutes for every inch of thickness. However, often whole fish fillets (fillets not cut into serving-size pieces) will take a bit longer to cook. The fish is done when it is opaque and just begins to flake.

5 While the baked fish rests, heat the butter in a light-colored saucepan over medium heat. This is so you can see the butter brown. When the butter melts, stir often until butter begins to froth. Just as the froth dissipates, you'll see brown flecks of butter fat on the bottom of the pan. Remove the pan from the heat and stir in the tarragon, lemon juice, honey, and garlic.

6 Season the honey tarragon butter with salt and pepper to taste and then drizzle it over the fish. Serve immediately with or without the citrus slices.

Note

Another method to keep fish from drying out during baking is to cut a piece of parchment paper to fit the inside of the baking dish. Once the fish is placed in the unlined dish and has been oiled and seasoned, gently lay the parchment over the top of the fish and bake as directed.

Side Dish Suggestions

rice, quinoa, couscous, or pearled couscous ✦ risotto or orzo ✦ new potatoes, winter squash, or sweet potatoes ✦ roasted, sautéed, or steamed vegetables

Roasted Teriyaki Sole with Shelled Edamame and Cilantro-Lime Rice

SERVES 3 OR 4

The word sole can cover quite a few types of finfish. However, for this recipe, you need the very thin, delicate fillets of fish often referred to as Dover sole. This type of sole shows up in my market now and again, and I love using it for this dish. The sole is mild, flaky, slightly sweet, and cooks quickly in the oven.

Thin sole fillets are great for stuffing and rolling, or just simply rolling and roasting as I do in this recipe. Paired with a homemade teriyaki sauce, it makes an easy and delicious meal. I've gone a step further and added some pan-seared edamame and cilantro lime rice for a great "bowl" meal. Or you can serve it with stir-fried rice for another delicious option.

I've listed my homemade teriyaki sauce recipe, which is super easy. But if you are short on time, feel free to use your favorite store-bought teriyaki sauce.

TERIYAKI SOLE

½ cup tamari or soy sauce

¼ cup water

¼ cup dark brown sugar

2 garlic cloves, minced

1 teaspoon minced fresh ginger

1 tablespoon rice vinegar

1 tablespoon cornstarch, plus 1 tablespoon cold water

1½ pounds Dover sole fillets (2 to 3 fillets per person), removed from the refrigerator about 15 minutes prior to cooking

Salt and freshly ground black pepper

Sesame seeds for garnish (optional)

Sliced green onions for garnish (optional)

EDAMAME

2 tablespoons high-heat oil (avocado, sunflower, safflower, etc.)

8 to 12 ounces frozen shelled edamame, thawed

Salt and freshly ground black pepper

CILANTRO-LIME RICE

2 cups cooked jasmine rice

¼ cup finely chopped fresh cilantro

2 teaspoons freshly squeezed lime juice

CONTINUES ➡

1. Make the sole: Preheat the oven to 400°F.
2. Stir together the tamari, water, brown sugar, garlic, ginger, and rice vinegar in a saucepan over medium heat. Bring to a slow boil and then lower the heat to a simmer.
3. Whisk together the cornstarch and water in a small bowl, and then whisk the cornstarch slurry into the teriyaki sauce. Bring it to a boil until the sauce thickens. Remove from the heat.
4. Season the sole fillets with just a pinch each of salt and pepper. Beginning at the narrow end of a fillet, roll it up and place it, seam side down, in a baking dish. Do this with each fillet.
5. Pour half to three-quarters of the teriyaki sauce over the fish. Reserve the remaining sauce to serve with the finished dish.
6. Place the baking dish in the oven and roast for about 10 minutes, or until the fish is done and opaque. Fish will cook through in about 10 minutes for every inch of thickness. Because the fillets are rolled, it might take a few minutes longer.
7. While the fish cooks, heat the high-heat oil in a sauté pan over medium-high heat. When the oil is hot, add the edamame, stirring them for just a few seconds. Let the edamame sit in the pan over the heat. This will slightly char the edamame on one side. Then, stir the edamame to finish heating them through. Season with a pinch each of salt and pepper.
8. Make the rice: Place the warm, cooked rice in a bowl and stir in the cilantro and lime juice.
9. To serve, divide the edamame and rice among three or four bowls and then top with the teriyaki baked sole. Garnish with sesame seeds and sliced green onions (if using) and serve with the remaining teriyaki sauce.

Mediterranean Roasted Fish Fillets with Parmesan Polenta

SERVES 4

There is no doubt that Mediterranean flavors pair perfectly with seafood. I adore this simple dish prepared in one pan and finished in the oven. I typically make this recipe with whatever local or regional white fish I have on hand—rockfish, halibut, lingcod—and each time, it's just as delicious.

To round things out, we have a creamy polenta that I've created with two parts whole milk, one part water, and a touch of grated Parmesan for extra flavor and texture. This seafood meal tastes so indulgent, no side dishes are needed. But if you decide to make this for dinner guests, a salad of mixed greens with a balsamic vinaigrette is perfect.

FIND YOUR FISH: Most any mild white fish will work here: snapper, branzino, rockfish, cod, pollack, haddock, halibut, flounder, whatever is fresh in your market. However, on occasion I'll find wahoo (ono), mahi-mahi, or swordfish, in my local market and use them in this recipe. Because these lower-fat fish cook in the sauce, they stay moist and tender and absorb all the delicious flavors. I don't cook with these three fish very often, but when I do, it's quite a treat. If you're unsure about which white fish to choose from your market, go to www.seafoodwatch.org to decide on the best possible choice.

1½ pounds skinless white fish, cut into 3 or 4 pieces, removed from the refrigerator at least 15 minutes prior to cooking

Salt and freshly ground black pepper

2 to 3 tablespoons extra-virgin olive oil

1 medium onion, thinly sliced

3 to 4 garlic cloves, minced

6 to 8 canned tomatoes, slightly drained and coarsely chopped

1 tablespoon chopped fresh parsley

½ teaspoon smoked paprika

⅓ cup sliced Kalamata olives

1 to 2 small lemons, thinly sliced

Chopped fresh basil for garnish (optional)

POLENTA

2 cups whole milk

1 cup water

1 cup quick-cook polenta

¼ cup grated Parmesan

Salt and freshly ground black pepper

CONTINUES ➡

1. Season the fish with salt and pepper; set aside.
2. Preheat the oven to 400°F.
3. Heat the olive oil in a large oven-safe skillet over medium heat and then add the onion. Cook just until soft and wilted. Then, stir in the garlic and cook for 1 minute longer.
4. Stir in the tomatoes, parsley, paprika, and olives.
5. Nestle the fish in the sauce and top with the lemon slices.
6. Place the skillet in the oven and roast for 10 to 15 minutes, depending on the thickness of the fish. Fish cook through in about 10 minutes for every inch of thickness. Most fish fillets are ½ to 1 inch thick, so I find 10 to 15 minutes is a good range for this dish, since it's being cooked in a sauce.
7. Remove the skillet from the oven and let the fish rest for a few minutes before serving. Garnish with basil, if desired.
8. Make the polenta: Combine the milk and water in a saucepan over medium-high heat. When the liquid comes to a boil, slowly stir in the polenta.
9. Continue to stir until it thickens and is soft and creamy, adjusting the heat as necessary. Remove from the heat and fold in the Parmesan. Season to taste with salt and pepper.

Roasted Furikake Salmon

SERVES 4

If you have never made fish seasoned with furikake, you're in for a treat. Furikake is a dry Japanese seasoning typically made with white or black sesame seeds, nori, and sometimes salt and sugar. However, it can come in variations with all sorts of ingredients, such as bonito flakes and wasabi powder. It's considered the salt and pepper of Japanese cooking and is typically sprinkled over rice. In fact, the meaning of furikake is "to sprinkle."

With a total of just six ingredients, this recipe is easy and flavorful. It makes a quick weeknight meal that is delicious and satisfying.

1 to 1½ pounds salmon fillets, cut into 4 pieces, removed from the refrigerator 15 minutes prior to cooking

2 tablespoons mayonnaise (this keeps the furikake from falling off the salmon)

Pinch of freshly ground black pepper

3 tablespoons furikake

Chopped fresh chives for garnish

Tamari or soy sauce for drizzling

CONTINUES ➡

1 Preheat the oven to 400°F.

2 Place the fillets, skin side down, on a parchment-lined baking sheet. Some fillets will be thin at one end and thick at the other end. When this happens, I tuck the thin end under, which will help the fish cook more evenly.

3 Brush the fillets with mayonnaise and then sprinkle with a little pepper.

4 Sprinkle furikake over each fillet and then transfer the baking sheet to the oven.

5 Bake for about 10 minutes, depending on the thickness of the salmon. Fish cook through in about 10 minutes for every inch of thickness. For the salmon in the photo, I roasted it for about 12 minutes as they were thicker pieces.

6 Once the fish is done, remove it from the oven and serve sprinkled with chopped chives and drizzled with tamari, if desired.

Side Dish Suggestions

sticky, jasmine, or brown rice ✦ steamed broccoli

Za'atar-Spiced Fish with Orange Cumin Vinaigrette and Fresh Greens

SERVES 4

Za'atar seasoning, a staple of Middle Eastern cuisine, exploded onto the American seasoning scene several years ago and I immediately jumped on that bandwagon. It's a lovely blend of sesame seeds, dried sumac, salt, thyme, and oregano. Some of the blends I've purchased also include ground cumin.

Like the Japanese seasoning furikake, za'atar is used for all types of recipes. But I really like to use it on seafood for the quick and easy layers of flavor that it provides. Here, I've mixed it with olive oil and ladled it over local rockfish, which is roasted in the oven.

Because the seasoning pairs deliciously with orange flavors, I add the finished fish to a salad of fresh greens and then top both the fish and the salad with an Orange Cumin Vinaigrette. Vinaigrettes make excellent "sauces" for a seafood dinner because they are quick to prepare and add a touch of additional flavor and texture.

FIND YOUR FISH: Although I usually use rockfish for this recipe, any mild, flaky white fish will work (cod, petrale sole, tilapia, flounder, haddock, or snapper). I think salmon would be lovely here, too. Grilled or pan-cooked fish would also make a nice alternative.

1½ pounds skinless white fish, either in 1 piece or cut into 4 pieces, removed from the refrigerator about 15 minutes prior to cooking and check for pin bones

Salt and freshly ground black pepper

3 tablespoons extra-virgin olive oil

1 tablespoon za'atar seasoning

VINAIGRETTE

Zest of 1 orange

¼ cup freshly squeezed orange juice

3 tablespoons Champagne vinegar

1 teaspoon sugar

1 garlic clove, minced

1 tablespoon minced shallot

½ teaspoon ground cumin

1 teaspoon Dijon mustard

¾ cup extra-virgin olive oil

SALAD

5 to 6 ounces fresh baby greens

Chopped fresh chives for garnish (optional)

CONTINUES ➡

1 Preheat the oven to 375°F.

2 Cut a piece of parchment roughly the size of the inside of your baking dish (don't worry about making it perfect), then set aside.

3 Place the fish in the unlined baking dish and season both sides with salt and pepper.

4 Whisk together the olive oil and za'atar seasoning in a small bowl and then spread it over the top of the fish.

5 Gently lay the parchment over the fish. It doesn't need to touch the fish; the objective is to keep in some of the moisture. Then, place the baking dish in the oven.

6 Bake for 10 to 15 minutes, depending on the thickness of the fish. Fish will cook through in 8 to 10 minutes for every inch of thickness. My fish fillet for this photo was a little over 1 inch thick, so it cooked for about 14 minutes. Once the fish is done, remove it from the oven and let it rest for a few minutes.

7 While the fish cooks, prepare the vinaigrette: Whisk together the orange zest and juice, vinegar, sugar, garlic, shallot, cumin, Dijon, and olive oil in a bowl until nicely combined. Season to taste with salt and pepper.

8 Toss the greens with a tablespoon or two of vinaigrette and then divide the dressed greens among four plates. Place the fish over the greens, drizzle a little vinaigrette over the fish, and garnish with chopped chives (if using). Serve immediately.

Chile-Spiced Rockfish with Summer Peach and Jalapeño Quinoa Salad

SERVES 4

Summer peaches are one of my favorite stone fruits, and when I'm not using them for desserts, I love to use them in savory recipes, such as this quinoa salad, and then top it with a beautiful fillet of fish.

I've chosen to roast the fish in the oven, which makes it an easy weeknight meal. However, I think this recipe would also work well with grilled fish.

FIND YOUR FISH: For this recipe, I've used rockfish, which is commonly found where I live. But you can substitute most any mild-flavored, medium-firm white fish that you like.

2 cups cooked quinoa

1 to 2 medium jalapeño peppers, seeded and diced

1 to 2 ripe fresh peaches, pitted and sliced

¼ cup chopped fresh cilantro or mint

¼ cup finely sliced green onion

Juice of 1 lime

3 to 4 tablespoons extra-virgin olive oil

Salt and freshly ground black pepper

1 to 1½ pounds rockfish, cut into 4 individual pieces, removed from the refrigerator 15 minutes prior to cooking

2 teaspoons chile lime seasoning, Mexican Tajín seasoning, or Chile con Limon from Spiceology (if you can't find the chili citrus combination, substitute the juice of 1 lemon and chili powder)

1 Preheat the oven to 400°F.

2 Prepare the salad first so the flavors have time to meld. Combine the quinoa, jalapeño, sliced peaches, cilantro, green onion, and lime juice in a large bowl and toss.

3 Drizzle with 1 to 2 tablespoons of the olive oil, toss and then season to taste with salt and pepper.

CONTINUES ➡

4 To prepare the fish, place the fish in a baking dish and brush with the remaining olive oil. Season with a pinch of salt and pepper.

5 Then, season the fish with the chile lime seasoning. If you can't find chile lime seasoning, drizzle the juice of 1 lemon over the fish and sprinkle with chili powder. Be sure to taste the chili powder before using. Not all chili powder blends are equally spicy. Many are mild, but some brands have a high level of heat.

6 Put the baking sheet in the oven and roast the fish for about 10 minutes for every inch of thickness. This will be based on the thickest part of your fish. The fish is done when it is opaque and flakes slightly with a fork.

7 If you'll notice in the photo, you can see some flaky separation in the fish fillets. This is one way you'll know it's done.

8 Plate the quinoa salad and then top with the cooked fish. Serve immediately.

Hoisin Five-Spice Sauce Baked Fish with Ramen Noodles and Broccolini

SERVES 3 TO 4

This recipe can easily be made in under 30 minutes. While the fish cooks, prepare the ramen and broccolini, and slice the green onions for garnish. When the fish is done, assemble the meal and dinner is ready.

I've kept the cooking method simple here, for those who want either a quick meal or are still learning to cook fish. However, for additional flavor and color, the fish can be seared in an oven-safe skillet, the sauce poured over the fish, and the skillet placed in the oven to finish cooking. This pan-searing method is ideal for pieces of fish ¾ to 1½ inches in thickness. Find instructions for this method in the "Seafood 101" section (page 14).

4 ounces hoisin sauce

1 tablespoon tamari or soy sauce

1 garlic clove, minced

1 teaspoon grated fresh ginger

½ teaspoon Chinese five-spice powder (start with ¼ teaspoon and taste; add add another ¼ teaspoon if you like the flavor)

Pinch of cayenne pepper

1 to 1½ pounds mild flaky white fish (rockfish, cod, halibut, flounder, petrale sole, or any other mild-flavored white fish), cut into 4 pieces, removed from the refrigerator 15 minutes prior to cooking, and patted dry with a paper towel

1 tablespoon extra-virgin olive oil

Salt and freshly ground black pepper

Cooked ramen noodles

Roasted or steamed broccolini

Sliced green onions for garnish

1 Preheat the oven to 400°F.

2 Combine the hoisin, tamari, garlic, ginger, five-spice powder, and cayenne in a small bowl.

3 Place the white fish in a baking dish. Brush it with the olive oil and season with a little salt and pepper. Pour half to three-quarters of the sauce over the fish, saving the rest for drizzling when serving.

4 Place the baking dish in the oven and let the fish cook for 10 to 12 minutes, until done. If your fish was at or near room temperature prior to baking and it's less than 1 inch in thickness, it should be done at around 10 minutes. To test for doneness, place a fork

at an angle, at the thickest part of the fish, and give it a little tug. If the fish begins to flake and looks opaque, it is done. If not, let it cook for a few minutes longer. Fish will continue to cook a bit more once it's been removed from the oven.

5 Remove the fish from the oven and plate with ramen noodles and broccolini. Garnish with sliced green onions and serve with the leftover hoisin mixture or soy sauce.

Basic Pan-Cooked Salmon with Lemon Dill Crème Fraîche and Persian Cucumber

SERVES 3 OR 4

In my opinion, pan cooking is one of the best methods for preparing fish. Although it can seem intimidating at first, once you get the hang of it, you will find that it's effortless and quick.

It makes dinner as simple as cooking a piece of fish on the stovetop and then serving it with a sauce, salsa, pesto, or dressing of some kind. Sometimes I simply pair it with a mélange of roasted veggies, aromatics, and fresh herbs. And on occasion, just a squeeze of fresh lemon juice works perfectly.

Because roasting and baking do most of the work for us, we can include more ingredients in such recipes. Pan cooking, however, needs our undivided attention and time, so I like to keep pan cooked recipes a little simpler. But simplicity shouldn't mean a lack of flavor. This dish is filled with bright notes from the crème fraîche and lemon, complementary textures, and fragrant herbs.

4 ounces crème fraîche

1 tablespoon chopped fresh dill

1 tablespoon freshly squeezed lemon juice

1 to 1½ pounds salmon, either skinless or skin on, cut into 3 or 4 pieces, patted gently with a paper towel to remove any excess moisture, and any visible pin bones removed (read how to remove pin bones in the "Seafood 101" section, page 14)

Extra-virgin olive oil for brushing

Salt and freshly ground black pepper

1 to 2 tablespoons ghee or high-heat oil

3 to 4 Persian cucumbers, cleaned and thinly sliced

1 Mix together the crème fraîche, dill, and lemon juice in a small bowl. Set aside.

2 Brush a little olive oil over the salmon pieces and then season with salt and pepper

3 Heat a large skillet over medium-high heat.

4 Add the ghee to the skillet. When the ghee is hot, add the salmon, flesh side down. Let the salmon cook for 3 to 4 minutes without moving so it can brown. You'll notice the edges of the salmon becoming golden brown and the flesh closest to the bottom of the pan turning opaque.

5 Then, flip the salmon over to be skin side down and let cook for another 3 to 4 minutes; cook longer for a thicker piece of salmon. Most fish cook through in about 10 minutes for every inch of thickness.

6 Once the salmon is done, transfer to plates.

7 Fold the sliced cucumber into the crème fraîche mixture and season to taste with salt and pepper.

8 Top the salmon with dollops of the cucumber mixture and serve.

Side Dish Suggestions

pearled couscous, lemon orzo, or jasmine rice ✦ roasted or steamed broccoli ✦ roasted asparagus with balsamic vinaigrette ✦ a salad of fresh greens, tomatoes, and olives with a lemon vinaigrette

Simple Fish Meunière

SERVES 4

Meunière is one of the first seafood dishes I learned to prepare in culinary school. It's super easy—an excellent recipe to practice the pan-cooking method—and still one of my go-to weeknight meals. Although this classic recipe is perfectly wonderful when prepared in the traditional method, which is simply butter, parsley, and lemon, I've given this sole meunière a bit of a modern twist with the addition of wine, garlic, and capers. The wine lightens the richness of the butter, and the garlic and capers season the sauce to perfection.

Be sure to have all ingredients ready because this recipe does move quickly. The good news is that when you have your method down, this dish can transition from skillet to table in less than 30 minutes. I highly recommend using a flexible fish spatula, which you can find online or in most kitchen stores. For more information about fish spatulas and pan cooking, refer to page 39.

FIND YOUR FISH: Most fish can be used in this recipe. However, I find that a very thin fillet of fish, such as Dover sole, petrale sole, some cod fillets, trout fillets, tilapia, haddock, branzino, or even thin fillets of snapper and rockfish, work well here. ("Cheek meat" can also be used in this recipe; read more about cheek meat on page 19.)

1½ pounds thin, filleted white fish, removed from the refrigerator at least 15 minutes prior to cooking
Salt and freshly ground black pepper
½ cup all-purpose flour
4 to 5 tablespoons ghee
3 tablespoons chopped fresh parsley, plus more for garnish
½ cup dry white wine
1 garlic clove, minced
1 lemon, halved
1 tablespoon capers, rinsed and patted dry
4 to 6 tablespoons (½ to ¾ stick) cold unsalted butter, diced
Lemon wedges for garnish

1 Pat the fish dry and season with salt and pepper. Place the flour in a large bowl.

2 Heat a large heavy-bottomed cast-iron, ceramic-coated, or non-stick fish-friendly skillet over medium-high heat and then add 2 to 3 tablespoons of the ghee, making sure to coat the entire surface of the pan. Add more as needed.

CONTINUES ➡

3 Just before the ghee is hot and sizzling, dust the fish in the flour and shake off the excess. Place the fillets on a baking sheet.

4 Place the fish fillets in the hot ghee, being careful not to splatter yourself, and sauté for a minute or two on each side, or until the fish is opaque, springy to the touch and cooked through. You may need to do this in two batches, depending on the size of your skillet.

5 Transfer the cooked fish to a platter and sprinkle with 1 tablespoon of the parsley.

6 Once the fish fillets are cooked, let the skillet cool, then wipe it down a bit with a paper towel; no need to wash it. You just want to remove the burned bits of flour.

7 Place the skillet back over medium heat and add the wine. Just as the wine begins to simmer, stir in the garlic, the remaining 2 tablespoons of parsley, the juice of one lemon half, and the capers. Let the wine simmer until it's reduced by half.

8 Then, whisk in the cold, diced butter. When the butter has melted and the sauce feels silky, 1 to 2 minutes, remove from the heat and season to taste with salt and pepper. *Don't allow the sauce to boil.* Add additional lemon juice from the remaining lemon half, if desired.

9 Plate the fish fillets on individual plates or one large platter. Pour the sauce over the top of the fish, and garnish with chopped parsley. Serve warm with lemon wedges.

Side Dish Suggestions

roasted green beans ✦ new red potatoes ✦ wilted spinach ✦ lemon risotto ✦ sauteed mushrooms ✦ orzo

Pan-Cooked White Fish with Papaya Red Pepper Salsa

SERVES 4

Vibrant colors and fresh flavors are front and center in this lovely pan-cooked white fish recipe. When done right, fruit with fish can be an exceptional flavor combo, especially when using tropical fruit, such as papaya. Papaya doesn't have an intense sweetness but just enough to complement the fish and other savory ingredients in the salsa.

For the best flavor, choose papaya that is yellow or orange and soft to the touch. Cut it in half, then scoop out and discard the seeds. I divide my papaya into four sections lengthwise and then cut those into wedges. I remove the skin with a small knife and then cut the wedges into diced pieces about the size of the tip of my pinkie finger. Try to do the same with the onion and red pepper so that the three main ingredients are uniform in shape.

For this recipe, I've chosen to lightly dust the fish with flour or cornstarch. This gives the fish a very light crust and helps it stay together during the pan-cooking process. If a fillet does break during flipping, it's okay! Just keep cooking. It'll still taste great.

1 tablespoon lime juice

1½ teaspoons honey

½ teaspoon chili powder

1 medium to large red bell pepper, seeded and diced

½ cup diced red onion

1 jalapeño pepper, finely minced

1 handful fresh cilantro, chopped

1 cup peeled, seeded, and diced papaya (about 1 medium papaya)

Salt and freshly ground black pepper

Drizzle of extra-virgin olive oil

1½ pounds flaky white fish (halibut, flounder, rockfish, snapper, haddock, cod, sole, or any white fish that is less than 1-inch in thickness), cut into 4 pieces and removed from refrigerator 15 minutes prior to cooking

½ cup all-purpose flour or cornstarch

2 tablespoons ghee or high-heat oil

2 tablespoons unsalted butter

Lime wedges for garnish

1 Prepare the salsa: In a medium bowl, whisk together the lime juice, honey and chili powder. Then add the bell pepper, red onion, jalapeno, and cilantro. Toss to combine. Gently fold in the papaya and then season to taste with salt and black pepper. Give it just a drizzle of olive oil. Set aside.

CONTINUES ➡

2 Pat the fish fillets with a paper towel to remove any excess moisture. Then, sprinkle with a little salt and black pepper and lightly dust in the flour. Place them on a baking sheet.

3 Heat a large skillet over medium-high heat, add the ghee, then add the butter to the center of the skillet.

4 Once the butter is melted and the oil is hot and slightly smoking, add the fish fillets and let them cook, undisturbed, for 3 to 5 minutes. You should notice the bottom edges becoming golden brown. The fish will be ready to flip when it easily comes off the bottom of the pan. If it feels like it's stuck, just let it sit for 30 seconds longer, adjusting the heat as needed.

5 Flip the fish over and let cook for another 3 to 4 minutes, until flaky and golden brown on the bottom.

6 Transfer to a platter or plates and ladle some salsa over each piece. Garnish with lime wedges and serve immediately.

Side Dish Suggestions

Orzo, couscous, pasta salad, wild rice, or a caprese salad is lovely with this recipe. Extra helpings of this salsa can also make a wonderful appetizer with chips.

Pan-Seared White Fish with Sauce Verte

SERVES 4

Thus far we've covered baking, roasting, steam cooking, and pan cooking. For this recipe, I've chosen a method called pan searing. It's basically pan cooking, only the dish is finished in the oven.

To pan sear, we prepare the fish in the same method as pan cooking, but once we've flipped the fish, we place the oven-safe skillet in a preheated oven to finish cooking. This method works well with thicker cuts of fish, such as a thicker piece of halibut, cod, rockfish, or salmon. It allows for nice browning on the fish, which adds flavor, but finishing it in the oven will help keep a thicker piece of fish tender and moist.

Once the fish is done, it's topped with a fragrant and flavorful sauce verte. The sauce includes a variety of fresh herbs and aromatics, such as garlic, and citrus—flavors that are deliciously complementary to most seafood. Although there are several versions of sauce verte, I prefer this simpler one. It makes a perfect canvas for a delightful pan-cooked fish dish.

1 anchovy, finely minced

1 garlic clove, finely chopped

2 tablespoons finely chopped fresh parsley

1 tablespoon finely chopped fresh basil

1 tablespoon finely chopped fresh chives

1 teaspoon minced capers

Zest of 1 lemon

1½ teaspoons freshly squeezed lemon juice

⅓ cup extra-virgin olive oil

Salt and freshly ground black pepper

1½ pounds fish (halibut, salmon, or thicker pieces of fish work well here), cut into 4 or 5 pieces, removed from the refrigerator at least 15 minutes prior to cooking and patted dry with paper towels

2 to 3 tablespoons high-heat oil or ghee

1 Preheat the oven to 400°F.

2 Mash the anchovy with the garlic in a medium bowl. Then, whisk in the parsley, basil, chives, capers, lemon zest and juice, and olive oil. Season to taste with salt and pepper.

3 Brush the fish with a little high-heat oil and season with salt and pepper.

CONTINUES ➡

4 Heat 2 tablespoons of the ghee in a large oven-safe skillet over medium-high heat. Be sure the ghee coats the surface of the skillet.

5 When the ghee is hot and slightly smoking, add the fish, flesh side down. Let the fish cook for 3 to 4 minutes, until the bottom edges become golden brown. The fish will be ready to flip when it easily comes off the bottom of the pan. If it feels like it's stuck, just let it sit for 30 seconds longer.

6 Flip the fish, remove from the heat, and transfer the skillet to the oven. Let the fish finish cooking in the oven for 4 to 5 minutes, or longer depending on its thickness. To check for doneness, take a fork and pierce the thickest part of the fillet. If it flakes easily or if it looks opaque, your fish is done. Fish will cook a bit longer once it is removed from the oven.

7 Remove the skillet from the oven and let the fish rest for 1 to 2 minutes. Place the fish fillets on a platter or individual plates and ladle with a little of the sauce verte. Serve immediately.

Side Dish Suggestions

roasted new or fingerling potatoes ✦ mashed potatoes ✦ roasted or steamed haricots verts ✦ sautéed greens, such as spinach or Swiss chard

Grilled Salmon Caesar Salad with Parmesan Garlic Bread Crumbs

SERVES 4

Perhaps a testimony to its universally satisfying flavors, this was probably one of the most frequently used recipes in my kitchen while my girls were growing up. It was absolutely one of their favorites, especially during the summer months when grilling outdoors was a must.

It's simple to make, but a guaranteed crowd-pleaser—easy enough for a weeknight but certainly delicious enough to serve dinner guests for a casual weekend gathering. I fancied up the recipe a bit by adding Parmesan garlic bread crumbs rather than croutons. Because in my house, every recipe needs a topping.

If grilling salmon isn't an option for you, pan searing and finishing in the oven, or pan cooking the salmon will work just as well. For instruction on pan searing and pan cooking, refer to the "Seafood 101" section (page 14). If you're short on time, feel free to use your favorite bottle of prepared Caesar dressing, but if you'd like to use homemade, I've included the recipe.

CAESAR DRESSING

2 garlic cloves

6 anchovy fillets

1 teaspoon Worcestershire sauce

1 teaspoon Dijon mustard

2 tablespoons freshly squeezed lemon juice

½ teaspoon freshly ground black pepper

2 large egg yolks, at room temperature

½ cup extra-virgin olive oil

Salt

PARMESAN GARLIC BREAD CRUMBS

1 tablespoon extra-virgin olive oil

¼ cup bread crumbs

1 garlic clove, minced

¼ cup grated Parmesan

FISH

1½ pounds salmon (skin on), paper towel dried, cut into 4 pieces and removed from refrigerator at least 15 minutes prior to cooking

1 to 2 tablespoons high-heat oil

Salt and freshly ground black pepper

1 large head romaine lettuce, washed, dried, and chopped

Lemon wedges for garnish

CONTINUES ➡

1. Make the dressing: Combine the garlic, anchovies, Worcestershire, Dijon, lemon juice, pepper, egg yolks, and olive oil in a food processor or blender. Blend until smooth and creamy. Add water to thin, if desired. Add salt to taste, if desired.
2. Make the bread crumbs: Heat the olive oil in a medium sauté pan over medium heat. Add the bread crumbs and slowly let them become golden.
3. Then, stir in the garlic and let the bread crumbs toast just a bit longer, about 30 seconds. Don't let the garlic get too browned or it will be bitter.
4. Remove the pan from the heat and then pour the bread crumbs into a bowl. When the bread crumbs cool, stir in grated Parmesan and set aside.
5. Next, prepare the fish: Preheat a grill to 425°F. Be sure your grill grates are as clean as possible. This will help prevent sticking.
6. Brush each salmon fillet with high-heat oil on all sides and season with a sprinkle of salt and pepper.
7. Place the salmon pieces, flesh side down, diagonally on the grill, this will also help the fish flip easier. Close the lid and let salmon cook for 5 to 7 minutes, checking on the fish every few minutes.
8. Then, using your tongs, try to ease the fish up off the grill grates. If they don't budge, wait 30 seconds longer, or as needed. Once the fish come up off the grill easily, flip the fish to be skin side down and cook for another 3 to 4 minutes, until the fish are done. Remember, most fish cook through in about 10 minutes for every inch of thickness. The fish should be opaque and flake with a fork.
9. Once the fish are done, transfer to a platter. The fish will usually slide right off the skin, leaving the skin on the grill. However, if the skin comes off the grate with the fish, you can either leave it on, or remove it from the fish.
10. Place the chopped lettuce in a large bowl and toss with a little of the dressing. Divide the dressed lettuce among four plates and top with a tablespoon or more of the bread crumbs. Then, place a fillet of grilled salmon over each salad. Garnish with lemon wedges and serve with the remaining dressing and bread crumbs.

Pan-Cooked Fish with Summer Blackberry Orange Relish

SERVES 3

When I think of summer berries, my mind typically turns to all the pies, tarts, and baked goods I'm going to make. But, did you know that berries are one of the most complementary ingredients to pair with fish?

Most berries have a slightly sweet, sometimes tart, tangy flavor that is mingled with an unmistakable berry fragrance. This combination of flavor and fragrance is a delicious balance to the buttery flakiness of fish. Especially when the fish is mild flavored, such as rockfish, haddock, cod, sole, flounder, halibut, and more. (For additional examples of mild-flavored white fish, refer to the Seafood Chart starting on page 22.)

1 pound mild-flavored thin white fish fillets, cut into 3 to 4 pieces, removed from the refrigerator at least 15 minutes prior to cooking

Salt and freshly ground black pepper

1 tablespoon extra-virgin olive oil

2 tablespoons finely chopped shallot

2 tablespoons honey

1 teaspoon chopped fresh thyme, plus more for garnish

Zest of 1 medium to large orange

8 ounces lightly chopped fresh blackberries

2 tablespoons high-heat oil or ghee

1 tablespoon unsalted butter

1. Pat the fish dry with paper towels and season with salt and pepper. Set aside.
2. Heat the olive oil in a medium saucepan over medium-low heat.
3. Stir in the shallot and cook just until tender and translucent.
4. Mix in the honey, thyme, and orange zest. Remove the pan from the heat and transfer the shallot mixture to a medium bowl.
5. Fold in the blackberries and season to taste with salt and pepper. Set aside while you cook the fish.
6. Heat the high-heat oil and butter in a large skillet over medium-high heat.
7. Stir the butter with the oil, and when mixture is hot, add the fish, flesh side down.
8. Let cook, undisturbed, for 3 to 5 minutes. You should notice the bottom edges becoming golden brown. The fish will be ready to flip when it easily comes off the surface of the pan. If it feels like it's stuck, just let it sit for 30 seconds longer.

9 Flip the fish and let it finish cooking for another 3 to 5 minutes, depending on thickness. The fish is done when it easily flakes with a fork or is opaque. (Alternatively, the pan-searing method can be used here; for more information about that method, see the "Seafood 101" section, page 14, and the recipe for Pan-Seared White Fish with Sauce Verte, page 99.)

10 Once the fish is done, transfer to plates or a platter. Top with the berry relish and garnish with chopped thyme. Serve immediately.

Side Dish Suggestions

farro, pearled barley, pearled couscous, wild rice, orzo, or quinoa ✦ a mixed green salad with buttermilk dressing

Easy Whipped Pimiento Sauce with Pan-Cooked Fish

SERVES 4

I adapted this dish from one of my grandmother's recipes. The sauce was basically whipped cream and pimientos, but I decided to elevate it a bit by adding cream cheese, along with garlic and green onion to complement the pimientos. It's an easy sauce to make for any grilled, pan-cooked, or roasted fish. For this recipe, I've chosen to pan cook the fish, as that is typically my go-to cooking method for fish.

The sauce is also a lovely base for grilled shrimp over crostini or paired with grilled chicken and roasted potatoes. One can never have enough sauce recipes!

4 ounces cream cheese, at room temperature

4 ounces heavy cream

1 to 2 garlic cloves, minced

One 4-ounce jar diced pimientos, strained

3 tablespoons sliced green onion

1 teaspoon freshly squeezed lemon juice

Salt and freshly ground black pepper

Oil for pan cooking

1½ pounds fish (such as cod, rockfish, haddock, halibut, snapper, petrale sole, or flounder), cut into 4 to 6 pieces, patted dry with a paper towel, removed from the fridge for at least 15 minutes before cooking

Cornstarch or all-purpose flour for dusting

1. Whip the cream cheese in a stand mixer fitted with the whisk attachment or in a bowl with a handheld mixer until soft, and then add the heavy cream. Continue to whip until light and fluffy.
2. Fold in the garlic, pimientos, green onion, and lemon juice. Season to taste with salt and pepper.
3. Place a large skillet over medium-high heat. Add enough oil to coat the skillet, about 2 tablespoons.
4. Season the fish with salt and pepper, then lightly dust it with cornstarch. Shake the excess off the fish.

5 When the oil is hot but not smoking, add the fish (flesh side down if it has skin on it) to the skillet. If the skillet is too hot, lower the heat.

6 Let the fish brown on the bottom, allowing it to cook at least two-thirds of the way through, 5 to 6 minutes depending on the thickness of the fish. You'll see it become slightly opaque on the sides. Remember the rule of thumb: Fish cook through in about 10 minutes for every inch of thickness.

7 With a fish spatula, gently lift the fish off the pan and flip to the other side. Let cook until golden on the bottom and the fish begins to flake or separate a bit on the top. Transfer to plates or platter and serve with a dollop of the pimiento sauce.

Side Dish Suggestion

fresh salad greens and citrus vinaigrette ✦ shaved root vegetable salad ✦ lightly braised garlicky greens, spinach, or Swiss chard ✦ roasted or steamed broccoli, cauliflower, zucchini, or yellow squash ✦ roasted new potatoes ✦ white rice

Easy Curry Poached Fish with Mango Ginger Pearled Couscous

SERVES 4

Poaching is one of the easiest ways to prepare fish. It's a mostly fuss-free method that produces a flavorful and tender result. Poaching liquid can range from a simple broth or white wine to butter, olive oil, or as in this recipe, coconut milk.

Here, I've included curry powder as the anchor flavor, but I've also added garlic and lime juice, and combined the coconut milk with fish broth for added umami. This combination pairs deliciously with the mango ginger couscous for one tasty meal.

If I have time, once I remove my fish from the poaching liquid, I'll bring it to a boil and simmer it until reduced by half. I taste for seasoning and then serve it alongside the fish and couscous.

COUSCOUS

2 cups cooked pearled couscous, prepared according to package directions

1 to 2 ripe mangoes, peeled and diced

⅓ cup sliced green onion

1 teaspoon grated fresh ginger

Salt and freshly ground black pepper

FISH

1 tablespoon olive or coconut oil

1 garlic clove, smashed and lightly chopped

1 tablespoon curry powder

One 14-ounce can full-fat coconut milk (do not use light)

Juice of 1 lime

1½ cups warm water plus 1½ teaspoons Better Than Bouillon Fish Base (see Note), OR 1½ cups seafood stock

¼ teaspoon salt

¼ teaspoon freshly ground black pepper

1½ pounds firm white fish (such as rockfish, cod, halibut, Arctic char, turbot, tuna, or striped bass), cut into 2 or 4 pieces

Additional diced mango and sliced green onions for garnish (optional)

CONTINUES ➡

1 Make the couscous: Gently combine the couscous, diced mango, green onion, and ginger in a large bowl, and then season to taste with salt and pepper. Set aside.

2 Prepare the fish: Heat the oil in a large saucepan over medium heat. When the oil is hot, stir in the garlic and curry powder and sauté for about 30 seconds to 1 minute.

3 Stir in the coconut milk, lime juice, prepared fish bouillon, salt, and pepper. Bring to a boil and then lower the heat to a simmer. Simmer for about 5 minutes.

4 Add the fish to the poaching liquid. Over low heat, allow the fish to poach for 7 to 10 minutes, depending on the thickness of the fish. You don't want to boil your fish, just cook at a very gentle simmer.

5 Once the fish is done, remove it from the poaching liquid and serve it over the couscous. Garnish with additional mango and sliced green onions, if desired.

Note

My go-to fish stock or seafood stock is the Better Than Bouillon brand Fish Base and Lobster Base, respectively. For more information about these products and where to purchase, refer to the Resources (page 315).

Side Dish Suggestions

steamed or roasted vegetables, such as eggplant, zucchini, or cauliflower

Simple Brazilian Fish Stew

(MOQUECA)

SERVES 4

I've added this stew to this chapter because everyone should have an easy fish stew recipe in their back pocket. There are days when a stew just hits the dinner spot, and seafood is one of the quickest cooking ingredients for this purpose.

The ingredient list looks a bit longer than some of the other recipes here, but I assure you it's not terribly time consuming and you'll love the result!

I recommend using your favorite white fish for this stew, but if you love shrimp, this is also another delicious addition. I use red palm oil as is traditional in a moqueca. However, if you don't have it on hand or you can't find it, the smoked paprika and tomato paste will give the stew its traditional pinkish color.

2 tablespoons red palm oil, coconut oil, ghee, or vegetable oil

1 medium onion (red, yellow, or white), small diced (about 1 cup)

1 red bell pepper, seeded and small diced

3 garlic cloves, minced

One 15-ounce can full-fat coconut milk

2 cups water plus 1 teaspoon each Better Than Bouillon Fish Base and Lobster Base (see Note), OR 2 cups seafood stock

1½ teaspoons smoked paprika

1 tablespoon tomato paste

Pinch of red pepper flakes or hot sauce (optional)

1 pound white fish, checked for bones, skinned, and cut into 1-inch cubes or bite-size pieces

⅓ cup thinly sliced green onion

½ cup chopped fresh cilantro

Squeeze of lime juice

Salt and freshly ground black pepper

Cooked jasmine or basmati rice or warm crusty bread for serving

1 Place a large soup pot over medium heat and add the oil.

2 When the oil is hot, stir in the onion and bell pepper and cook until soft and the onion is translucent, about 5 minutes.

3 Then, stir in the garlic and cook for 1 minute longer.

CONTINUES ➡

4 Add the coconut milk, prepared fish and lobster bouillon, paprika, tomato paste, and red pepper flakes (if using).

5 Bring to a boil, then lower the heat to low and simmer, uncovered, for about 10 minutes.

6 Gently stir in the fish and let the stew come back to a slow simmer. Cook for about 5 minutes, or until the fish is opaque and flaky. Do not boil the broth.

7 Remove the stew from the heat and stir in the green onion, cilantro, and squeeze of lime juice. Season to taste with salt and black pepper.

8 Serve over jasmine or basmati rice. Or you can serve the stew with warm crusty bread for dunking.

Note

My go-to fish stock or seafood stock is the Better Than Bouillon Fish Base and Lobster Base, respectively. For more information about these products and where to purchase, refer to the Resources (page 315).

Basque-Style Tuna and Potato Stew

(MARMITAKO)

SERVES 3 OR 4

This lovely yet hearty Basque-style stew is simple, flavorful, and so perfect for a cool fall, winter, or spring day.

Using a high-quality fish stock is key here. The more flavorful the broth, the more flavorful the stew. In addition to using a high-quality fish stock, if you have time, roasting the bell pepper will also give the stew additional flavor. If time is of the essence, use a few jarred roasted peppers.

> FIND YOUR FISH: I've kept this recipe traditional, using raw tuna that I source sustainably off the Pacific Coast. Be sure to check www.seafoodwatch.org to find out whether tuna found in your area is sustainably sourced. If not, I've listed multiple resources for purchasing sustainable seafood on page 14. The good news is that this stew can also be prepared with other types of firm-textured fish, such as halibut, grouper, haddock, snapper, or cod. Just be sure to pull the pin bones before cooking.

- **2 tablespoons extra-virgin olive oil or your favorite oil**
- **1 large yellow or white onion, chopped**
- **1 large orange or red bell pepper (roasted first, if possible), chopped**
- **3 garlic cloves, finely diced**
- **1 tablespoon chopped fresh parsley**
- **1½ teaspoons smoked paprika**
- **½ cup white wine**
- **3 cups water plus 3 teaspoons Better Than Bouillon Fish Base (see Note), OR 3 cups high-quality or Homemade Seafood Stock (page 224), plus more as needed**
- **8 ounces jarred or canned tomatoes, lightly crushed with a fork**
- **Pinch of crushed red pepper flakes (optional, but adds some nice flavor)**
- **1 pound new potatoes, halved or cut into bite-size pieces (no need to peel)**
- **1½ pounds raw tuna, albacore, or skipjack, cut into 1- to 2-inch cubes**
- **⅓ cup sliced green onion**
- **Squeeze of lemon juice (about 1 tablespoon)**
- **Drizzle of good extra-virgin olive oil for serving**
- **Warm, crusty bread for serving**

CONTINUES ➡

1. Heat the oil in a soup pot or Dutch oven over medium heat and add the onion and bell pepper.
2. Cook the vegetables over medium or medium-low heat until they are somewhat caramelized, about 10 minutes. Add another drizzle of oil, if needed.
3. Stir in the garlic, parsley, and smoked paprika. Cook for 1 minute longer.
4. Mix in the white wine and let the mixture reduce by half.
5. Stir in the prepared fish broth, tomatoes, red pepper flakes (if using), and potatoes.
6. Bring to a simmer and cook until the potatoes are soft, about 15 minutes.
7. Once the potatoes are soft, lower the heat to low and add the tuna.
8. Bring the stew back to a very gentle simmer and then turn off the heat. You want to gently cook the tuna. Tuna is lean and can become dry if overcooked.
9. Stir in the sliced green onion, squeeze of lemon juice and season to taste with salt and black pepper.
10. Serve with a drizzle of good olive oil and warm, crusty bread for soaking up the broth.

Note

My go-to fish stock is the Better Than Bouillon brand Fish Base. For more information about this product and where to purchase, refer to the Resources (page 315).

Basic Pan-Cooked Sea Scallops with Miso Ginger Butter

SERVES 2 OR 3

Pan-cooked scallops are quick, delicious, and pair well with all sorts of ingredients. Often on weeknights, I'll pan cook scallops and serve them over a salad of fresh baby greens with a dash of ponzu and olive oil, seasoned rice wine vinegar, or a ginger sesame dressing. And sometimes I serve them with one of the many compound butters that I have stashed in my freezer.

Compound butter is basically soft butter combined with assorted herbs, spices, and other fresh ingredients to make a quick and delicious "sauce" or topping for seafood, meat, poultry, and vegetables. For this recipe, I've included a miso ginger butter. It's easy to whip up and it can be stored in the freezer for up to three months. It's also good over grilled fish.

If miso or ginger aren't your favorite flavors, you can combine ½ cup of room-temperature unsalted butter with some minced garlic, lemon zest, and a tablespoon of chopped fresh herbs.

It's important to purchase "dry-packed" scallops, which have been shipped packed on ice. Some sea and bay scallops are packed in a solution containing phosphate, which keeps the scallops white and fresher longer. But when they are "wet packed" in this solution, they soak up additional water and will resist forming that beautiful crust, which will result in loss of flavor and texture.

I think scallops taste best when cooked in ghee. Ghee is a type of clarified butter, and it acts much like oil because it has no milk solids. It's also shelf stable. Ghee is now widely available in most markets, but you can also make it at home. I've included a recipe here.

MISO GINGER BUTTER

¼ cup white miso paste

4 tablespoons (½ stick) unsalted butter, at room temperature

1 teaspoon grated fresh ginger

1 small clove garlic, minced

SCALLOPS

1 pound dry-packed sea scallops, patted dry, and their "foot" (adductor muscle) removed (it's easily pulled off without a knife; for more information on purchasing and prepping scallops, refer to the "Seafood 101" section, page 14)

Salt and freshly ground pepper

3 tablespoons ghee, or as needed

1 tablespoon chopped fresh chives for garnish

CONTINUES ➡

1 Make the miso ginger butter: Whisk together the butter, miso paste, ginger, and garlic in a small bowl. To store, place the miso butter on a piece of plastic wrap or waxed paper and form into a small log. Roll it up in its wrapper and store in the freezer. Slice small thin coins to top scallops or grilled fish.

2 Make the scallops: Season the scallops with salt and pepper.

3 Heat the ghee in a large skillet over high heat.

4 When the ghee is hot and smoking, place the scallops in the pan, one at a time, making sure they don't touch. Don't overcrowd the pan or the scallops won't brown properly. You may need to cook the scallops in two batches. Because we are using ghee, it won't burn.

5 Cook the scallops for 1 to 2 minutes, until you see a golden-brown crust forming on the bottom.

6 Flip the scallops (tongs work best here) and let them cook for another 1 to 1½ minutes. The top and the bottom should be opaque and golden brown. Every stovetop is different, so adjust the heat and cook time as needed.

7 Transfer to a plate or platter and dollop each scallop with a little miso ginger butter and garnish with chopped chives. Serve immediately.

Side Dish Suggestions

You could serve this dish as an appetizer, but for a complete meal, serve with a salad of baby greens tossed with ponzu and olive oil. Or serve over rice or ramen noodles with a dash of seasoned rice wine vinegar and steamed broccolini.

How to make ghee at home: Place 1 pound (4 sticks) of unsalted butter in a small saucepan over low heat. Leave it over the heat for about 10 minutes. Don't stir. It will go through several stages. A froth will form and then disappear, and when you see golden bits on the surface of the pan, it will be ready to strain.

Remove it from the heat and then, using a piece of cheesecloth or a paper towel, line a mesh colander and strain the butter into a bowl. When the butter is cool enough, transfer to a glass jar with a lid. Once all the milk solids are gone, the ghee is now shelf stable and can live in a cabinet with your oils. The warmer it is, the more liquid the ghee will be. The colder it is, the ghee will solidify. This is completely normal.

Note

You can also use this recipe as a guide for pan-cooked scallops in other recipes in this book, using only steps 2 through 6.

Salmon Fried Rice

SERVES 3 TO 4

This is another quick-cooking dish, so it's important to have all your ingredients prepped and ready (everything cubed, sliced, minced, and measured) before you start. This is what we call mise en place and it allows you to be organized and timely in your approach to cooking.

When rice is chilled, the starch firms and the rice dries out. When reheated in oil, it becomes tender again, but not mushy. However, if you want to make this at the last minute, do not fret! You can still use warm cooked rice, but the fried rice dish texture will be a bit denser and not as fluffy as the rice had it been cold.

I recommend using a wok for this recipe; however, a large sauté pan or skillet will also work. Don't be afraid of the oil. I've included a total of 4 tablespoons in the recipe as this is a "fried" rice dish. Feel free to adjust the measurements, using more or less as needed. And although I kept the ingredient list to a minimum, feel free to add peas, carrots, and/or corn along with the green onions, if desired. The pickled ginger and cilantro will bring all the flavors together and really complement the richness of the salmon.

1 pound salmon, cut into 1-inch bite-size cubes, removed from refrigerator 15 minutes prior to cooking

Salt and freshly ground black pepper

4 tablespoons high-heat oil

2 large eggs, whisked

½ cup thinly sliced green onion

1 garlic clove, minced

2 cups cold cooked rice

Toasted sesame seeds for garnish

Handful of chopped fresh cilantro for garnish

Pickled ginger for serving

Good-quality tamari or soy sauce for serving

1 Season the salmon with salt and pepper.

2 Heat 1 tablespoon of the high-heat oil in a wok or deep sauté pan over medium-high heat.

3 When the oil is hot, add the cubed salmon and let it brown on opposite sides until opaque or flaky, 4 to 5 minutes. Don't overcrowd the pan. You may need to do this in two batches.

4 When the salmon is done, transfer to a plate. Remove the pan from the heat and wipe it out with a paper towel, removing any burnt bits.

5 Place the pan back over medium-high heat and add 2 tablespoons of the remaining oil.

6 When the oil is hot, stir in the eggs. When the eggs are done, about 1 minute, transfer to a plate.

7 Keeping the pan over medium or medium-high heat, add the green onion and garlic to the pan and cook for 30 seconds to 1 minute. Be careful not to burn the garlic.

8 Add the last tablespoon of oil and then add the cold rice, stirring constantly to combine the green onion and garlic with the rice.

9 When the rice is hot, add the eggs back to the pan and break them up with a spatula to combine with the rice.

10 Remove the pan from the heat and gently fold in the salmon.

11 Transfer to a platter or plates and garnish with toasted sesame seeds and chopped cilantro.

12 Serve with pickled ginger and good-quality tamari or soy sauce.

Pan-Cooked Shrimp with Lemon, Garlic, and Fresh Herbs

SERVES 2 TO 4

Pan-cooked shrimp is one of the easiest shellfish to prepare. Feel free to use the recipe as a guide to create your own pan-cooked shrimp with your favorite signature flavors.

Most often I include garlic because garlic and shrimp were made for each other. But shallot or sweet onion also works well, and on occasion, I use sliced green onion and fresh grated ginger just for fun.

The key to preparing succulent and tender shrimp is to not overcook them. Shrimp need only 1 to 2 minutes of cook time when prepared in a skillet or sauté pan. Because shrimp cook so quickly, I always opt for real butter. And because I use butter, I typically keep my gas burner at medium heat. If using electric or induction heat, you may need to adjust the heat between medium and medium-high. After preparing shrimp with this method several times, you'll get the hang of it and become a pro!

1 pound shrimp (21/30 or 16/20 count; see Notes) peeled and deveined, tails on or off, whatever you prefer (for more information on prepping and deveining shrimp, refer to the "Seafood 101" section, page 14)

1 tablespoon oil

Salt and freshly ground black pepper

4 tablespoons (½ stick) unsalted butter, plus 2 tablespoons if searing in 2 batches

Squeeze of lemon juice

3 garlic cloves, minced

Pinch of crushed red pepper flakes (optional)

1 tablespoon assorted chopped fresh herbs, such as parsley, thyme, and chives

1. Place the shrimp in a large bowl and toss with the oil and a pinch each of salt and black pepper. Let sit for 5 to 10 minutes.
2. Place a large skillet or sauté pan over medium-high heat and add 2 tablespoons of the butter.
3. Once the butter is melted, add the shrimp in a single layer. Don't overcrowd your pan, or the shrimp will steam rather than sear. You may need to cook your shrimp in batches.
4. If you end up pan-cooking shrimp in two batches, the butter may burn slightly, and you may need to replace the butter before searing the second batch. To do this, remove

the burned or browned butter, wipe the pan with a paper towel and add the new butter and your second batch of shrimp.

5 Let the shrimp cook for 1 to 2 minutes per side, adjusting the heat as needed. The shrimp will be done when they have turned opaque and are white and orange.

6 Remove the pan from the heat and then transfer the shrimp to a platter.

7 Place the pan back over low heat and stir in the lemon juice and the remaining 2 tablespoons of butter.

8 Once the butter is melted, add the garlic and red pepper flakes, if using, and cook for about 1 minute. Then, remove the pan from the heat.

9 Add the chopped herbs to the pan.

10 Add the shrimp back to the pan and let them bathe in the warm garlic and herb butter.

Notes

I prefer large or jumbo shrimp for this recipe. Large shrimp are typically 21/30 count and jumbo are 16/20 count, meaning that in 1 pound of shrimp, you will get 21 to 30 large shrimp or 16 to 20 jumbo shrimp.

You can also use this recipe as a guide for pan-cooked shrimp in other recipes in this book. Omit the garlic and herbs.

Serving Suggestions

in a large bowl with fresh bread ✦ over pasta with fresh chopped summer tomatoes or cherry tomatoes and fresh basil ✦ with a dollop of ricotta on crostini

Classic White Wine–Steamed Clams with Garlic and Herbs

SERVES 2 TO 4

There are times I crave a big bowl of steamers with loads of crusty fresh bread to dip in the broth. For me, this is pure food joy. And making this recipe couldn't be simpler!

It's important to choose fresh clams, never frozen clams, for this dish. Be sure to rinse and scrub the clams before cooking, and if the clams feel extra sandy, place them in a bowl of cool water with a few tablespoons of salt to soak for about an hour. This will help the clams release the sand and grit. Be sure to give them another rinse before cooking.

This recipe will serve two as an entrée along with a salad, pasta, and or vegetables. But it also makes a delicious appetizer for four.

2 pounds fresh clams (littlenecks, cherrystone, quahog, or steamers)
4 tablespoons (½ stick) unsalted butter
3 garlic cloves, minced
1 tablespoon chopped fresh herbs, such as parsley and chives
2 thyme sprigs
Pinch of crushed red pepper flakes
1 cup dry white wine
½ cup clam broth or clam juice
Salt and freshly ground black pepper
2 tablespoons melted butter
Squeeze of lemon juice
Fresh warm, crusty bread for dipping

1 Place the clams in a colander and rinse thoroughly in cold water to make sure there is no extra sand or grit.

2 Place the butter in a medium to large pot over medium heat and let it melt.

3 When the butter has melted, stir in the garlic, herbs, and red pepper flakes. Cook for about 1 minute.

4 Then, add the wine, clam broth, and a pinch each of salt and pepper and bring to a simmer.

5 Stir in the clams and then cover with a lid. Cook over medium heat for 5 to 7 minutes, shaking the pot a bit so the clams have room to open.

6 Remove the lid and give the clams a stir. If some of the clams haven't opened, place the lid back on for 1 minute longer. Sometimes, I remove the pan from the heat and let them sit for 1 minute. The hot liquid and steam will help the remaining clams to open.

7 At this point, check for clams that have not opened and discard them.

8 Stir in the melted butter and lemon juice.

9 Pour the clams, along with the broth into a large bowl and serve immediately with warm, crusty bread.

Note

You can also use this recipe as a basic guide for steamed clams that are used in other recipes in this book. Follow the steps but omit the garlic and herbs.

CHAPTER TWO

Show Off Those Skills!

This chapter includes flavorful recipes that utilize techniques from the previous chapter, but also offers expanded ingredient lists, and recipes that will require a little more active prep time. These are dishes that explore more adventurous flavor profiles or new cuts of fish, offer variations of traditional recipes, and help you practice all the skills you've mastered. The goal is to build continued confidence in cooking seafood.

If you've cooked your way through the last chapter, you've become familiar with a variety of cooking techniques and seafood. Unlike that chapter, however, the recipes in this one are arranged according to *type of seafood*. This makes it easy to browse them based on what you have on hand, what seafood you might be craving, or what is in season in your local fish market or community-supported fishery.

We begin with all things shellfish, continue on to salmon, then to ahi tuna, swordfish, and anchovies. The last half of this chapter's recipes are prepared with white fish, the last recipe being a decadent butter-poached halibut.

As always, if you need additional instructions or information, refer to the "Seafood 101" section (page 14).

Classic Crab Cakes with Tangy Dipping Sauce

MAKES ABOUT TWELVE 3-INCH PATTIES

The key to this recipe is purchasing fresh lump crabmeat. Because crab is seasonal, I usually plan to make these crab cakes as soon as the season begins. This is also when lump crabmeat is least expensive.

You can also purchase whole crabs and crack them for the meat. This works just as well, and sometimes we make an evening of it along with a crisp white wine for sipping while we work. I live on the Pacific Coast, so one medium Dungeness crab can produce 5 to 6 ounces of meat. I usually purchase four or five crabs. This will allow us to snack on some of the crabmeat while cracking the crabs, and then we save the rest for the crab cakes.

These crab cakes are easy to make, but when frying, be sure to watch the heat. I give directions to begin over medium heat; however, if the oil gets too hot and starts to over-brown the crab cakes, lower the heat to medium-low. I find that when I make these crab cakes, I adjust the heat often.

FIND YOUR FISH: Several types of edible crab are found in the United States; the most common are Dungeness, snow, blue, stone, and king crab. They are all delicious and work well in this recipe.

CRAB CAKES

⅓ cup mayonnaise

2 teaspoons seafood seasoning, such as Old Bay, or another local brand that you love

1 heaping teaspoon lemon zest

1 teaspoon freshly squeezed lemon juice

2 teaspoons Dijon mustard

1½ tablespoons chopped fresh flat-leaf parsley

⅓ cup thinly sliced green onion

Salt and freshly ground black pepper, if needed

1 large egg, whisked

1 pound fresh crabmeat, picked through for shells and squeezed with a cheesecloth or paper towels to eliminate extra moisture

¼ cup panko bread crumbs, plus 1 cup for rolling

High-heat oil for frying

DIPPING SAUCE

½ cup mayonnaise

2 teaspoons chopped fresh flat-leaf parsley

1 teaspoon Worcestershire sauce

2 teaspoons chili sauce

2 tablespoons freshly squeezed lemon juice

1 garlic clove, minced

1. Prepare the crab cakes: Whisk together the mayonnaise, seafood seasoning, lemon zest and juice, Dijon, parsley, and green onion in a large bowl. Season to taste with salt and pepper.
2. Stir in the whisked egg, then fold in the crabmeat and ¼ cup of panko bread crumbs.
3. Place the remaining cup of panko bread crumbs in a plate or bowl.
4. Form the crab mixture into twelve 3-inch patties, then coat in the reserved panko bread crumbs and place on a parchment-lined baking sheet. Refrigerate for 30 minutes.
5. While the crab cakes are in the refrigerator, make the dipping sauce: Whisk together the mayonnaise, parsley, Worcestershire, chili sauce, lemon juice, and garlic in a small bowl. Season to taste with salt and pepper. Set aside.
6. Heat a large skillet over medium heat and add about ¼ inch of high-heat oil. When the oil is hot and shimmering, but not smoking, add the crab cakes. Don't overcrowd the pan or it'll be hard to flip the cakes. I typically pan cook the crab cakes in two batches, six per batch.
7. Cook the crab cakes until golden brown on the bottom, adjusting the heat as needed. Sometimes, I turn my heat to medium-low to finish the first side so that the crab cakes don't brown too quickly.
8. Then, gently flip to the other side. Continue to cook until the bottom is golden brown, again adjusting the heat as needed. (Tip: After the first batch, if a lot of the bread crumbs escaped and have started to burn in the skillet, strain the oil, gently wipe out the skillet with a paper towel, and add back the oil [plus more, if needed] and begin step 6 again for the second batch.)
9. Transfer the crab cakes to a paper towel–lined plate or cooling rack. Serve warm with dipping sauce.

Imperial-Style Crab Dip

SERVES 6 TO 8

I've tasted many versions of this traditional East Coast crab dip. The recipe varies from chef to home cook, and I admit, all versions I've sampled are delicious.

Some versions include sautéed onion or shallot; others, roasted, diced red pepper. I favor pimientos paired with crab and shrimp, so I've included them in this recipe. With crab and shrimp, I also prefer green onion versus diced yellow onion or shallot. This dip is truly a matter of taste, so have fun and play around with it and create your favorite version.

I make this recipe in a sourdough bread bowl and serve it with bread cubes. But it's also delicious baked in a baking dish.

This is another recipe when fresh crabmeat is best. For more information about the types of crabmeat and where to source it, refer to page 128.

1 round sourdough bread (optional)

½ cup mayonnaise

One 4-ounce jar pimientos, drained

1 tablespoon chopped fresh parsley

¼ cup finely sliced green onion

Zest and juice of 1 lemon

1 teaspoon Worcestershire sauce

1 teaspoon Dijon mustard

1 teaspoon Old Bay seasoning or your favorite seafood seasoning

Splash of good-quality sherry, about 1 or 2 teaspoons (optional, but it adds a lovely flavor)

Dash of hot sauce (optional)

Salt and freshly ground black pepper

1 pound fresh lump, jumbo lump, or backfin crabmeat

1 large egg, whisked

½ cup shredded white Cheddar

ALTERNATIVE TOPPING

½ cup crushed saltines or buttery crackers, such as Ritz, plus more uncrushed for serving

3 tablespoons melted unsalted butter

1 Preheat the oven to 375°F.

2 If using the bread bowl, cut a round thin slice off the top of the bread and hollow out the rest, leaving about ½ inch of bread on the bottom and sides of the bread bowl.

3 Cut the discarded bread into cubes and use it to serve with the dip.

4 Combine the mayonnaise, pimientos, parsley, green onion, lemon zest and juice, Worcestershire, Dijon, seafood seasoning, sherry (if using), and hot sauce (if using). Taste for salt and pepper.

5 Gently fold in the crabmeat (you don't want to break it up too much) and whisked egg until nicely combined.

6 Pour the crab mixture into the bread bowl or a 1- to 1½ quart baking dish. Sprinkle the shredded Cheddar over the top, or use the alternative cracker topping. To make the alternative topping, combine the cracker crumbs and melted butter in a small bowl and stir until evenly mixed.

7 Bake for 15 to 20 minutes, until the crab is heated through and the cheese is melted and bubbly, or the crushed crackers are golden brown and toasted.

8 Remove from the oven and serve with cubed bread or your favorite crackers.

Crab Louis–Style Salad

SERVES 4 AS A FIRST COURSE AND 2 AS AN ENTRÉE

I have been a fan of this salad most of my adult life. For me, there is nothing more indulgent than sweet, flavorful jumbo lump crabmeat sitting on this gorgeous salad and drizzled with a slightly spicy rémoulade-style dressing.

Because lump or jumbo lump crabmeat can have a hefty price tag, I typically reserve this recipe for a special date night in, or as a starter salad for a small dinner party.

Fresh crabmeat is best for this salad. However, buying whole crab and cracking it at home is a bit more economical. For additional information about crabmeat, refer to page 128.

FIND YOUR FISH: This salad is best with crabmeat, but if crab is not in season or difficult to find, try using bay shrimp or grilled shrimp.

DRESSING

- **¼ cup chili sauce**
- **1 cup mayonnaise**
- **2 tablespoons sweet pickle relish**
- **1 garlic clove, finely minced**
- **1 tablespoon chopped capers**
- **1 teaspoon Worcestershire sauce**
- **1 tablespoon chopped fresh chives**
- **1 teaspoon freshly squeezed lemon juice**
- **Salt and freshly ground black pepper**

SALAD

- **1 head butter lettuce, cleaned, rinsed, and quartered**
- **2 small vine-ripened or summer tomatoes, quartered, or 1 cup cherry tomatoes, halved**
- **2 or 3 hard-boiled eggs, quartered or sliced**
- **12 to 16 ounces fresh lump or jumbo lump crabmeat**
- **½ cup quartered or sliced pitted black olives**
- **1 cucumber, peeled and sliced**
- **1 tablespoon chopped fresh chives**
- **Coarse or blended sea salt to finish**
- **Lemon wedges or slices for serving**

1 Make the dressing: Combine all the dressing ingredients in a medium bowl, seasoning to taste with salt and pepper. Keep in the refrigerator in a covered container for up to 5 days.

2 To assemble the salad, divide the lettuce among four or two plates, placing the lettuce on one side of each plate.

3 Then, stack tomatoes, cucumber, and hard-boiled egg on the other side of each plate.

4 Divide the crab among the plates, setting it in the center or on/near the lettuce.

5 Drizzle some of the dressing over the top and garnish with black olives and chopped chives.

6 Serve the salad with the remaining dressing on the side, along with the finishing salt and lemon wedges, if desired.

Crab and Boursin Cheese Quiche

SERVES 6

On a busy weekend, I found myself with leftover lump crabmeat, which is rare. I didn't want it to go to waste, so I thought it would be a lovely addition in a brunch quiche.

The problem was that I didn't have any cheese for the quiche, except a package of garlic and fine herb Boursin cheese. But it occurred to me how much I love crab with creamy cheese and fresh herbs, and so as they say, the rest is history.

I've given a piecrust recipe here because there is nothing like homemade piecrust. But if time is of the essence, feel free to use a ready-made piecrust of your choice.

Over the years, I've developed a lot of quiche recipes. My preferred ratio for a creamy quiche custard is four eggs to 1¾ cups heavy cream, using a deep-dish pie plate (about 2 inches deep). If the pie plate is a standard pie plate (1½ inches deep), reduce the heavy cream to 1½ cups. It'll still be delicious!

PIECRUST

1½ cups all-purpose flour, plus more for dusting

1 teaspoon salt

6 tablespoons unsalted butter, cold, cut into cubes

⅓ cup ice-cold water

QUICHE FILLING

6 ounces crabmeat

One 5.2-ounce package garlic and fine herb Boursin cheese

1 tablespoon chopped fresh chives

4 large eggs

1¾ cups heavy cream

1 teaspoon salt

½ teaspoon freshly ground black pepper

1 Make the piecrust: Combine the flour, salt and butter in a food processor and pulse until it forms crumbles. Then, while pulsing, add the cold water and pulse until the dough comes together. It'll be a bit shaggy. Roll out the dough on a floured surface and form a 10- to 11-inch disk. Cover with plastic wrap and refrigerate for at least an hour.

2 Preheat the oven to 350°F.

3 Roll out the chilled dough on a floured surface, to about a 12-inch round that is ⅛ inch thick. Fold the dough in half and place it in a 9-inch deep-dish pie plate, placing the fold in the center and then unfolding the dough. Press the dough down into the pie plate, trim the edges, and then pinch to form a pretty edge.

CONTINUES ➡

4 Make the quiche filling: Squeeze out all the excess liquid from the crab and paper towel it dry. Then, layer into the bottom of the piecrust. Next, layer the Boursin cheese over the crab and then sprinkle with the chopped chives.

5 Whisk together the eggs, heavy cream, salt, and pepper in a medium bowl and then pour it over the crab and cheese. Put the pie plate on a baking sheet and place it in the oven. Bake for about 45 minutes, or until the center is set. If needed, place a piece of parchment over the quiche to keep the crust from getting too brown. Or use foil to place around the edges of the exposed piecrust.

6 Once the quiche is done, remove from the oven and let sit for about 10 minutes. Serve warm or at room temperature.

Note

As always, fresh lump crabmeat is best in this recipe. For more information about crab, refer to page 128.

Side Dish Suggestion

This quiche is lovely with a salad of tossed greens or a classic Caesar salad.

New England–Style Clam Chowder

SERVES 4 TO 6

Clam chowder is a classic soup/stew that comes in a variety of preparations and recipes. I've found that most anyone who loves this chowder has an opinion about how to make it and what ingredients should be included. My family is no different.

Once I created this recipe, I couldn't change it. This is the recipe my family looks forward to every soup season. However, this doesn't mean you can't tweak it according to your own preferences. Recipes are guidelines and should be altered to suit our tastes.

Whatever you do, don't buy fancy smoked bacon, such as applewood smoked or the like, for this recipe. Otherwise, this type of bacon will overpower the flavor of your chowder. Just use regular bacon.

Traditional New England-style clam chowder calls for white pepper. I am not a fan, so I've listed black pepper in the recipe. Use whatever pepper makes your taste buds happy.

For the clams, I always purchase frozen chopped clams from my fish market or the freezer section of my local market. Then, I thaw them for the chowder. For more information on thawing seafood, refer to page 28. Although I think thawed frozen chopped clams taste best, if you can't find them, a can of high-quality chopped clams will work.

8 ounces uncooked bacon, chopped

1 medium to large yellow onion, small-diced

2 celery stalks, small-diced

2 garlic cloves, minced

6 tablespoons all-purpose flour

½ cup white wine or cream sherry

4 cups clam juice or chicken stock, or a mixture of both, if you'd like

1 pound yellow potatoes, peeled and cut into ½-inch cubes (small bite-size)

2 thyme sprigs

1 bay leaf

¾ to 1 pound chopped clams with juice, thawed and removed from refrigerator 15 minutes prior to using

1 cup heavy cream, or more as desired

1 tablespoon chopped fresh parsley, plus more for garnish

Squeeze of lemon juice

Salt and freshly ground black pepper

Dash of Tabasco (optional)

Oyster crackers (optional)

Fresh warm bread for dipping (optional)

CONTINUES ➡

1. Place the chopped bacon in a large soup pot over medium-low heat and cook it slowly to render the fat. Once the fat has been rendered and the bacon is golden brown, remove the chopped bacon from the pot and transfer to a paper towel–lined plate.
2. Keep 4 tablespoons of the bacon fat in the pot and discard the rest. I know this seems like a lot, but we need the fat to make the roux for the chowder.
3. Turn the heat to medium and add onion and celery to the pot. Cook until wilted and translucent, about 5 minutes.
4. Add the garlic and cook for 1 minute longer. I always add garlic toward the end of cooking the aromatics. This is to keep it from getting too brown or burning.
5. Stir in the flour and let it cook for 30 seconds. Then, add the wine and stir, and then add the clam juice.
6. Let the liquid come to a simmer and then stir in potatoes, thyme, and bay leaf.
7. Continue to simmer over low heat, stirring occasionally, until the potatoes are soft, about 15 minutes.
8. When the potatoes are soft, stir in the clams.
9. Then, stir in the heavy cream, parsley, and lemon juice, and return the cooked chopped bacon to the pot.
10. Bring the chowder back to a simmer just until it's heated through. Do not boil.
11. Season the chowder with salt and pepper to taste and add a dash of Tabasco, if desired.
12. Remove the chowder from the heat and let sit for at least 10 minutes or longer. This will allow the flavors to deepen. Reheat over low heat before serving.
13. Garnish with additional chopped parsley and serve with oyster crackers or warm bread for dipping.

Side Dish Suggestions

An iceberg lettuce salad with buttermilk dressing is lovely with this chowder.

Spanish-Style Steamed Clams

SERVES 4 AS AN APPETIZER OR 2 AS AN ENTRÉE

This is a slightly traditional Spanish-style steamed clam dish and one that I absolutely adore. I have added ½ cup of diced, cooked chorizo, which lends a bit of heat, flavor, and zest to the steamers. But if you prefer, you can always use a vegan chorizo as a substitute.

The sweet paprika adds a depth to the broth along with the piquillo peppers and white wine. This recipe comes together quickly, so be sure to have everything in place and ready to go.

2 tablespoons unsalted butter

2 tablespoons extra-virgin olive oil

1 shallot, diced

½ cup small-diced cooked chorizo

2 garlic cloves, minced

2 jarred piquillo peppers, diced

½ cup white wine

½ cup water plus ½ teaspoon Better Than Bouillon Fish Base, OR ½ cup clam broth

1½ teaspoons sweet paprika

Zest and juice of 1 lemon

Salt and freshly ground black pepper

2 pounds small fresh clams, scrubbed and rinsed (discard any open clams or clams with broken shells)

1 tablespoon chopped fresh parsley

Warm, crusty bread for dipping

1. Heat the butter and olive oil in a large pot over medium heat.
2. When the butter is melted and the oil is hot, add the shallot and cook for about 1 minute, or until translucent.
3. Stir in the chorizo, garlic, and piquillo peppers and let cook for about 1 minute longer.
4. Add the white wine, prepared fish bouillon, paprika, and lemon zest and juice. Bring to a simmer. Season to taste with salt and black pepper.
5. Mix in the clams, cover, and cook over low heat for 5 to 7 minutes, until all the clams have opened. Discard any clams that do not open.
6. Gently toss with the parsley and pour into a large bowl, ladling the broth over the clams.
7. Serve immediately with warm, crusty bread for dipping.

Notes

When purchasing clams, they should be tightly closed and smell like the sea—briny and fresh. If they smell fishy, more than likely they are old and they won't taste good. For more information about the types of clams, and purchasing and preparing fresh clams, refer to page 124.

Some chefs recommend soaking your clams in salt water overnight to eliminate extra sand in the clams. Unless you've dug them up yourself, you won't need to do this. But clams should always be scrubbed and rinsed in cold water, or, alternately, while you prep ingredients for this recipe, you can always immerse the clams in cold water with a few tablespoons of salt. Then rinse them completely before cooking.

Sake-Steamed Mussels with Lemongrass and Lime

SERVES 3 TO 4 AS A STARTER OR 2 AS AN ENTRÉE

Steamed fresh mussels make a delightful entrée or starter, especially when prepared properly. This recipe is brilliant when made in a wok, but if you don't have one, a large pot will do. A flavorful broth is also key to this tasty dish, which is why I use a combination of Better Than Bouillon brand Lobster Base and Fish Base.

I started using these seafood bases in my soup, stew, and steamer recipes after learning about them from one of my favorite chefs and colleague, Enrique Sanchez-Rodriguez, of Local Ocean Seafood in Newport, Oregon. They are concentrated so it allows the home cook or professional chef to control seasoning. I've also listed additional information and purchasing options for these bases on page 316.

1 cup hot water plus ½ teaspoon each Better Than Bouillon Lobster Base and Fish Base (see Notes)

2 tablespoons ghee (for more information, refer to the "Seafood 101" section, page 14)

2 lemongrass stalks, split in half and chopped into thirds

1 tablespoon chopped fresh garlic (3 to 4 cloves)

1 teaspoon finely chopped fresh ginger

¼ teaspoon crushed red pepper flakes

1 cup medium-dry sake

Salt and freshly ground black pepper

2 pounds mussels, scrubbed cleaned, debearded, and rinsed

Juice of 1 lime

1 tablespoon chiffonaded fresh basil for garnish

Fresh bread for dunking

1 Combine the hot water with the lobster and fish bases. Set aside.

2 Heat a wok or large pot over medium heat and add the ghee.

3 Stir in the lemongrass, garlic, ginger, and red pepper flakes. Let them sauté for 30 seconds to 1 minute.

4 Then, add the sake and prepared lobster and fish bouillon. Heat to a simmer and continue to simmer, lowering the heat to low if needed, for about 5 minutes to allow all the flavors to infuse the broth.

5 Season to taste with salt and black pepper.

CONTINUES ➡

6 Gently stir in the mussels, cover, and let them cook for 3 to 4 minutes, until all have opened. Discard any mussels that did not open.

7 Transfer the mussels to a large bowl and squeeze the lime juice over them.

8 Then, ladle any remaining broth over the mussels and garnish with the chiffonaded basil. The lemongrass will be tough and inedible but will have flavored the broth; feel free to discard the lemongrass.

9 Serve immediately with fresh bread for dunking in the broth.

Notes

Make sure to purchase only fresh mussels. They should smell like the sea, briny and fresh, and should not smell overly fishy. The shells should be tightly closed, and any mussels with chipped or broken shells should be discarded.

As soon as you arrive home, place the mussels in a bowl in your refrigerator. Mussels are best used the same day they are purchased. Before the mussels are cooked, scrub and rinse them in cold water (do not soak them in a bowl of water) and tug at the little beard, or what is technically called the byssus, to remove it. I usually pull them off, but if they don't release just snip them off with a knife or scissors.

My go-to fish stock or seafood stock is the Better Than Bouillon Fish Base and Lobster Base, respectively. For more information about these products and where to purchase, refer to the Resources (page 315).

Side Dish Suggestions

fresh bread or garlic bread ✦ a crisp green salad with a Thai ginger dressing ✦ stir-fried rice

Southern-Style Shrimp and Cheesy Grits

SERVES 4

I spent my youth and young adult years in the southern part of the United States and this dish was a staple in many homes as well as community potlucks or social gatherings.

Over the years, I've experimented with the recipe, but ultimately, this is my preferred version. I found that a sweet onion works perfectly here, and because I love all things tomatoes, I added diced tomatoes along with fresh parsley, lemon, garlic, and green onion. The combination of flavors combined with the creamy cheesy texture of the grits tastes like one giant food hug in a bowl.

GRITS

3 tablespoons unsalted butter

1½ cups whole milk

1½ cups vegetable or chicken stock

1 cup yellow or white stone-ground or instant grits

1 cup shredded Cheddar

Salt and freshly ground black pepper

SHRIMP

4 to 6 slices uncooked bacon

2 tablespoons unsalted butter

1 small, sweet onion, diced

2 garlic cloves, minced

One 14-ounce can diced tomatoes

1 tablespoon freshly squeezed lemon juice

1 tablespoon chopped fresh parsley

1 pound shrimp (I use 26/30 count; see Note) shelled and deveined

½ cup sliced green onion

Dash of Tabasco (optional)

Salt and freshly ground black pepper

1 Make the grits: Combine the butter, milk, and stock in a large pot. When the liquid comes to a bowl, while whisking, add the grits. *It's important to whisk while adding grits to the broth so they don't clump.* Cook according to the package directions. Stone-ground grits should take 20 to 25 minutes to cook. However, when I can find only instant grits, they take about 5 minutes to cook.

2 When the grits are done, stir in the Cheddar plus salt and pepper to taste. Keep warm.

3 Make the shrimp: Place the bacon in a large skillet over medium-low heat. Cooking the bacon over medium-low heat will help render the fat, but also brown the bacon. Once the bacon is done, transfer to a paper towel–lined plate to cool. Crumble the cooked bacon into small pieces. Reserve 2 tablespoons of the bacon fat in the skillet.

CONTINUES ➡

4 Next, in the same skillet, add the butter to the reserved bacon fat over medium heat. Stir in the onion and cook until soft and wilted.

5 Add the garlic and cook for 1 more minute.

6 Then, stir in the diced tomatoes, lemon juice, and parsley. Bring to a simmer.

7 Add the shrimp and cook just until pink, 3 to 4 minutes.

8 Remove the skillet from the heat and stir in ¼ cup of the sliced green onion and dash of Tabasco, if desired. Season to taste with salt and pepper.

9 Ladle the grits into a large serving bowl or individual bowls. Top with the shrimp mixture and then garnish with the crumbled bacon and remaining sliced green onion. Serve immediately.

Note

This recipe calls for 1 pound of shrimp and I typically use 26/30 count, meaning you will typically get 26 to 30 shrimp per pound based on their size. This will give each person 6 to 8 shrimp. You can certainly use smaller or larger shrimp. If using frozen shrimp, refer to page 28 for thawing instructions.

English Prawn Cocktail

SERVES 4

Prawn mayonnaise is a classic component of an English-style prawn cocktail, originally prepared with a Marie Rose sauce. The history of the sauce is varied; however, everyone seems to agree the basic ingredients are typically mayonnaise, ketchup, and Worcestershire sauce. Over the years, chefs and home cooks alike have put their individual spin on this lovely recipe.

Which is exactly what I did. I wanted this to be a simple but elegant shrimp starter for family dinners and special occasions. And although this recipe is simple, I've used raw prawns (or shrimp) and poached them to tender perfection. Poaching might seem intimidating to some, but once you get the hang of it, it's easy. Because I love this dressing so much, I occasionally use it over seafood salads, and it makes a delicious topping for pan-cooked or grilled fish.

PRAWNS

1 pound raw prawns or shrimp (16/20 or 21/25 count; see Note on page 123), thawed if previously frozen, peeled, and deveined (for more instruction on deveining prawns and shrimp, refer to the "Seafood 101" section, page 14)

2 teaspoons salt

4 tablespoons (½ stick) unsalted butter

1 cup white wine

2 cups fish stock or more to cover prawns

DRESSING

½ cup mayonnaise

1 tablespoon fresh parsley

1 tablespoon chili sauce

1 teaspoon sugar

1 teaspoon freshly squeezed lemon juice, or more taste

1 garlic clove, minced

½ teaspoon Worcestershire sauce

1 teaspoon cream sherry or brandy (optional)

TO SERVE

Salt and freshly ground black pepper

Chopped fresh chives or microgreens for garnish

1 Poach the prawns: Toss the raw prawns with the salt. You want to let the prawns rest while you heat the poaching liquid. This is much like a brine and allows the prawns to maintain moisture after poaching. Do not rinse the prawns prior to adding them to the poaching liquid.

2 Combine the butter, white wine, and fish stock in a medium pot over high heat.

3 When the butter has melted and the liquid has just come to a low boil, lower the heat to low and add the prawns. Let the liquid come back to a gentle simmer for 2 to 3 minutes, until the prawns are opaque and have formed into a slight C shape.

4 Drain the prawns and then place them on a large platter and gently cover. Place in the refrigerator and let chill.

5 Make the dressing: Combine the mayonnaise, parsley, chili sauce, sugar, lemon juice, garlic, Worcestershire, and cream sherry (if using) in a small bowl.

6 Once the prawns have chilled, toss them in the dressing and season to taste with salt and pepper.

7 Divide the prawns among four cocktail glasses or small plates and garnish with chopped chives or microgreens and serve.

Shrimp Enchilada Soup with Lime Crema

SERVES 4 TO 6

Shrimp is one of the most popular seafoods, as its versatility seems to be never-ending. It also pairs well with most vegetables, herbs, spices, and fruit.

For this recipe, I've given shrimp a flavorful soup base of aromatics, herbs, spices, vegetables, and lime. To add just a little extra umami to the soup, I've included a can of mild enchilada sauce.

I also use my two favorite bouillon bases mixed with hot water to create the broth for this soup. I highly recommend stocking these bouillon bases in your pantry to keep on hand for soups, stews, and sauces. However, feel free to substitute another seafood stock, if desired.

I like a brothy soup, but my family loves a soup that is stuffed, so I've listed some optional add-ins.

SOUP

2 tablespoons extra-virgin olive oil

1 white onion, diced

3 garlic cloves, minced

1 jalapeño pepper, seeded and diced (optional)

12 ounces unpeeled potatoes, cut into 1-inch cubes (about 2 medium potatoes)

One 15-ounce can mild red enchilada sauce

3 cups water plus 1 teaspoon each Better Than Bouillon Lobster Base and Fish Base (see Notes), OR 3 cups seafood or fish stock

1 teaspoon ground cumin

1 teaspoon ground coriander

1 teaspoon dried oregano

Pinch of ground cinnamon (about ⅛ teaspoon)

Squeeze of lime juice (about 2 teaspoons)

Salt and freshly ground black pepper

1 pound medium to large shrimp (31/35 or 21/30 count; see Notes), peeled and deveined

½ cup sliced green onion

½ cup chopped fresh cilantro

Optional add-ins: 1 cup black beans, 1 cup roasted corn, or one 4-ounce can mild green chiles

CREMA

½ cup sour cream

Juice of 1 lime

TO SERVE

Shredded cheese

Lime wedges

Crushed tortilla chips

Sliced green onions

CONTINUES ➡

1. Heat the olive oil in a large soup pot over medium heat. When the oil is hot, stir in the onion and cook until soft and translucent, 3 to 5 minutes.
2. Then, stir in garlic and jalapeño and cook for 1 to 2 minutes more.
3. Add the potatoes, enchilada sauce, water, prepared lobster and fish broth. Bring to a boil and lower the heat to a simmer.
4. Stir in the cumin, coriander, oregano, cinnamon, and lime juice. Simmer the soup for about 20 minutes, or until the potatoes are soft and cooked through. Add additional water (or stock) in ½-cup increments, if needed.
5. Season to taste with salt and black pepper.
6. Add the shrimp and bring the soup back to a gentle simmer. Cook for 2 minutes, or until the shrimp are opaque and cooked through. Remove the soup from the heat.
7. Stir in the green onion and cilantro.
8. Make the crema: Mix together the sour cream and lime juice in a small bowl.
9. Serve the soup in individual bowls with a drizzle of the lime crema and topped with shredded cheese, lime wedges, crushed tortilla chips and additional sliced green onions.

Notes

This recipe calls for medium to large shrimp. Medium shrimp are typically 31/35 count and large are 21/30 count, meaning that in 1 pound of shrimp, you will get 31 to 35 medium shrimp or 21 to 30 large shrimp.

My go-to fish stock and seafood stock is the Better Than Bouillon brand Fish Base and Lobster Base, respectively. For more information about these products and where to purchase, refer to the Resources (page 315).

Grilled Shrimp Tacos

SERVES 4 TO 5

This is one of my most requested shrimp recipes. I've probably been making these tacos for at least 15 years. My kids grew up eating these tacos, and now when they come home to visit, this is one of the meals they ask me to prepare.

Grilling shrimp couldn't be easier. The key is to oil and season them at least 15 minutes prior to grilling. Skewering the shrimp also helps them stay put on the grill and cook evenly. Once the shrimp are grilled, they are added to a warm garlic butter with fresh cilantro and lime juice. They hang out in this luscious butter while the rest of the recipe is prepared.

By the time the tacos are ready to be assembled, the shrimp have absorbed loads of flavor. The pineapple cilantro slaw is both sweet and savory and is deliciously complementary to the grilled shrimp. Fresh avocado, Cotija cheese, sour cream, and salsa are served with the tacos for one delicious and festive meal.

QUICK-PICKLED RED ONIONS

1 red onion, thinly sliced

½ cup rice vinegar

1 cup water

1 tablespoon sugar

SHRIMP

1½ pounds large or jumbo shrimp (21/30 or 16/20 count; see Notes on page 123), peeled and deveined

1 tablespoon oil

Salt and freshly ground black pepper

1 teaspoon smoked paprika

4 tablespoons (½ stick) unsalted butter

3 garlic cloves, minced

1 tablespoon chopped fresh cilantro

Pinch of red pepper flakes

Juice of ½ lime

PINEAPPLE CILANTRO SLAW

1 tablespoon lime juice

½ cup mayonnaise

1 teaspoon sugar

Dash of your favorite hot sauce

Salt and freshly ground black pepper

4 cups shredded napa cabbage

1 small bunch cilantro, chopped

½ cup diced pineapple

TACOS

8 to 10 corn tortillas, steamed

1 cup crumbled Cotija cheese

Sour cream with an optional squeeze of lime juice

Sliced avocado

Lime wedges

1 cup salsa

CONTINUES ➡

1 Make the quick-pickled onions: Place the sliced red onion in a glass jar, large enough to hold all the slices. Then, combine the vinegar, water and sugar in a small saucepan and bring to a simmer over medium heat. Remove the pan from the heat, let cool for a minute or two, then pour the liquid over the onion. Let the slices rest in the liquid for about 30 minutes. They are now ready to use, or cover the jar with a lid and store in the refrigerator for up to 1 week.

2 Preheat a grill to 400°F. Have ready 6 to 8 metal skewers, or if using wooden, soak them in water for at least 30 minutes.

3 Make the shrimp: Place the shrimp in a bowl and toss with the oil. Combine ½ teaspoon of salt, ½ teaspoon of black pepper, and the smoked paprika, then toss with the shrimp to coat.

4 Melt the butter in a medium saucepan or skillet over medium heat.

5 Just when the butter is melted and frothy, add the garlic, cilantro, red pepper flakes, and a pinch each of salt and pepper. Turn off the heat, but keep everything on the stovetop. Once the shrimp are grilled, they will go into the butter.

6 The best way to grill shrimp is to skewer them. You'll want to leave a bit of space between each shrimp so that the heat can circulate and cook the shrimp evenly.

7 Thread the shrimp on the skewers, then place them on the grill to cook for 1 to 2 minutes on each side, just until they've turned color. Cooking them too long will make them tough.

8 Remove the shrimp from the grill and from the skewers.

9 Add the shrimp to the warm butter mixture and then add the lime juice. Let the shrimp sit in the butter mixture while you prepare the tortillas and the slaw.

10 Make the slaw: Whisk together the lime juice, mayonnaise, sugar, and hot sauce in a small bowl. Season to taste with salt and black pepper.

11 Combine the cabbage, cilantro, and pineapple in a large bowl and then toss with half of the dressing. Save the remaining dressing to serve with the tacos.

12 I like to serve this dish as a "make your own taco" dinner. Transfer the grilled shrimp to a bowl, along with the butter mixture.

13 Serve alongside the steamed tortillas, crumbled Cotija, pineapple cilantro slaw, sour cream, sliced avocado, salsa, and extra wedges of lime, and then let everyone assemble their tacos.

Shrimp, Black Bean, and Corn Chilaquiles

SERVES 4 TO 6

Chilaquiles is a fun and lip-smackingly good recipe that I love to serve as a communal starter or snack. Traditionally, this is a Mexican breakfast or brunch dish of torn or cut tortillas that are lightly fried, tossed in a red or green sauce, and then layered with assorted toppings, but most often, I find them served with a fried egg.

I'll be honest: I cut corners here by using canned enchilada sauce instead of making it from scratch. This is mostly because I usually whip this up on a whim when I've got last-minute guests or an impromptu summer gathering in my backyard.

I love this recipe when summer corn is in season. It's also excellent with small grilled shrimp as an alternative to cooked bay shrimp. Before grilling the shrimp, I toss it in the chile lime seasoning (or Tajín seasoning) with a dash of oil. Grilled shrimp instructions can also be found in my Grilled Shrimp Tacos recipe on page 153.

CREMA

8 ounces sour cream

1 teaspoon ground coriander

Juice of 1 to 2 limes

Salt

CHILAQUILES

8 ounces cooked bay shrimp or small cooked shrimp

1 teaspoon chile lime seasoning or Tajín seasoning

1 cup cooked or canned black beans, drained

1 cup cooked or grilled corn

2 tablespoons vegetable oil

½ red onion, thinly sliced

One 15-ounce can mild red enchilada sauce

8 ounces tortilla chips (about 8 cups)

Salt

1 bunch cilantro, chopped

½ cup Cotija

1 avocado, sliced, or dollops of guacamole

Pickled jalapeños (optional)

1. Make the crema: Whisk together the sour cream, coriander, and lime juice in a small bowl. Add salt to taste. Set aside.
2. Make the chilaquiles: Toss the cooked shrimp with the chile lime seasoning. Set aside until needed.
3. Heat the black beans and cooked corn and set aside until needed.
4. Heat the oil in a large skillet over medium heat. Add the red onion and cook until wilted and slightly golden.
5. Lower the heat and add the enchilada sauce and warm.

6 Remove the skillet from the heat and gently toss the chips with the sauce and onion. This will take a little time, to coat all the chips. Be sure to toss gently so the chips don't break. Season with a little salt, if needed.

7 Once the chips are well coated, let them sit for a few minutes to soak up the sauce.

8 Pour half of the chips onto a large platter and layer with some of the shrimp, black beans, and corn. Then, pour the rest of the chips over the top and layer with the remaining shrimp, black beans, and corn.

9 Top with chopped cilantro, Cotija, sliced avocado, and pickled jalapeños, if using. Drizzle with some of the lime crema and serve immediately.

My Favorite Shellfish Boil

SERVES 6 TO 8

At my house, shellfish boils happen most often during the summer months. When I serve this outdoors, I lay a heatproof paper or camping tablecloth on my patio table. Once the seafood is done, I drain it and pour it directly onto the table.

I place little bowls of melted butter on the table for each person, along with forks, paper plates, and bowls for shells. I typically include crab legs, shrimp, and clams. But on occasion, I'll toss in 4-ounce lobster tails that I've cut in half lengthwise. And if I can find them, I'll also include crawfish.

Although this is referred to as a "boil," the seafood should be gently simmered, much like a poach, adjusting the heat as needed. I added my shellfish boil to this chapter because it does require a few more ingredients and a bit more prep work. However, the end result is absolutely worth it.

¼ cup Old Bay seasoning, or one 3-ounce package shrimp and crab boil

2 small onions, quartered

5 to 6 garlic cloves, smashed

2 bay leaves

2 lemons, thickly sliced

2 to 3 pounds new potatoes, no need to peel (about 3 potatoes per person)

6 ears of corn, cut into thirds

2 pounds kielbasa or mild andouille sausages, or your favorite smoked sausages

3 to 4 pounds jumbo shrimp (16/20 count; see Notes on page 123) shells on

3 to 4 pounds crab legs

2 pounds clams

Four 4-ounce lobster tails, halved (optional)

2 pounds crawfish (optional)

TO SERVE

½ pound (2 sticks) salted butter, melted

2 garlic cloves, minced

1 tablespoon chopped fresh parsley

Hot sauce or Tabasco (optional)

1 Fill your largest pot two-thirds full of water and add the Old Bay seasoning, onions, garlic, bay leaves, and lemon slices.

2 Bring to a boil, and then lower the heat to low and let simmer for about 10 minutes. Add additional water and salt, if needed.

3 Add the potatoes and let them cook for about 5 minutes, adjusting the heat as needed.

4 Then, add the corn and the sausage. Cook for another 5 minutes.

5. Stir in the shrimp, crab legs, and clams and gently simmer for 5 minutes.
6. Next, if using, stir in the lobster tails and crawfish, then gently simmer for another 3 to 5 minutes. The total cook time should be 25 to 30 minutes.
7. To serve, combine the melted butter with the garlic and parsley. Pour into several small containers for dipping the seafood.
8. Drain the shellfish and scoop it into foil containers or large platters.
9. If serving this traditional style, pour the drained, hot shellfish down the center of the prepared table. Place little bowls of butter around the shellfish, along with your favorite hot sauce or tabasco. I highly recommend a lot of napkins.
10. If serving indoors, place the foil containers or large platters in the center of the table and surround with little bowls of the garlic butter and hot sauce (if using).

Note

For this recipe, I usually plan on ½ to 1 pound of shellfish per person. You can use an outdoor seafood steamer/boiler, but no need to go buy one. You can certainly do this indoors on your stovetop. I use a 16-quart stockpot, and if I need a second pot, I'll use my 10-quart as well. Be sure to divide your seasonings and ingredients appropriately if using more than one pot. If you're preparing a smaller seafood boil, one large stockpot (10- to 12-quart) will be fine.

Side Dish Suggestions

Sweet cornbread with honey butter is a lovely addition to this meal.

CONTINUES ➡

Preparing Lobster Tails for a Shellfish Boil

1 Place the thawed lobster tails on a cutting board, leg side up.

2 Cut the lobster tail lengthwise into two vertical pieces. Keep the lobster meat in the shell and add to the shellfish boil per instructions.

Spicy Salmon Poke Bowl

SERVES 4

While spending a little time on Maui, we discovered the coolest fish shop that made the best poke I've ever had. The flavors were so perfectly combined, bright and fragrant, and left me wanting a second serving. Since that time poke recipes have been flying all over the internet. And for good reason—poke is delicious.

I missed that fish shop poke so much I re-created it at home. It's not quite the same but it comes close, and that makes my taste buds very happy.

The bowl ingredients depend entirely on you and what you like with your poke. The bowl can be as simple as rice, poke, and sauce. Or slightly loaded like my recipe here. I listed our favorite bowl ingredients; however, diced mango, pineapple, seaweed salad, sugar snap peas, mung beans, and cilantro are just a few additional ingredients that are also delicious with poke. Don't be afraid to get creative!

FIND YOUR FISH: For the best poke, use quality, sushi-grade ahi tuna or salmon. For this recipe, I chose to use sushi-grade salmon, since it's easily found where I live. Either is fine, but be sure the fish looks bright in color with a little shimmer to the flesh. It should never smell fishy, just fresh like the ocean. For more information about thawing frozen fish, refer to page 28.

CONTINUES ➡

SALMON

- ⅓ cup tamari
- 1 tablespoon seasoned rice vinegar
- 2 garlic cloves, minced
- 1 teaspoon toasted sesame oil
- 1 teaspoon grated fresh ginger
- 1½ tablespoons Thai sweet chili sauce, such as Mae Ploy brand
- 1 tablespoon toasted sesame seeds
- Juice of 1 lime
- ¼ cup finely sliced or chopped green onion
- 1 pound sushi-grade salmon, cut into ½-inch cubes or very small bite-size pieces

SAUCE

- ½ cup mayonnaise
- 2 tablespoons Thai sweet chili sauce
- 1 tablespoon seasoned rice wine vinegar
- Squeeze of lime juice (about 1 tablespoon)
- Sriracha to taste (optional)

TO ASSEMBLE

- 2 cups cooked sticky rice, jasmine rice, or ramen noodles
- 1 cup steamed or pan-cooked edamame
- 1 large cucumber, sliced or quartered
- 1 red bell pepper, seeded and sliced
- Handful of baby spinach
- ½ cup sliced green onion
- Lime wedges and avocado slices for serving
- Toasted sesame seeds for garnish

1 Make the salmon: Combine the tamari, vinegar, garlic, sesame oil, ginger, sweet chili sauce, toasted sesame seeds, lime juice, and green onion in a large nonreactive or glass bowl.

2 Then, toss the salmon with the marinade and let it rest in the refrigerator for 30 minutes or up to 1 hour.

3 Make the sauce: Combine the mayonnaise, sweet chili sauce, vinegar, lime juice, and sriracha to taste (if using) in a small bowl.

4 To assemble, place the rice in a bowl and top with the salmon poke and additional toppings as desired. Drizzle with a little sauce and serve immediately.

Salmon Lox and Three-Cheese Puff Pastry Pinwheels

MAKES 20 TO 22 PINWHEELS

Salmon lox is salt cured or brined and has a salty flavor and buttery texture that makes it perfect in this recipe. Smoked salmon is typically salt brined and then either hot or cold smoked. Hot smoked salmon is meatier and flakier in texture and darker in color.

Lox works well here as it's usually found thinly sliced. Because of its salty flavor, it also pairs well with creamy cheese, such as this combination of goat cheese, Boursin, and cream cheese. And of course, the puff pastry seals the deliciousness.

2 ounces goat cheese, at room temperature

2 ounces cream cheese, at room temperature

2 ounces herb and garlic Boursin, at room temperature

1 sheet puff pastry, thawed according to package directions

All-purpose flour for dusting

4 ounces smoked salmon lox slices

1 large egg, whisked with 1 teaspoon cold water

1 Place the goat cheese, cream cheese, and Boursin in the bowl of a stand mixer fitted with the paddle attachment and mix at medium speed until smoothly combined.

2 Open the puff pastry onto a lightly floured cutting board or kitchen counter. Gently roll it out to about 11 by 15 inches, smoothing out the pastry and keeping it in a rectangular shape.

3 Spread the cheese over the puff pastry, leaving a ½-inch clear margin around all sides of the puff pastry.

4 Lay the smoked salmon slices on top of the cheese.

5 Beginning at the short side of the pastry, roll it up snugly but gently. Wrap in plastic wrap and refrigerate for 30 minutes.

6 Preheat the oven to 400°F.

7 Remove the pastry from the plastic wrap and, using a very sharp or serrated knife, cut into ½-inch slices.

8 Place the slices, cut side down, on a parchment-lined baking sheet, or two baking sheets if needed.

9 Brush each pinwheel with egg wash, and then place the baking sheet(s) in the oven.

10 Bake for 12 to 15 minutes, until golden brown.

11 Remove from the oven and let cool for about 5 minutes. Serve immediately.

Note

Because the pastry needs to be refrigerated, this recipe can be prepped a day in advance and kept in the refrigerator until needed.

Pasta with Brown Butter, Peas, Mint, and Salmon

SERVES 3 OR 4

Pasta recipes are the perfect base for grilled, roasted, or pan-cooked seafood. This lovely dish includes a pasta lightly bathed in brown butter, which is nutty and luscious. It's the perfect complement to sweet spring peas, fresh mint, and salmon. Although I love this served with spaghetti or linguine, strozzapreti and orecchiette are also delightful.

10 to 12 ounces spaghetti, linguine, or your favorite pasta, cooked according to package directions, ½ cup pasta water reserved

2 tablespoons ghee or high-heat oil

1 pound salmon, skinless or skin on, cut into 3 or 4 pieces

Salt and freshly ground black pepper

4 tablespoons (½ stick) good-quality unsalted butter

1 to 2 garlic cloves, thinly sliced

¾ cup cooked peas

Zest of 1 lemon

1 tablespoon freshly squeezed lemon juice

1 tablespoon chopped fresh parsley, plus more for garnish

¼ cup fresh mint, chopped

½ cup grated Parmesan

1 While the pasta is cooking, prepare the salmon.

2 Brush a little ghee over the salmon pieces and season with salt and pepper. Heat the remaining ghee in a large, light-colored skillet (so you can see the butter brown when making the sauce) over medium-high heat.

3 When the ghee is hot and shimmering, add the salmon, flesh side down. Let the salmon cook for 3 to 4 minutes without moving it, so it can brown. You'll notice the edges of the salmon becoming golden brown and the flesh closest to the surface of the pan turning opaque.

4 Flip the salmon over and let it cook for another 3 to 4 minutes, or longer for a thicker piece of salmon, adjusting the heat to medium, if needed. Most fish cook through in about 10 minutes for every inch of thickness. When the salmon is done, remove from the pan and set aside.

CONTINUES ➡

5 Let the skillet cool and clean it out with paper towels, just to remove the bits of salmon and ghee. Or use a different skillet, if needed. Then, place the skillet over medium-low heat and add the butter.

6 Move the pan around a bit as the butter melts; just before it browns, it will become frothy. Once the foam dissipates, you'll be able to see the milk solids begin to turn brown.

7 Stir in the garlic and let it cook for about 15 to 30 seconds (don't let it burn), then add the lemon juice and reserved pasta water.

8 Mix in the peas, lemon zest and juice, parsley, and mint. Then, toss with the pasta and ¼ cup of the Parmesan. Season to taste with salt and pepper.

9 To serve, divide the pasta among three or four bowls and top with the salmon. Serve with remaining Parmesan.

Note

I've pan cooked the salmon here, but roasted or grilled salmon will also work well. For more information on grilling or roasting fish, refer to the recipes in the previous chapter.

Side Dish Suggestions

If a first dish is required, I'd recommend a salad of fresh greens with lemon vinaigrette and crusty warm Italian bread.

Roasted Salmon with Savory Strawberry Sauce

SERVES 4

Strawberry season is ripe for all sorts of pies and desserts, but I especially love strawberries in unexpected dishes like this one. You may have seen salmon frequently paired with various citrus, as those sweet and sour flavors complement the fish so perfectly. But for me, salmon is most enjoyable when paired with fresh berries, as in this simple savory strawberry sauce.

I was inspired to create this sauce about 15 years ago after sampling something similar at a small restaurant tucked away on the northern coast of Washington State. That sauce was also served over salmon, and it was quite spicy, but so delicious I could have licked my plate. When I got home, I immediately went to work in my kitchen testing savory strawberry sauce recipes. This recipe has evolved over the years and this version is my favorite.

Black pepper is one of the most complementary spices to strawberries. Using freshly ground black pepper gives the sauce a little spice without it overpowering the flavor of the berries. I've added pinot noir as an homage to my home state of Oregon, and of course a strawberry sauce wouldn't be complete without a dash of good-quality, aged balsamic vinegar.

1½ pounds salmon, cut into 4 or 5 pieces

1 to 2 tablespoons high-heat oil

Salt and freshly ground black pepper

2 tablespoons unsalted butter

2 tablespoons finely minced shallot

1 pound fresh strawberries, trimmed and sliced

1 tablespoon sugar

1 teaspoon chopped fresh thyme

½ cup pinot noir

½ teaspoon cornstarch plus ½ teaspoon cold water

1 teaspoon high-quality aged balsamic vinegar, plus more if needed

1 Preheat the oven to 400°F.

2 Place the salmon in a baking dish or on a baking sheet and brush with the high-heat oil. Season with salt and pepper.

CONTINUES ➡

3 Place the salmon in the oven and roast for about 10 minutes, depending on the thickness of fish. Most fish cook through in about 10 minutes for every inch of thickness. (For more information on roasting fish, refer to the "Seafood 101" section, page 14.)

4 While the salmon is roasting, prepare the sauce.

5 Heat the butter in a saucepan over medium heat. Once the butter is melted, add the shallot and cook for 1 minute, or until soft.

6 Stir in the strawberries, sugar, thyme, pinot noir, ½ teaspoon of pepper, and a pinch of salt. Bring to a simmer and let cook for about 10 minutes over low heat.

7 Stir together the cornstarch and cold water (this is called a cornstarch slurry). Increase the heat so the strawberry sauce is at a lively simmer and then stir in the cornstarch slurry. Simmer for 15 to 30 seconds to slightly thicken. Some strawberries exude more liquid than others, so if the sauce is still too thin, repeat with another round of cornstarch slurry.

8 Take the saucepan off the heat and taste the sauce for salt and then stir in the balsamic vinegar.

9 Taste the sauce again and add an additional teaspoon of balsamic vinegar, if desired.

10 Once the salmon is done, remove it from the oven and transfer to a platter or individual plates. Top with the strawberry sauce and serve.

Note

I've used roasted salmon here, but this recipe is lovely with grilled or pan-cooked salmon as well. You'll find instructions for both grilled and pan-cooked salmon in the previous chapter.

Side Dish Suggestions

pearled couscous, quinoa, or wild rice ✦ a salad of spring greens tossed in a honey balsamic vinaigrette ✦ roasted spring asparagus

Grilled Salmon with Pistachio Lemon Pesto

SERVES 4

Grilled salmon is one of the great joys of summer. It pairs well with just about all summer produce and is one of the easiest fish to grill due to firm texture and higher fat content than other fish. The pesto will keep in the refrigerator for about three days and can also be used on grilled or roasted vegetables.

FIND YOUR FISH: Although I've used salmon fillets in the recipe, this is lovely with fish steaks and meaty or firm fish, such as tuna, swordfish, or mahi-mahi.

2 cups packed fresh basil leaves

1 garlic clove

¼ cup pistachios

3 tablespoons freshly squeezed lemon juice

1 tablespoon chopped fresh parsley

⅔ cup extra-virgin olive oil

3 tablespoons grated Parmesan

Zest of 1 lemon

Salt and freshly ground black pepper

1½ pounds salmon fillet, skinless or skin on, cut into 4 servings, removed from refrigerator 15 minutes prior to cooking

1 to 2 tablespoons high-heat oil

Chopped pistachios for garnish

Basil sprigs for garnish

1 Combine the basil, garlic, pistachios, lemon juice, parsley, and olive oil in a food processor or blender and puree until smooth.

2 Pour into a bowl and stir in the Parmesan and lemon zest. Season to taste with salt and pepper, then set the pesto aside.

3 Preheat a grill to 400°F or to medium-high heat. Be sure your grill grates are as clean as possible. This will help prevent sticking.

CONTINUES ➡

4 Brush each salmon fillet with high-heat oil on all sides and season with a sprinkle of salt and pepper.

5 Place the salmon pieces, flesh side down, diagonally on the grill; this will also help the fish flip easier. Close the lid and let the salmon cook for 6 to 7 minutes, checking on the fish every few minutes.

6 Then, using your tongs, try to ease the fish up off the grill grates. If they don't budge, wait 30 seconds longer, or as needed. Once the fish comes up off the grill easily, flip the fish to be skin side down and cook for another 3 to 4 minutes, until the fish is done. Remember, most fish cook through in about 10 minutes for every inch of thickness. The fish should be opaque and flake with a fork.

7 Once the fish is done, transfer to a platter. The fish will usually slide right off the skin, leaving the skin on the grill. However, if the skin comes off the grate with the fish, you can either leave it on, or remove it from the fish.

8 To serve, plate the salmon, top with pesto, and garnish with additional chopped pistachios and basil sprigs.

Side Dish Suggestions

orzo, farfalle, quinoa, or farro ✦ scalloped potatoes ✦ roasted or grilled vegetables

Grilled Fish Steaks with Blueberry Ginger Butter

SERVES 3 OR 4

Compound butter is always a delicious way to finish a fish dish. I usually have a selection of them hanging out in my freezer. They are perfect toppings for grilled, roasted, or pan-cooked fish, meat, and vegetables.

Compound butter is soft butter that has been mixed with an assortment of ingredients and can be sweet or savory. Or it can be a little bit of both, such as this blueberry ginger butter that I've paired with grilled fish steaks.

I have found that fish steaks are best suited to grilling, and honestly, they make a summer evening meal simple to achieve. For more information about fish steaks, refer to page 18.

In this recipe, I have used salt and pepper for seasoning on the fish. Although I do like some seafood seasoning, I think that salt and pepper complement the fish as well as the compound butter.

8 tablespoons (1 stick) salted butter, at room temperature
1 garlic clove, minced
1 to 2 teaspoons fresh grated ginger
½ cup chopped fresh blueberries
3 or 4 fish steaks (salmon, halibut, etc.)
2 tablespoons high-heat oil
Salt and freshly ground black pepper
2 tablespoons chopped fresh mint
Lemon wedges

1 Place the butter in the bowl of a stand mixer fitted with the whisk attachment, and whisk on medium speed for about 5 minutes, or until creamy and smooth.

2 Whisk in the garlic and ginger until combined. Then, scrape any excess butter off the whisk and fold in the chopped blueberries until evenly distributed. It will feel a bit clumpy but that's okay.

3 Pour the blueberry butter onto a sheet of plastic wrap or waxed paper and form a log about the same size as a stick of butter. Then, roll it up, twist the ends, and refrigerate for at least 1 hour.

CONTINUES ➡

4 Just before grilling the fish, remove the butter from the refrigerator, unwrap, and place on a plate. Cut several slices. The butter can be rewrapped and kept in the freezer for 1 month.

5 Preheat a grill to 400°F or to medium-high heat. Make sure the grates are clean.

6 Brush the fish steaks with the high-heat oil and then season with salt and pepper on both sides.

7 When the grill is hot, add the steaks to the grill, placing them on a diagonal. This will help keep them from sticking and will also make them look pretty. Grill the steaks for 3 to 5 minutes, and when the fish lifts off the grill easily and has some nice grill marks, flip it over to the other side. Close the lid and continue to cook for another 3 to 5 minutes.

8 Fish steaks will cook through in about 10 minutes for every inch of thickness, just like fish fillets. However, some fish steaks can be 1½ to 2 inches thick, so cook accordingly. Salmon steaks are good to begin with because they can be very forgiving when grilled, due to their meaty texture and higher fat content. Note that halibut steaks, also delicious in this recipe, will require constant attention as they can dry out quickly.

9 As soon as the fish is done, transfer to a platter and place one or two coins of the compound butter on each steak. Allow the butter to melt and then garnish with chopped mint. Serve immediately with lemon wedges.

Side dish suggestions

summer vegetable chopped salad ✦ grilled zucchini and yellow squash ✦ grilled eggplant ✦ pasta salad ✦ broccoli salad ✦ watermelon feta salad

Seared Ahi Tuna Wonton Tacos with Mango Pico de Gallo

SERVES 8 AS A STARTER OR 4 AS AN ENTRÉE

This is a recipe I like to prepare while everyone is hanging out in the kitchen, either for a family dinner or festive dinner party with friends. Once the ingredients are ready, I set them out "taco bar" style so everyone can make their own tacos. I think this dish tastes best served as soon as it's finished, whether you're standing around the kitchen counter or sitting outside at the patio table.

Pan-seared ahi tuna is typically cooked rare as it only needs to be seared or browned on both sides. The center will remain pink. Begin with high heat, and when the oil just begins to smoke, that's when the tuna is added. Let it form a brown crust on the bottom before flipping. Often I only get one side of my tuna nicely browned, which is absolutely fine! The other side is typically more golden because I want to keep the center of the tuna a nice pink color.

If you want to skip frying the wonton tacos, the tuna is also lovely when served à la carte topped with the mango pico de gallo and then drizzled with the lime crema. Garnish with a few avocado slices.

MANGO PICO DE GALLO

2 ripe mangoes, peeled and small-diced (about 1 cup small-diced)

½ cup small-diced white onion

1 to 2 jalapeño peppers, seeded and diced

4 Roma tomatoes, seeded and diced

1 bunch cilantro, chopped

Zest and juice of 1 lime

Salt and freshly ground black pepper

SPICY LIME CREMA

¼ cup mayonnaise

½ cup sour cream

Juice of 1 to 2 limes to taste

1 chipotle chile in adobo, finely diced

1 tablespoon warm honey

WONTONS

12 to 15 wonton wrappers

High-heat oil for frying

AHI TUNA

1 pound ahi tuna, removed from refrigerator at least 15 minutes prior to cooking, and patted dry with paper towels

2 teaspoons chile lime seasoning or Tajín seasoning

Salt and freshly ground black pepper (optional)

2 to 3 tablespoons high-heat oil as needed

CONTINUES ➡

Note

If you can't find wonton wrappers, small or street taco corn tortillas are a good substitute.

1. Make the mango pico de gallo: Combine the diced mango, onion, jalapeño, tomatoes, cilantro, and lime zest and juice in a medium to large bowl. Toss to mix and season to taste with salt and black pepper.
2. Make the crema: Combine the mayonnaise, sour cream, lime juice, diced chipotle pepper, and warm honey in a small bowl. Toss well, then set aside.
3. Make the wonton taco shells: Place a few paper towels over a cooling rack. Then, heat about ½ inch of high-heat oil in a medium skillet or wok over medium to medium-high heat, adjusting the heat as needed.
4. When the oil is hot, holding one corner of a wonton wrapper with tongs, add it to the oil and gently fold into a triangle. Don't allow it to seal. You will need to hold it open with your tongs to form the "taco" shell.
5. Once one side of the folded wonton is golden brown, roll to the other side and cook until golden. Then, transfer to the paper towel–lined cooling rack. Repeat until all wontons are fried. I always end up breaking a few, which is why I've called for 12 to 15 wonton wrappers.
6. Make the ahi tuna: Season the tuna with the chile lime seasoning and salt and black pepper, if needed.
7. Heat 2 tablespoons of high-heat oil in a large skillet over high heat. Add more oil if needed.
8. When the skillet is hot but not quite smoking, add the tuna and let it sear for about 1 minute.
9. Then, lower the heat to medium-high and continue to cook for 1 to 1½ minutes longer, until the bottom edges form a brown crust.
10. Using a fish spatula or tongs, flip the tuna and sear the other side for 1 to 3 minutes, until the bottom is golden or golden brown and the center is still pink. This will cook the tuna to rare or medium rare, depending on the thickness of the tuna.
11. Remove the tuna from the skillet and place it on a cutting board.
12. Let it rest for a few minutes and then slice on the diagonal into thin slices.
13. Place cooked ahi tuna strips in the wonton taco shells, top with a drizzle of crema, and then garnish with mango pico de gallo. Serve immediately.

Grilled Swordfish with Elote-Style Corn and Roasted Poblanos

SERVES 4

One of the very first fish I sampled was grilled swordfish. It was recommended because swordfish is a mild-flavored fish with a meaty texture. It makes an excellent fish to try if you're not sure you like seafood.

This is a dish I like to make during the summer months with my plethora of garden poblanos and local farmers' market corn. It has several prep steps, but once they are done, it comes together easily. I roast the poblanos in the oven for this recipe. However, you can also roast them on a grill or under the broiler. I prefer the oven method so I can use that time to prep the additional ingredients.

3 to 4 poblano peppers

Salt and freshly ground black pepper

1 to 2 teaspoons chile lime seasoning or chili powder (check for heat)

½ cup mayonnaise (soy-free Vegenaise brand makes the best base for sauces)

½ to 1 teaspoon Tajín seasoning or chile lime seasoning

Juice of 1 lime

1½ pounds swordfish, cut into 3 or 4 pieces

1 tablespoon high-heat oil

1½ to 2 cups grilled or pan-cooked corn

½ cup crumbled Cotija

½ cup chopped fresh cilantro

Lime wedges for serving

1. Preheat the oven to 400°F.
2. Roast the poblano peppers: Place the peppers on a baking sheet with space between them. Put the baking sheet on the center rack of the oven and roast for about 20 minutes, flipping them once or twice until they are charred on the outside.
3. Remove the baking sheet from the oven and cover with foil. This will help the peppers sweat and the skin will be easier to remove.
4. When the peppers are cool, peel off the skin, make a vertical cut in each pepper, and remove the seeds, veins, and stems. Do not wash the peppers. Flatten them out and lay them on a plate.

CONTINUES ➡

5 To make the crema, whisk together the mayonnaise, Tajín seasoning to taste, and lime juice. Set aside.

6 Brush the fish with the high-heat oil and season with Tajin or chile lime seasoning. If the seasoning does not contain salt, also season with a sprinkle of salt. Let the fish rest while you preheat a grill.

7 Preheat the grill to 400°F. Be sure the grill grates are clean and well oiled. (For more tips on grilling fish, refer to the "Seafood 101" section, page 14).

8 When the grill is hot, place swordfish on the grill, close the lid, and let cook for 3 to 5 minutes, depending on thickness. Then, flip the fish, close the lid, and cook for another 3 to 4 minutes, until the fish is done. Transfer to a plate.

9 To assemble, divide the poblano peppers among four plates, placing them flat on the plate. Top with a piece of grilled swordfish, then top with corn.

10 Drizzle with the seasoned lime crema and sprinkle with crumbled Cotija and cilantro. Serve immediately.

Note

For the latest information on purchasing sustainable swordfish, refer to the seafood watch websites in the Resources (page 315).

Side Dish Suggestions

pasta salad ✦ broccoli salad ✦ fresh tomato caprese salad ✦ tropical fruit salad

Spaghetti with Anchovies and Olives

SERVES 4

Anchovies are a versatile little fish that create depth of flavor in many recipes. For this recipe, the anchovies are melted into the oil and then combined with aromatics, white wine, tomatoes, and herbs. It's finished with a bit of lemon zest and a handful of sliced olives.

I've called for whole canned tomatoes here as most often they are canned at the peak of flavor. However, some canned tomatoes are "brighter" in flavor than others. If you feel the sauce is a bit too acidic or bright, try adding ¼ to ½ teaspoon of sugar. This will neutralize some of the acidity and bring those flavors back in check.

This recipe comes together quickly, so be sure to have everything ready mise en place (in its place) before cooking.

12 ounces uncooked spaghetti
¼ cup extra-virgin olive oil
6 to 8 canned flat anchovy fillets, preferably unsalted
1 small to medium yellow onion, small diced
3 garlic cloves, minced
½ white wine to deglaze
One 28-ounce can whole tomatoes with juice
1 tablespoon chopped fresh flat-leaf parsley
Pinch of crushed red pepper flakes
Zest of 1 lemon
½ cup sliced Kalamata olives or green olives, or both
Salt and freshly ground black pepper
Chopped fresh parsley for garnish
Grated pecorino or Parmesan for serving

1 Fill a large pot with water and season with 2 tablespoons salt. Bring to a boil and add the spaghetti. Cook according to the package directions, then drain, reserving ½ cup of pasta water. Set the cooked pasta aside. (I like to start the pasta as soon as I'm ready to make the sauce. It will take a few minutes to come to a boil and cook. By the time the spaghetti is done, the sauce should be ready.)

2 Combine the olive oil and anchovies in a large skillet over medium-low heat. It is important to keep the heat low to allow the anchovies to "melt" or break apart into the oil. Stirring slowly, cook for 1½ to 2 minutes, until the anchovies are nicely combined with the oil. Be careful as there may be some splatter while the anchovies are in the oil.

3 Stir in the onion and cook until soft and wilted. Then, add the garlic and cook for about 1 minute longer.

4 Remove the pan from the heat and whisk in the white wine until the ingredients are combined. Place the pan back over the heat and cook until the wine has reduced by half.

5 Stir in the tomatoes, parsley, and red pepper flakes. Let simmer over low heat for about 5 minutes, adjusting the heat as needed.

6 Add the lemon zest and olives, remove the pan from the heat, and season to taste with black pepper, plus salt if needed. I find that I rarely need additional salt in this recipe, but black pepper is complementary.

7 Add ¼ cup of the reserved pasta water to the sauce and then, using tongs, add the cooked spaghetti and toss in the sauce until nicely combined. Use the remaining ¼ cup of the pasta water, if needed.

8 Serve in pasta bowls and garnish with chopped parsley and grated pecorino or Parmesan.

Side Dish Suggestions

You can serve this with a salad of fresh greens and light buttermilk dressing alongside a mélange of roasted vegetables. But most of the time, I serve this à la carte with a glass of wine.

Basic White Fish Ceviche

SERVES 4 TO 6

Ceviche is a seafood dish in which fresh fish is "cooked" in freshly squeezed lime juice or some sort of citrus and then combined with various fresh ingredients. This recipe is my basic version and one that I make often.

During the warm summer months, though, I might add ½ cup of diced cucumber or sliced radishes. And, sometimes, I yearn for a sweeter flavor and mix the ceviche with a little diced pineapple or mango. However you decide to adjust the ingredients, it's important to begin with the freshest fish possible for the tastiest ceviche.

1 pound fresh saltwater fish (such as halibut, cod, turbot, haddock, pollack, rockfish, flounder, or any other mild-flavored white fish), pin bones removed, cut into ½-inch cubes

Juice of 10 to 12 limes, or enough to cover the diced fish

½ to ⅔ cup small diced white onion

4 to 5 Roma tomatoes, seeded and diced

1 jalapeño pepper, seeded and finely diced

½ cup coarsely chopped fresh cilantro

Salt and freshly ground black pepper

Good-quality extra-virgin olive oil (optional)

Tortilla chips for serving

Sliced avocado for serving (optional)

Fresh cilantro for serving (optional)

1. Combine the diced fish and lime juice in a large nonreactive or glass bowl. Make sure the lime juice covers the fish.
2. Cover the bowl with a lid and chill in the refrigerator for 30 to 45 minutes, stirring occasionally if needed. The fish should look opaque but still be tender.
3. Once the fish is "cooked," drain the lime juice, but don't rinse. We want all that lime flavor.
4. Toss the fish with the onion, tomatoes, jalapeño, and cilantro. Season to taste with salt and black pepper.
5. This is certainly not traditional, but I like to drizzle a tiny bit of good-quality olive oil and a little fresh lime juice over the ceviche and give it a good toss.
6. Place the ceviche in a bowl and serve with tortilla chips or patacones (fried plantains). Or for a festive look, serve the ceviche in martini glasses, topped with sliced avocado and garnished with cilantro.

Easy Acqua Pazza

(FISH IN CRAZY WATER)

SERVES 4

Like so many recipes, there are countless versions of acqua pazza. It can include a much longer list of ingredients with several additional prep and cooking steps. However, for this recipe, I kept the ingredients simple to allow the fresh fish to shine.

I've included fennel rather than onion in this dish. Slicing it thinly with a mandoline keeps the slices uniform and allowing the fennel to slightly caramelize adds so much flavor, I don't even miss the onion.

This comes together quickly, so be sure to have everything mise en place (in its place). I garnish with the lemon zest and olives for extra umami. The lemon brings all the flavors together and the salt from the olives is highly complementary. But don't forget the warm, crusty bread—it's a must for dipping in the flavorful broth.

FIND YOUR FISH: Most any flaky white fish will work here, such as cod, rockfish, snapper, or even tilapia.

¼ cup extra-virgin olive oil

1 fennel bulb, thinly sliced

3 garlic cloves, thinly sliced

Pinch of crushed red pepper flakes

2 cups canned whole tomatoes with juice, smashed a bit with a fork

1 cup dry white wine; sauvignon blanc works well here

2 cups water

1 tablespoon chopped fresh flat-leaf parsley

1 tablespoon chopped capers

Salt and freshly ground black pepper

1½ pounds fish fillets, cut into 4 or 5 pieces, removed from refrigerator at least 15 minutes prior to cooking

1 teaspoon lemon zest for garnish

½ cup sliced Kalamata olives for garnish

1 tablespoon chopped fresh parsley for garnish (optional)

Warm, crusty bread slices for dipping

1 Heat the oil in a Dutch oven or large, deep skillet over medium heat.

2 When the oil is hot and shimmering, add the fennel and slowly cook until wilted and slightly caramelized, adjusting the heat as needed.

3 Stir in the garlic and cook for 1 minute longer.

4 Add the red pepper flakes and the tomatoes, white wine, water, flat-leaf parsley, and capers. Bring to a gentle simmer and cook for about 10 minutes. Season to taste with salt and pepper.

5 Keeping the heat on medium-low, place the fish fillets in the broth and let them cook for about 5 minutes, or until the fish is opaque and begins to flake.

6 Remove the pan from the heat and divide the fish and broth among four shallow bowls. Garnish with lemon zest, olives, and additional chopped parsley (if using).

7 Serve with warm, crusty bread for dipping.

Spiced Butter Fish

SERVES 4

One of the lovely things about seafood is that it plays well with all types of world cuisine. I adore the traditional North Indian dish butter chicken (chicken makhani), which features an array of enchanting flavors. However, I wanted to create a seafood version similar in flavor profile but simple enough to be prepared on a weeknight.

Taking notes from my favorite butter chicken recipe, I used it as a guide for creating this one. The fish does not need to be marinated, and onion and garlic are added. I include traditional Indian spices, tomatoes, and yogurt instead of heavy cream. It's served over basmati rice for a fragrant and comforting seafood meal. Just be very gentle when stirring in the fish, so it doesn't fall apart before being served.

FIND YOUR FISH: I've listed white fish in this recipe, such as cod, halibut, flounder, or rockfish. But I do think shrimp would be delicious instead. Or even a mixture of both. I typically use local rockfish, but most any mild-flavored white fish will be delicious. For more information and recommendations about mild-flavored white fish, refer to the "Seafood" 101 section (page 14).

2 tablespoons ghee or coconut oil

½ teaspoon ground cumin

1 teaspoon garam masala

1 teaspoon mild curry powder

Pinch of cayenne pepper (optional)

1 sweet onion, diced

1 teaspoon minced fresh ginger

2 to 3 garlic cloves, minced

One 28-ounce can whole tomatoes with juice

½ cup clam broth or seafood stock

Salt and freshly ground black pepper

1 pound mild white fish, cubed and checked for bones

½ cup plain Greek yogurt

½ cup chopped fresh cilantro

Cooked basmati rice for serving

½ cup sliced green onion for garnish

1. Heat the ghee or coconut oil in a soup pot over medium heat.
2. Then, stir in the cumin, garam masala, curry powder, and cayenne (if using). Let the spices warm and combine with the oil for about 1 minute.

CONTINUES ➡

3 Add the onion and cook until wilted and soft, adjusting the heat lower or higher as needed.

4 Stir in the ginger and garlic and cook for 1 minute longer.

5 As you continue to stir, add the whole tomatoes with juice and the clam broth.

6 Bring the mixture to a simmer and let cook for about 15 minutes over low heat. Partially cover with a lid, if needed.

7 Season to taste with salt and black pepper.

8 Gently stir in the cubed white fish and bring the mixture to a gentle simmer. Cook over low heat for about 5 minutes, or until the fish is done and opaque. This won't take long.

9 Add the yogurt to a small bowl and then slowly whisk in ½ cup of the hot liquid into the yogurt. This is to temper the yogurt so it doesn't curdle.

10 Remove the pot from the heat and gently stir in the cilantro and Greek yogurt.

11 Serve over basmati rice and garnish with sliced green onion.

Fish Taco Buddha Bowls with Creamy Blender Chimichurri

SERVES 4

Bowl food feels festive, I think due to all the delicious ingredients involved. This bowl is prepared with spicy roasted fish, veggies, and herbs and topped with a flavorful creamy blender chimichurri sauce. I've listed various ingredients, such as rice, black beans, pico de gallo, and cabbage, but feel free to replace these or add other items to the bowl. Whatever makes your food heart happy.

I've listed instructions for roasting the fish while you prep the additional ingredients. This makes dinner a cinch after a busy day. However, the fish can also be pan cooked or pan seared and then finished in the oven. I give instructions for these methods in the recipes for Pan-Cooked White Fish with Papaya Red Pepper Salsa (page 95) and Pan-Seared White Fish with Sauce Verte (page 99).

Sometimes I place all the ingredients in serving bowls on the kitchen counter. Then, I let my family assemble their bowls with the ingredients they love best.

CREAMY BLENDER CHIMICHURRI

½ cup packed fresh flat-leaf parsley leaves

1 cup packed fresh cilantro (you can include some stems)

3 green onions, root end trimmed, coarsely chopped

2 garlic cloves, smashed

Leaves from two 4-inch oregano sprigs

Pinch of crushed red pepper flakes

1 teaspoon ground cumin

Squeeze of lime juice

1 tablespoon Champagne vinegar or white wine vinegar

¾ cup extra-virgin olive oil

¼ cup crème fraîche

Salt and freshly ground black pepper

FISH TACO BUDDHA BOWLS

1 teaspoon chili powder

½ teaspoon ground cumin

½ teaspoon ground coriander

Squeeze of lime juice

1 tablespoon oil

1 pound white fish (such as halibut, flounder, haddock, pollack, snapper, cod, rockfish, or turbot), removed from refrigerator 15 minutes prior to cooking and pin bones removed

2 cups cooked rice

1 to 2 cups thinly sliced napa cabbage

1 to 2 tablespoons rice vinegar

1½ cups black beans, heated

1 cup pico de gallo

1 avocado, sliced (optional)

⅓ cup sliced green onion

⅓ cup chopped fresh cilantro

Lime wedges for serving

CONTINUES ➡

1. Prepare the chimichurri: Combine the parsley, cilantro, green onions, garlic, oregano leaves, red pepper flakes, cumin, lime juice, and vinegar in a blender or food processor.
2. Pulse a few times, then, while the blender is running, add the oil. Blend until the sauce is smooth.
3. Remove the sauce from the blender and season to taste with salt and black pepper. Stir in the crème fraîche. Keep in the refrigerator until you need it.
4. Prepare the Buddha bowls: Preheat the oven to 425°F.
5. Combine the chili powder, cumin, coriander, lime juice, and oil. Season the fish with salt and black pepper and then rub the spice mixture over the fish.
6. Place the fish in the oven and roast for 10 to 12 minutes, until opaque and flaky. Most fish cook through in about 10 minutes for every inch of thickness.
7. Once the fish is done, remove from the oven and let sit for a few minutes. Flake the fish into bite-size pieces. Be sure to check for bones.
8. To assemble, combine the sliced napa cabbage with the rice vinegar.
9. Divide the rice among four bowls. Then, add the black beans, cabbage, and roasted fish to each bowl, topped by the pico de gallo, avocado if using, green onion, and cilantro.
10. Drizzle the chimichurri over the top and serve immediately with lime wedges.

Crispy White Fish Burgers with Smoked Provolone and Special Sauce

MAKES 4 BURGERS

Do you remember those crispy fish sandwiches we used to get years ago at the "fast-food place I shall not name"? Oddly, when I was a kid, I really liked those fish sandwiches. I always thought melted cheese over the fish was brilliant, and combined with the sauce and squishy soft bun, made for loads of great texture.

This is not that sandwich. But it takes all the things I loved about it and rolled them into something fresh and flavorful with loads of great texture. I've created a "special" sauce that reminds me of a rémoulade or Thousand Island dressing, along with quick-pickled red onions that add a burst of tang to the recipe. The fish is coated in panko and fried, and I've topped it with smoked provolone. If you can't find smoked provolone, a smoked Cheddar or even just a slice of creamy provolone or Havarti will be delicious.

FIND YOUR FISH: I've used rockfish for the recipe, but cod, snapper, or any mild-flavored white fish will work.

SPECIAL SAUCE

1 cup mayonnaise

⅓ cup chili sauce

⅓ cup sweet pickle relish

2 garlic cloves, finely minced

1 teaspoon soy sauce

½ teaspoon freshly ground black pepper

QUICK-PICKLED RED ONIONS

½ medium red onion, sliced

½ cup seasoned rice wine vinegar, or more as needed

FISH

2 to 3 tablespoons cornstarch

2 large eggs whisked with 1 tablespoon water

1 cup panko bread crumbs

1 pound rockfish, cut into 4 pieces (make sure there are no bones)

Salt and freshly ground black pepper

½ to 1 cup high-heat oil, or more if needed

4 slices smoked provolone

TO ASSEMBLE

4 pub buns or brioche buns, buttered and toasted if you prefer

4 pieces green leaf or red leaf lettuce

4 to 8 slices tomato

Sliced pickles

CONTINUES ➡

1. Make the special sauce: Combine the mayonnaise, chili sauce, sweet pickle relish, garlic, soy sauce, and pepper in a small bowl. Set aside.
2. Make the quick-pickled red onions: Place the sliced red onion in a 16-ounce jelly jar or a glass bowl. Heat the vinegar in a small saucepan, and when warm, pour over the slices (be sure there is enough vinegar to cover them). Let them hang out for about 15 minutes or so, or while you're preparing the fish. You can store the remaining pickled slices in a covered glass jar or container in the refrigerator for up to 1 week.
3. To make the fish, set up three plates or bowls, one with the cornstarch, one with the egg wash, and one with the panko.
4. Season both sides of the fish with salt and pepper, then dust in the cornstarch. Next, dip into the egg wash, and finally, toss in the panko. Place the fish on a baking sheet or plate. Repeat until all the fish are coated.
5. Heat a large skillet over medium or medium-low heat and add enough high-heat oil to cover the surface of the skillet.
6. Once the oil is hot and shimmering, but not smoking, place the fillets gently in the skillet and let each piece cook until golden brown on both sides. You may need to adjust the heat if your fish browns too quickly. Depending on the thickness of your fish, it should take 3 to 4 minutes on each side to cook the fish through. Typically, fish will cook through in 8 to 10 minutes for every inch of thickness. I find that rockfish cooks just a little faster.
7. Once your fish is done, transfer to a fish rack over a baking sheet or a paper towel–lined plate. Top with the provolone. This will give the cheese time to melt a bit. I like using a fish or cookie rack as this keeps both sides of the fish nice and crispy.
8. Assemble the burgers: If you wish, spread a little butter on the inside of each bun and then toast them in a pan over medium heat or on a baking sheet under the broiler for just a few seconds, just until golden. Toasting the buns gives additional flavor and texture to the sandwich.
9. Once the buns are toasted, add special sauce to each inner side of the bun. Place a provolone-topped fish fillet on the bottom bun. Layer with pickled red onion, lettuce, tomato, pickles, and the top of the bun. Skewer with party picks or toothpick to keep everything together prior to serving. But you'll want to serve these immediately.

Side Dish Suggestions

macaroni, pasta, or potato salad ✦ corn on the cob ✦ potato chips ✦ sweet potato fries ✦ roasted cheesy new potatoes

Salt and Vinegar Potato Chip–Crusted Fish Fingers with Dipping Sauces

SERVES 4

When my youngest daughter was in elementary school, we learned that she is gluten intolerant. I thought she might be the most upset about not being able to eat my homemade chocolate chip cookies. However, it turned out crispy fish fingers were what she would miss the most. Honestly, I was going to miss them, too.

I didn't want my daughter to miss out on the crunchy goodness of crispy fish fingers, so I started to substitute potato chips for the bread crumbs. In the beginning, I used regular potato chips, eventually branching out to her favorite barbecue chips. But then one trip to the market, she grabbed salt and vinegar chips and asked me whether I could use them for her fish fingers. It was such a delicious idea that we've been making them this way ever since.

As an alternative, these can be baked at 425°F for about 10 minutes, if desired, but I think they are best when panfried.

FIND YOUR FISH: Most any kind of white fish works for this recipe and especially a firmer fish, such as cod or rockfish. Be sure to remove any bones before cooking.

1 large egg whisked with 1 tablespoon cold water

Pinch of cayenne pepper (optional)

One 8.5-ounce bag salt and vinegar potato chips (about 2 cups finely crushed)

1 pound mild-flavored white fish, cut into 1-inch-thick strips (as you would for chicken or fish fingers)

Salt and freshly ground black pepper

2 tablespoons cornstarch

High-heat oil for frying

CONTINUES ➡

1 Whisk together the dipping sauce or sauces (see sidebar). If making a double batch of these fish fingers, it's always fun to set out all three sauces.

2 Set out two bowls, one with the egg wash whisked with a pinch of cayenne, if using, and the other with the crushed potato chips.

3 Place the fish fingers in a large bowl and sprinkle with salt and black pepper. Then, dust with the cornstarch, making sure each fish finger is nicely dusted. Shake off any excess cornstarch and lay the fish fingers, in a single layer, on a parchment-lined baking sheet.

4 Next, dip each fish finger into the egg wash, and then coat in crushed potato chips. Lay them back on the baking sheet.

5 Add ¼ to ½ inch of high-heat oil to a large, deep skillet over medium heat. When the oil is hot and shimmering, but not smoking (about 325°F), add the fish fingers in a single layer, so they are not overlapping.

6 Once the fish begins to brown on the bottom, 1½ to 2 minutes, flip the fish to the other side, using a fish spatula or tongs. If you notice the potato chips are browning too quickly, lower the heat to medium-low. Adjusting the heat and adding additional oil as needed is key to perfectly golden-brown fish.

7 The fish should be done once both sides are golden brown. Transfer to a paper towel-lined baking rack or a cooling rack. This will keep the potato chip crust crisp. If you have thicker pieces of fish, you will need to continue to cook a minute or two longer.

8 Once the fish is done, serve immediately with the dipping sauces.

Side Dish Suggestions

coleslaw or iceberg lettuce wedge with buttermilk dressing ✦ loads of dipping sauce

Dipping Sauces

Lemon Garlic Aioli

½ cup mayonnaise
Zest and juice of 1 lemon
1 garlic clove, minced
1 teaspoon finely chopped parsley

Mix all the ingredients together in a small bowl. Will keep in the refrigerator for up to 3 days.

Tartar Sauce

¾ cup mayonnaise
1 teaspoon prepared horseradish
¼ cup sweet pickle relish
1 garlic clove, minced
1 tablespoon chopped fresh parsley
1 tablespoon freshly squeezed lemon juice
Dash of Worcestershire sauce
Salt and freshly ground black pepper

Mix all the ingredients together in a small bowl, adding salt and pepper to taste. Will keep in the refrigerator for up to 3 days.

Panko Panfried Fish with Japanese-Style Tartar Sauce and Kimchi Slaw

SERVES 4

I have created and cooked hundreds of fish recipes over the last 20 years, from simple to fancy to everything in between. But panko panfried fish is the dish that my husband requests most. The panko creates a light and crispy texture on the outside and keeps the fish moist and tender. It's a method of cooking that pairs well with most any fish or seafood. The result can be served with an assortment of sauces and side dishes.

Japanese-style tartar sauce is one of my favorite sauces with fried fish. It's almost like a saucy egg salad, and I love egg salad. So, this sauce totally works for me. It's also delicious with kimchi slaw, which has a little tang and spice.

FIND YOUR FISH: I recommend Pacific cod in this recipe, but most any fish fillet will work, such as rockfish, catfish, hake, halibut, snapper, bass, or grouper. I've kept the seasoning simple, but feel free to use your favorite seafood seasoning on the fish.

TARTAR SAUCE

- **¾ cup mayonnaise (Japanese mayonnaise if you can find it)**
- **¼ cup finely chopped sweet onion**
- **⅓ cup sweet pickle relish**
- **2 hard-boiled large eggs, finely chopped**
- **1 tablespoon chopped fresh parsley**
- **Juice of 1 lemon**
- **Salt and freshly ground black pepper**

KIMCHI SLAW

- **3 cups shredded cabbage (I prefer savoy or napa cabbage, but green or red cabbage works as well)**
- **1 cup of your favorite kimchi, lightly chopped**
- **½ cup chopped fresh cilantro**
- **2 tablespoons mayonnaise**
- **Juice of 1 lime**
- **Salt and freshly ground black pepper**

PANKO PANFRIED FISH

- **2 large eggs, whisked with 2 teaspoons cold water**
- **1 cup panko bread crumbs**
- **Salt and freshly ground black pepper**
- **2 to 3 tablespoons cornstarch**
- **High-heat oil for panfrying**
- **1½ pounds white fish fillets, patted dry and cut into about 6 pieces, removed from refrigerator at least 15 minutes prior to cooking and checked for bones**

1 Prepare the tartar sauce: Combine the mayonnaise, sweet onion, pickle relish, chopped eggs, parsley, and lemon juice in a medium bowl. Season to taste with salt and pepper. Set aside. This can be made a day in advance and kept in the refrigerator.

2 Prepare the kimchi slaw: combine the cabbage, kimchi, and cilantro in a medium to large bowl.

3 Whisk together the mayonnaise and lime juice in a small bowl and toss it with the slaw mixture. Season with salt and pepper to taste. Refrigerate until needed.

4 Prepare the fish: Set out two bowls, one with the whisked eggs, and the other with the panko.

CONTINUES ➡

5 Place the fish fillets in a large bowl and sprinkle with salt and pepper. Then, dust with the cornstarch, making sure each fillet is nicely dusted. Shake off any excess cornstarch and lay the fillets, in a single layer, on a parchment-lined baking sheet.

6 Next, dip each piece into the egg wash and then coat in panko. Lay the fish back on the baking sheet.

7 Add ¼ to ½ inch of high-heat oil to a large, deep skillet over medium heat. When the oil is hot and shimmering, but not smoking, add the fish so they are not overlapping. I use a 12-inch skillet and can usually fit 1 to 1½ pounds of fish fillets into that skillet. But if you have a smaller skillet, you'll need to panfry the fillets in two batches.

8 Once the fish begins to brown on the bottom, 2 to 3 minutes, using a fish spatula or tongs, flip the fish to the other side. If you notice the panko browning too quickly, lower the heat to medium-low. Adjusting the heat and adding additional oil as needed is key to perfectly golden-brown fish.

9 The fish should be done once both sides are golden brown. Transfer to a paper towel–lined baking rack or cooling rack. This will keep the panko crisp. If you have thicker pieces of fish, you will need to continue to cook a minute or two longer. Be sure to lower the heat so you don't burn the panko.

10 Once the fish is done, it's time to serve! Panko panfried fish is best served immediately. Serve the fish with the kimchi slaw and Japanese tartar sauce on the side.

Simple Oven-Roasted Whole Fish

SERVES 2

Whole roasted fish might seem a little intimidating at first, but following just a few steps makes it quite easy. I usually make this recipe on a weekend night and serve it with roasted potatoes, a salad of fresh greens, and warm, crusty bread, along with a bottle of our favorite white wine. It's the perfect meal for date night at home!

I serve the fish whole on large dinner plates, rather than separating the fish from the bones and flesh. This way, everyone at the table can take their time to eat their way through the fish. I also like to serve my roasted fish with either a good drizzle of my special herbed olive oil or warm butter that I've infused with some chopped fresh herbs and garlic.

Some methods of roasting whole fish call for making three diagonal slices, ½ inch deep, through the outside of the fish and stuffing it with herbs, salt, pepper, lemon slices, or other ingredients. I give instructions for this, but sometimes, I skip this part. Mostly because I'm in a hurry and I just want to get the fish in the oven and dinner on the table. It will still taste just as delicious!

Flavor combinations for whole roasted fish are endless. That said, I've listed my top three just in case you need inspiration.

One last reminder: have fun; don't worry about it looking fabulous the first time you make the recipe. Just be sure to choose quality whole fish and use fresh ingredients for optimum flavor.

FIND YOUR FISH: I typically make this recipe with trout, rockfish, mackerel, or steelhead because that's what I find fresh most often. But any whole round fish can be used, such as snapper, sea bass, branzino, or whatever type of fish is sourced in your area.

When selecting whole fish, the skin and fins should be shiny, and the eyes clear and bulging, not sunken. The whole fish should smell like the ocean, clean and briny. Be sure to ask your fishmonger to clean and scale the fish and remove the gills and fins. It'll make it easier for you when you get home to prepare the fish.

CONTINUES ➡

2 whole fish, 1 to 1½ pounds each, scaled, cleaned, gills and fins removed

Good-quality extra-virgin olive oil

Salt and freshly ground black pepper

1 garlic clove, chopped or sliced, plus more, minced, for butter sauce

Assorted fresh herbs, such as thyme, parsley, and chives

Lemon slices

½ pound (2 sticks) salted butter for butter sauce

Coarse sea salt for finishing (optional)

Flavor Combination #1

Thyme sprigs

Parsley sprigs

Fresh chives

Lemon slices

2 to 3 garlic cloves, sliced

Good-quality extra-virgin olive oil

Salt and freshly ground pepper

Flavor Combination #2

Thinly sliced fennel

Thinly sliced shallot

Thinly sliced garlic cloves

Lemon slices

Parsley sprigs

Salt and freshly ground pepper

Good-quality extra-virgin olive oil

Flavor Combination #3

Thinly sliced garlic

Minced fresh ginger mixed with a few tablespoons ponzu or soy sauce

Cilantro sprigs

Fresh chives

Slices of lime and orange

Freshly ground black pepper

Good-quality extra-virgin olive oil

1 Preheat the oven to 450°F.

2 With a sharp knife, make three diagonal cuts, about ½ inch deep, on one side of the outside body of the fish. This is optional but it is pretty and does allow more of the seasoning into the meat.

3 Place the fish on a baking sheet and brush inside and out with olive oil. Season with salt and pepper inside and out and be sure to get some of the seasoning into the three sliced areas on the outside of the fish.

4 Add the garlic, assorted fresh herbs, and lemon slices to the cavity of the fish, or use one of the flavor combinations that I have listed here. (Note: If using flavor combination #3, you won't need to salt the inside of the fish.) If I've super stuffed the fish, sometimes I'll tie the fish closed with kitchen twine in two or three places around the belly of the fish, just to keep the stuffing in while roasting. This is optional, but it can be helpful.

5 Place half a lemon slice in each of the sliced areas on top of the fish or just lay a few lemon slices on top. Drizzle again with a little olive oil and place the baking sheet in the oven. Bake for about 20 minutes, or until the internal temperature is 140° to 145°F.

6 When the fish is done, remove from the oven and place the whole fish on individual plates or a platter. Just remove any twine or lemon slices and then peel back the skin. You will reveal tender and flavorful fish. Watch for bones and don't forget to eat the cheek meat, which is found just below the eye.

7 To make a butter sauce, heat the butter in a small saucepan over low heat. When the butter is melted and warm, stir in the garlic and fresh chopped herbs. Remove the pan from the heat and let the herbs and garlic rest in the warm butter.

8 Serve the herb and garlic butter with the fish along with extra wedges of lemon and a finishing salt, if desired.

Moroccan-Style Roasted Fish

SERVES 4

Flavor abounds in this delicious roasted fish recipe with fresh herbs, spices, and citrus. The fish is topped with a chermoula-like herb mixture and roasted for an easy seafood meal. I've included smoked paprika in the topping, which gives the dish a hint of spice but complements all the other flavors.

FIND YOUR FISH: I use whatever fish I have on hand or find fresh in season at my local fish market or co-op. Rockfish, flounder, cod, hake, turbot, and halibut are some of the white fish that I use here, but most any mild-flavored white fish will work. For more information about white fish, refer to page 18.

⅓ cup packed fresh cilantro leaves

¼ cup packed flat-leaf parsley leaves

1 tablespoon capers

2 garlic cloves, smashed

1½ teaspoons smoked paprika

1 teaspoon grated fresh ginger

1 tablespoon freshly squeezed lemon juice

Pinch of red pepper flakes or cayenne pepper (optional)

3 tablespoons extra-virgin olive, or your favorite oil

1½ pounds white fish, with skin or skinless, paper towel dried and cut into 4 fillets

Salt and freshly ground black pepper

4 lemon slices

Lemon wedges for serving

1 Preheat the oven to 400°F and line a baking sheet with parchment.

2 Finely chop the cilantro and parsley and place in a medium bowl.

3 Then, lightly chop the capers and finely mince the garlic. Add them to the herb mixture.

4 Stir in the smoked paprika, ginger, lemon juice, red pepper flakes, and olive oil. Season to taste with salt and black pepper.

5 Season the fish with salt and black pepper and lay the fish, skin side down (if with skin), on the prepared pan.

6 Spread the herb mixture evenly over the top of the fish fillets and place a lemon slice on each piece of fish.

7 Then, place the baking sheet in the oven and roast for 8 to 10 minutes depending on the thickness of your fish. For every inch of thickness, the cooking time is about 10 minutes.

8 When the fish is done, flaky, and opaque, remove from the oven and either place on a platter to serve or on individual plates. Garnish with additional fresh lemon wedges.

Side Dish Suggestion

pearled couscous with dried apricots and toasted pine nuts ✦ roasted fennel and tomatoes

Fish Amandine

SERVES 4

When I find beautiful fish fillets, such as petrale sole, at my fish market, I snag them for this recipe. This is another recipe for which all the ingredients should be prepped and ready to go ahead of time. But once everything is mise en place (in its place), this recipe comes together quickly.

Contrary to what you might think, this recipe doesn't begin with dusting the fish in cornstarch or flour. The fish is seasoned, dredged through the egg wash and the almond panko mixture, and then quickly panfried. Then it is topped with additional almonds, garlic, and herbs when served.

Pan cooking fish takes practice and it's also a bit intuitive. I give heat and cook times but use your judgment to make adjustments. Every stovetop and every skillet heats differently, so the more you pan cook on the stovetop, the quicker you'll learn to adjust heat and cook times according to your equipment.

When I'm making this at home, sometimes I'll pan cook the fish first, clean out my skillet, and then make the almond topping. However, the skillet is quite hot after pan cooking the fish. So, in this recipe, I've recommended using two different pans.

FIND YOUR FISH: I find thinner fish fillets work best in this recipe—not delicate fish, but sturdier thinner fillets, such as cod, flounder, trout, catfish, or thin fillets of halibut. Trout is the traditional fish used but I really do love this prepared with petrale sole. You can use skin on or skinless; however, I prefer skinless fish unless it's salmon.

1 cup sliced raw almonds

½ cup panko bread crumbs

2 teaspoons chopped fresh parsley, plus more for garnish (optional)

2 teaspoons chopped fresh chives

8 tablespoons (1 stick) butter

1 garlic clove, minced

1 large egg, whisked with 1 tablespoon water

Salt and freshly ground black pepper

1½ pounds fish fillets, removed from refrigerator 15 minutes prior to cooking and patted dry with paper towels

2 to 3 tablespoons high-heat oil

1 lemon, cut into wedges

CONTINUES ➡

1 Combine ½ cup of the almonds with the panko, 1 teaspoon of the parsley, and 1 teaspoon of the chives in a food processor. Process until coarse crumbs appear.

2 Heat the butter in a saucepan or skillet. When the butter has just melted, add the remaining ½ cup of almonds, garlic, and remaining teaspoon of parsley and teaspoon of chives to the pan. Cook for a minute or two, or until the almonds are golden, and then remove from the heat. Transfer to a plate.

3 Salt and pepper the fish fillets. Set out two bowls, one with the egg wash, and one with the panko mixture.

4 Heat the high-heat oil in a large skillet over medium to medium-high heat.

5 When the oil is hot and shimmering, but not smoking, dredge the seasoned fillets through the egg wash and then through the panko mixture.

6 Add the fillets to the skillet and cook for 1 to 2 minutes, lowering the heat, if needed. Once the fish is browned on the bottom, flip to the other side and continue to cook until done. Thin fillets should take 4 to 6 minutes, but always adjust the time and temperature as needed.

7 Transfer the fish to a platter or plates and drizzle with a squeeze of lemon over each fillet.

8 Top with the toasted almond mixture and serve immediately with the lemon wedges. Garnish with additional chopped parsley if desired.

Side Dish Suggestions

a baby arugula salad lightly dressed in lemon or French vinaigrette ✦ rice or wild rice ✦ roasted potatoes ✦ additional lemon wedges

Orange, Fennel, and Avocado Salsa with Pan-Cooked Fish

SERVES 4

Oranges and fennel are a classic pairing with seafood. It's found in a multitude of recipes, and it is delicious with fish no matter how it's prepared. And, because I've always been a "topping" person, what better way to top fish than with a salsa of oranges, fennel, and avocado? Fresh and light and so perfect with most any fish.

For this recipe, I used halibut cheek meat. Fish cheeks are the small bit of meat just below the eyes of the fish. These tender morsels are considered one of the best parts of the fish, with a sweeter flavor and delicate texture. You'll find cheek meat most often from larger fish, such as halibut, grouper, snapper, or lingcod. So, if you happen to see it in your local fish market, snag some and pan cook them just like any other fish fillet.

I've dusted the fish in a little flour (or cornstarch) to give it a nice crust, which is a delightful contrast to the textures in the salsa. This is optional, however; it's not only tasty but often makes pan cooking fish fillets easier.

FIND YOUR FISH: Most any type of fish works here. Mild, flaky, medium-textured, a little more flavorful, even salmon works in this recipe. I've paired this salsa with lingcod, black cod, skate, halibut cheeks, and rockfish with mouthwatering results.

1 small to medium bulb fennel, thinly sliced with a mandoline, then lightly chopped

2 medium to large oranges, segmented and lightly chopped, 1 tablespoon of juice reserved (in a pinch, you could use a jar or two of mandarins, drained)

1 tablespoon chopped fresh flat-leaf parsley

1 tablespoon chopped fresh mint

½ cup thinly sliced green onion

1 tablespoon good-quality extra-virgin olive oil

Salt and freshly ground black pepper

Pinch of cayenne pepper (optional)

1 medium to large avocado, diced

1½ pounds fish fillets, removed from refrigerator at least 15 minutes prior to cooking, checked for bones

2 to 3 tablespoons all-purpose flour or cornstarch

2 to 3 tablespoons ghee or high-heat oil

Toasted sliced almonds for garnish (optional)

CONTINUES ➡

JACOBSEN
SALT

1 Combine the fennel, orange segments and reserved juice, parsley, mint, and green onion in a medium to large nonreactive or glass bowl. Toss with the olive oil and season to taste with salt and pepper, and a pinch of cayenne (if using).

2 Then, gently toss with the diced avocado. Cover and keep in the refrigerator while you prepare the fish.

3 Make the fish: Season each fillet with salt and pepper. Spread the flour in a bowl and lightly dredge the fillets through the flour, dusting them off lightly and placing them on a baking sheet or plate. If you don't want to use flour, cornstarch is a good alternative. The flour or cornstarch gives the fish a very light crust and helps it stay together during the cooking process.

4 Heat a large skillet over medium-high heat and add enough ghee to lightly coat the surface of the skillet.

5 When the ghee is hot but not smoking, add the fish to the skillet. Let the fillets cook for 3 to 4 minutes, until the bottom of the fish looks golden brown. With a fish spatula or a wide spatula, flip each fillet to the other side and cook for another 2 to 4 minutes, until the fish is cooked through. If the fish won't flip or if it feels stuck, let it sit for another 30 seconds or so, adjusting the heat as needed. When the fish is ready, it should flip easily. Most fish will cook through in 10 minutes for every inch of thickness. Fish will continue to cook when removed from the pan, so keep this in mind when cooking.

6 When the fish is done, transfer to plates or a platter and ladle with the fennel salsa. Serve immediately.

Side Dish Suggestions

orzo, couscous, pearled couscous, quinoa, or farro ✦ white or brown rice ✦ roasted asparagus

Pan-Cooked Fish with Herbed Gremolata and White Beans

SERVES 4

The blend of fresh herbs and lemon in this gremolata harmonizes deliciously with most any white fish and makes a flavorful and satisfying fish dinner. A gremolata is often used as a garnish to finish a dish. But here, I've used it much like a sauce that complements the fish as well as the white beans.

This is another great recipe to practice pan cooking fish. I've given detailed instructions here, but for more information about skillets and other equipment, refer to page 39.

FIND YOUR FISH: I recommend white fish here (halibut, rockfish, snapper, cod, pollack, bass, grouper, or haddock) but I've also used more flavorful fish for this recipe, such as black cod, blue fish, or sea bass. The fresh flavors of the herbs and lemon balance the richness of these fish.

3 tablespoons plus 1 teaspoon chopped fresh flat-leaf parsley

3 tablespoons chopped fresh chives

3 tablespoons chopped fresh basil

1 tablespoon chopped fresh mint

1 garlic clove, finely minced or pressed

Zest of 1 lemon

1 tablespoon freshly squeezed lemon juice

¼ cup extra-virgin olive oil

Salt and freshly ground black pepper

One 15-ounce can white beans, drained

Pinch of dried oregano or chopped fresh

1½ pounds white fish, cut into 4 pieces, bones removed, patted dry with paper towels

3 tablespoons all-purpose flour or cornstarch

2 to 4 tablespoons ghee or high-heat oil

1 Prepare the gremolata: Combine 3 tablespoons of the parsley plus the chives, basil, mint, garlic, and lemon zest and juice in a small bowl. Then, stir in the olive oil and season to taste with salt and pepper. Set aside.

CONTINUES ➡

2 Place the white beans in a small pan and heat over low heat. Stir the oregano, a drizzle of olive oil and the remaining teaspoon of parsley. When the beans are hot, remove the pan from the heat and season with salt and pepper. Cover and keep warm.

3 Prepare the fish: Season each fillet with salt and pepper. Spread the flour in a bowl and lightly dredge the fillets through the flour, dusting them off lightly and placing them on a baking sheet or plate.

4 Heat a large skillet over medium-high heat and add enough ghee to lightly coat the surface of the skillet.

5 When the ghee is hot and shimmering, but not smoking, add the fish to the skillet. Let the fillets cook for 2 to 3 minutes, until the bottom of the fish looks golden brown.

6 With a fish spatula or a wide spatula, flip each fillet to the other side and cook for another 2 to 3 minutes, until the fish is cooked through. If the fish won't flip or if it feels stuck, let it sit for another 30 seconds or so. When the fish is ready, it should flip easily. Most fish will cook through in 8 to 10 minutes for every inch of thickness. The fish is done when it reaches 140°F and it begins to flake.

7 To serve, divide the white beans among plates, top with a fillet or two of fish, and then sprinkle with a tablespoon of gremolata. Serve immediately.

Side Dish Suggestions

roasted or steamed vegetables, such as asparagus, broccoli, sautéed spinach, or Swiss chard

Butter-Poached Halibut with Roasted Cherry Tomatoes, Leeks, and Potatoes

SERVES 4

In the traditional French method of butter poaching, called beurre monté, a splash of water is heated in a saucepan, and then butter is whisked in. This allows the butter to remain stable and not separate until it gets to a higher temperature.

I've incorporated the technique into this recipe, but I put a little spin on it. I'm using white wine to begin, and after the butter is whisked in, I add the aromatics and herbs. I've listed seafood stock just in case additional liquid is needed.

Butter poaching is an excellent cooking method to use for lean cuts of fish, lobster, or shrimp. But I especially like to use this method with halibut.

FIND YOUR FISH: If you can't find halibut, flounder, fluke, or turbot are delicious options.

4 small to medium leeks, white to light green, halved and washed (they often have sand between the layers), then quartered

4 tablespoons extra-virgin olive oil

1 teaspoon chopped fresh thyme

Salt and freshly ground black pepper

12 ounces cherry tomatoes

2 medium potatoes, diced into ½-inch cubes

¼ cup white wine

1 pound (4 sticks) unsalted butter, cut into cubes

3 garlic cloves, smashed

1 tablespoon chopped fresh parsley, plus more for garnish

2 thyme sprigs

1 lemon, sliced

1½ pounds halibut, cut into 4 or 5 pieces

1 cup warm seafood stock, if needed

Coarse or blended sea salt for finishing

Lemon slices for garnish

1 To roast the vegetables, preheat the oven to 400°F.

2 Place the leeks in a large bowl and toss with 1½ tablespoons of the olive oil and chopped thyme, then season with salt and pepper. Pour them out in a single layer onto half of a baking sheet, leaving room for the tomatoes.

CONTINUES ➡

3 Then, toss the tomatoes in 1½ tablespoons of the olive oil and season with salt and pepper. Pour them out onto the other side of the same baking sheet as the leeks. Place the baking pan in the oven and roast for 15 to 20 minutes, until the leeks are soft and golden.

4 Toss the potatoes in a bowl with the remaining tablespoon of olive oil and sprinkle with salt and pepper. I place these in a small baking or roasting pan and pop them in the oven with the leeks and tomatoes. Let them also roast for 15 to 20 minutes.

5 To poach the halibut, heat the wine in the bottom of a medium pot, or one large enough to hold the fish, over medium-low heat.

6 When the wine just begins to simmer, whisk in the butter, a little at a time, until all the butter has been incorporated.

7 Then, stir in the garlic, parsley, thyme sprigs, lemon slices, and pinch of salt and pepper.

8 Bring the liquid to a gentle simmer and then carefully add the halibut to the poaching liquid. The liquid should just cover the fish. If you need additional liquid, add ¼ to ½ cup of warm seafood stock at a time until the fish is covered.

9 Let the fish cook for 7 to 10 minutes. Do not let the broth boil. You just want a very gentle, slow simmer. Just when the fish starts to flake, it should be done. Using a spider strainer, transfer the fish to a plate and set aside.

10 Strain the poaching liquid and add it back to the pot. Place the pot back over low heat and let it simmer for about 5 minutes. Turn off the heat and let it rest. Just before serving, skim off the flavorful clarified butter that has settled on the top and transfer to a bowl.

11 Once the vegetables are done, arrange them on a platter or divide among plates. Top with a piece of halibut, season with a little finishing salt, if desired, and garnish with chopped parsley and lemon slices. Serve with the clarified butter on the side.

CHAPTER THREE

A Little Fancy

Sometimes, I need a seafood meal that feels a little fancy. A meal that tastes indulgent, or uses an assortment of lush ingredients, or even a meal that feels like a warm, cozy blanket in a bowl. These are the recipes I turn to when I have a little extra time to spend in the kitchen or I want to prepare a recipe that will wow my dinner guests.

Many of these recipes I prepare for family dinners, weekend gatherings, date night in, special occasions, or celebrations. The active prep time and cook time is a bit more involved, and either there is a longer ingredient list or there are a few new or special ingredients. This chapter also includes recipes that deliciously incorporate fish into a dish rather than serving a whole fillet, such as the Halibut and Leek au Gratin (page 311) and the Curried Fish Cakes with Lime and Mint Yogurt Sauce (page 303).

I started this chapter with a recipe for Homemade Seafood Stock (page 224). I know that doesn't sound indulgent or fancy, but it makes my food heart happy when I've got homemade stock on hand to use in a special recipe.

Also in this chapter, I've included my versions of traditional favorites, such as the Shrimp and Sausage Jambalaya (page 237), Seafood Risotto (page 268), and Coconut Shrimp with Sweet and Spicy Apricot Glaze (page 225). But I've also added a few eclectic recipes such as the Pan-Seared Scallops with Tomato Ginger Jam (page 253) and the Sablefish with Creamy Piquillo Pepper Sauce and Lemon Cream (page 305). These are recipes that sound quite elaborate, but with practice and anticipation, they can be super easy. And if you've already cooked your way through the previous two chapters, you're ready for a challenge!

So, dive in, show off those cooking skills, and cook something a little fancy.

Homemade Seafood Stock

MAKES ABOUT 2 QUARTS

After a shellfish boil (such as my recipe on page 158) or an evening of cracking crab, I save all the shells, place them in a sealed bag, and put them in the freezer. When I've collected about a pound or more of shells, I make seafood stock.

I keep some of the stock in the refrigerator if I know I'll need it. Otherwise, I divide the stock among 1-cup containers and store them in the freezer. This is a good use for all those discarded shells and a great way to keep seafood stock on hand.

I like to add aromatics, herbs, and a little tomato paste to the stock to deepen the flavor and give it a richer color. If I'm in a hurry, I'll throw everything in the pot, add water, and start simmering. If I have more time, I'll sauté the vegetables and shells in oil, which gives the stock good flavor. Either way, it's delicious and will be a lovely complement to any seafood recipe. I would especially recommend it in the Seafood Risotto (page 268), and Irish-Style Fish Chowder (page 293).

3 tablespoons extra-virgin olive oil

1 large onion, thickly sliced

1 carrot, coarsely chopped

2 celery stalks, coarsely chopped

2 garlic cloves, smashed

1 to 1½ pounds shells from crab, shrimp and/or lobster, big pieces broken up

2½ quarts filtered water

2 tablespoons tomato paste

1 bay leaf

2 thyme sprigs

1 tablespoon coarsely chopped flat-leaf parsley

6 to 8 black peppercorns

2 teaspoons salt

1 Heat a large stockpot over medium heat and add the oil, onion, carrot, celery, garlic, and shells. Cook for about 10 minutes, stirring occasionally.

2 Add the filtered water, tomato paste, bay leaf, thyme, parsley, peppercorns, and salt. Simmer for about 1 hour.

3 Remove from the heat, let cool, and then strain the stock through a sieve, being sure to press down on the shells and vegetables to release all the stock.

4 Store in airtight containers in the refrigerator for up to 3 days. Otherwise, store in the freezer and thaw when needed.

Coconut Shrimp with Sweet and Spicy Apricot Glaze

SERVES 4

These savory, sweet coconut shrimp have been in my recipe repertoire for at least 15 years. I never tire of this scrumptious dish and it's always a crowd-pleaser.

To make coating the shrimp easier, I place the panko and coconut in a food processor and give a few pulses. This grinds the coconut a little finer and it blends better with the panko. If you don't have a food processor, I recommend giving the coconut a good chop before combining with the panko.

Try not to rush the coating process. It's a bit tedious but worth taking time to fully coat each shrimp. Once they are coated, I recommend keeping them on a parchment-lined baking sheet for about 10 minutes before frying.

I panfry in high-heat oil, but if you have a deep fryer, that also works well. The sauce is luscious, but if you prefer not to make a sauce, serve these with Thai sweet chili sauce or mango chutney.

SHRIMP

1 cup shredded sweetened coconut

½ cup panko bread crumbs

½ cup all-purpose flour

2 large eggs whisked with 1 teaspoon water

1 pound shrimp (21/30 or 16/20 count; see Notes on page 123), peeled and deveined (leave tails on), patted dry with paper towels

Salt and freshly ground black pepper

High-heat oil

SAUCE

1 cup apricot preserves or jam

1 teaspoon grated fresh ginger

1 teaspoon Thai roasted red chili paste

1 teaspoon rice vinegar

¼ cup white wine or water

1 Combine the coconut and panko in a food processor and pulse a few times until the coconut is lightly chopped and nicely combined with the panko. Then, transfer the coconut panko to a medium bowl.

2 Place the flour in a bowl and the whisked egg in another bowl. Line up the bowls in this order: flour, egg, and coconut panko.

3 Line a baking sheet with parchment.

CONTINUES ➡

4 Season the shrimp with salt and pepper and toss with the flour.

5 Holding a shrimp by the tail, dust the excess flour off the shrimp, dip into the egg, and then gently roll in the coconut panko mixture, coating all sides but leaving the tail uncoated. Place the shrimp on the prepared baking sheet and repeat until all the shrimp are coated.

6 While the shrimp rest, whisk together the jam, ginger, roasted red chili paste, vinegar, and wine or water in a small saucepan over low heat. Bring to a simmer and then remove from the heat. Set aside to cool. When cool, transfer to a small bowl to serve with the fried shrimp.

7 To fry the shrimp, heat a large skillet over medium heat and add high-heat oil to about 2 inches deep.

8 When the oil is shimmering and reaches 350°F, add the shrimp in batches; don't overcrowd the shrimp. Let them cook for 1 to 1½ minutes on each side, turning them if needed and adjusting the heat as needed. Once they are golden brown, transfer to a paper towel–lined plate or platter.

9 Once all the shrimp are done, serve immediately with the sauce.

Butter Lettuce with Grilled Shrimp, Avocado, Bacon, and Creamy Herb Dressing

SERVES 2 AS AN ENTRÉE OR 4 AS A SIDE SALAD

It's not often that I make a salad on constant repeat. But this is so luscious, it's the salad that I serve at most of our family Sunday dinners.

Chives, parsley, and basil are three of my favorite herb flavor combinations and make a flavorful dressing for this salad. I also use vegan mayonnaise as a base for the dressing, rather than conventional mayonnaise. The flavor and texture work well with the herbs and I find that it is saucier than mayonnaise.

Although this salad happens year-round, it's especially fun to make and eat during the warm summer months. Shrimp are easy to grill, and the grilling method enhances the shrimp flavor. During winter months, I often use a grill pan on my stovetop. It's not quite as "grilled" in flavor, but it does the trick.

DRESSING

1½ tablespoons chopped fresh chives

1½ tablespoons chopped fresh parsley

1 tablespoon chopped fresh basil

1 garlic clove, minced

1 cup vegan mayonnaise, preferably Follow Your Heart brand soy-free Vegenaise

1 tablespoon extra-virgin olive oil

1 teaspoon apple cider vinegar

1 teaspoon spicy brown or Dijon mustard

2 to 3 tablespoons water

Salt and freshly ground black pepper

SALAD

1 pound shrimp, peeled, deveined, with or without tails on, patted dry with a paper towel

1 to 2 tablespoons extra-virgin olive oil

Salt and freshly ground black pepper

1 head butter lettuce, leaves separated and lightly torn, if desired

1 to 2 avocados, sliced

8 ounces bacon, cooked and chopped

1 tablespoon chopped fresh chives for garnish

1 Make the dressing: Place the chives, parsley, basil, garlic, mayonnaise, olive oil, vinegar, and mustard in a food processor and pulse until nicely combined. You should still see specks of the fresh herbs. Whisk in 1 to 2 tablespoons of water for your desired consistency. Season to taste with salt and pepper.

CONTINUES ➡

2 Alternatively, you can put all the dressing ingredients in a bowl and whisk to combine. Then, season to taste with salt and pepper. However, the food processor combines the ingredients more thoroughly, which allows a stronger herb flavor.

3 Preheat a grill to 400°F. Have ready 6 to 8 metal or wooden skewers. If using wooden, be sure to soak them in water for 20 minutes prior to using.

4 Toss the shrimp with 1 to 2 tablespoons of olive oil and then season with salt and pepper.

5 Thread the shrimp on the skewers, leaving a little space between each shrimp.

6 Once the shrimp are skewered, place them on the grill to cook for 1½ to 2 minutes and then turn them over and grill for another 1 to 1½ minutes. When they are done, they will be pink and opaque.

7 Remove the shrimp from the skewers.

8 Assemble the salad: Divide the butter lettuce among your serving plates. Top with the shrimp, avocado, and chopped bacon.

9 Drizzle the dressing over the salad and garnish with chopped chives, if desired. Serve immediately with extra dressing on the side.

Shrimp Panzanella Salad with Basil Vinaigrette

SERVES 4 TO 6

While traveling through Tuscany, I must have eaten my weight in panzanella salad. Each salad was composed of assorted vegetable variations and paired with or without a protein. But they all included bread, which makes this salad so appealing. Sometimes, the bread was marinated in vinegar and oil, and other times, it was made soft by the liquid from the vegetables. Every version was heaven on a plate.

I love this salad so much I have turned it into an entrée dish paired with grilled shrimp. This is one of my spring and summer salads that can be simply prepared as written, or additional summer garden vegetables added for a heartier version.

Some chefs and home cooks like to toast the bread cubes or fry them in oil. I like them plain but at least a day or two old. The dry bread soaks up all the delicious flavors of the roasted vegetables, which complements the grilled shrimp and basil vinaigrette.

Although I serve this as an entrée salad, it is lovely as a side dish for weekend dinner guests.

BASIL VINAIGRETTE

1 cup packed fresh basil

½ cup extra-virgin olive oil

¼ cup grated Parmesan

2 tablespoons white wine vinegar or Champagne vinegar

2 tablespoons freshly squeezed lemon juice

1 small garlic clove

Salt and freshly ground black pepper

SHRIMP

1 pound shrimp, peeled, deveined, tails off

1 to 2 tablespoons extra-virgin olive oil

Salt and freshly ground black pepper

SALAD

12 ounces cherry tomatoes

1 large shallot, sliced

2 tablespoons extra-virgin olive oil

Salt and freshly ground black pepper

1 large loaf day-old or dry ciabatta bread, cubed (6 to 8 cups)

½ cup torn or coarsely chopped fresh basil, plus more for garnish

8 ounces mozzarella, ciliegine, or pearls

Squeeze of lemon juice (about 1 teaspoon)

CONTINUES ➡

1 Make the vinaigrette: Combine the basil, olive oil, Parmesan, vinegar, lemon juice, and garlic in a blender or food processor. Pulse until smooth. Season to taste with salt and pepper. Set aside.

2 Grill the shrimp: Preheat a grill to 400°F. Have ready 6 to 8 metal or wooden skewers. If using wooden, be sure to soak them in water for 20 minutes prior to using.

3 Place the shrimp in a bowl, toss with the olive oil, and season with salt and pepper.

4 Thread the shrimp on the skewers, leaving a little space between each shrimp.

5 Once the shrimp are skewered, place them on the grill to cook for 1½ to 2 minutes, then turn them over and grill for another 1 to 1½ minutes. When they are done, they will be pink and opaque.

6 Remove the shrimp from the skewers and place in a bowl. Toss the warm shrimp with a few tablespoons of the basil vinaigrette. Set aside.

7 Make the salad: Preheat the oven to 400°F.

8 Toss the tomatoes and sliced shallot with the olive oil and season well with salt and pepper.

9 Arrange the tomatoes and shallot in a single layer on a baking sheet and place in the oven. Roast for 8 to 10 minutes, until the tomatoes are wilted and slightly golden.

10 Remove the tomatoes and shallot from the oven and let cool.

11 Then, place the bread cubes in a large bowl and toss with the tomatoes, shallot, basil, mozzarella, lemon juice, and a few tablespoons of the vinaigrette. Season to taste with salt and pepper. Let the salad marinate for about 15 minutes before serving.

12 Pour the salad onto a platter and top with the shrimp. Garnish with chopped basil and serve with the remaining vinaigrette on the side.

Shrimp Po'boy with Spicy Cajun Dressing

MAKES 4 SANDWICHES

Living in Louisiana for several years was a culinary adventure and one that made a lasting impression on my memories and my taste buds. Po'boy sandwiches are iconic in this area and were said to originate in 1929 when the Martin brothers invented this recipe and handed them out to the striking streetcar drivers, who they called the "poor boys." Po'boys, as these sandwiches became known, can be found on most menus in Louisiana, and now on many menus across the country.

Po'boys are typically prepared with a fried seafood or meat that is combined with assorted condiments and sauce. I've had them made with fried oysters, crawfish, crab, fish, and chicken. But I've also seen them on menus made with alligator, sausage, beef, and veggies. Each loaded with local and seasonal ingredients and sauces that range from sweet and mild to spicy and hot.

I love to make these festive sandwiches for game days, weekends with the family, and on occasion, I'll make them for days we spend outdoors hiking, kayaking, or fishing at the lake. I package the ingredients separately and then let everyone assemble their po'boys when we gather for lunch.

For an extra treat, I sometimes butter and toast the inside of the hoagie rolls. But truly, these sandwiches are just as delicious without toasting the rolls.

SAUCE

¾ cup mayonnaise

1 teaspoon Cajun or Creole seasoning

2 tablespoons freshly squeezed lemon juice

1 garlic clove, minced

¼ cup chili sauce

¼ cup sweet pickle relish

¼ cup chopped green onion

Dash of Tabasco (optional)

Salt and freshly ground black pepper

SHRIMP

1 pound raw small to medium shrimp (31/40 count; see Note on page 123), peeled, deveined, and patted dry with paper towels

2 to 3 teaspoons Cajun or Creole seasoning (depending on heat level)

½ to 1½ teaspoons salt

1 cup buttermilk

1 cup finely ground cornmeal

½ cup all-purpose flour

½ teaspoon garlic powder

½ teaspoon freshly ground black pepper

Oil for frying

TO ASSEMBLE SANDWICHES

Four 8-inch hoagie rolls

2 to 3 cups shredded iceberg or romaine lettuce

Sliced dill pickles (sandwich slices)

Sliced tomatoes (optional)

Lemon wedges

CONTINUES ➡

1 Make the sauce: Combine the mayonnaise, Cajun or Creole seasoning, lemon juice, garlic, chili sauce, pickle relish, green onion, and Tabasco (if using) in a small bowl. Season to taste with salt and pepper. Set aside.

2 Prepare the shrimp: Toss the shrimp with 1 to 2 teaspoons of the Cajun or Creole seasoning and 1 teaspoon of the salt (if the seasoning doesn't contain salt). Let them sit for about 10 minutes in the seasoning. I use this time to prep the lettuce and slice the tomatoes, if I'm using them.

3 Pour the buttermilk into a bowl and then gently add the shrimp.

4 Combine the cornmeal, flour, garlic powder, black pepper, the remaining teaspoon of Cajun seasoning, and the remaining ½ teaspoon of salt in a medium bowl.

5 Place a piece of parchment on a baking sheet. Take each shrimp from the buttermilk, letting the excess drip off a bit, and coat in the cornmeal mixture, gently shaking off any excess, and place it on the baking sheet.

6 Pour the oil to about 2 inches deep in a large skillet over medium heat and heat to about 350°F. Working in batches, fry the shrimp until golden brown on both sides, 2 to 3 minutes; adjust the heat as needed. Place the shrimp on a paper towel–lined cooling rack or plate.

7 To assemble the sandwiches, spread the sauce on the inside of a bun and layer with lettuce, pickle slices, and tomatoes (if using), and then top with shrimp. Squeeze a little lemon juice on top. Serve with extra sauce and dig in!

Side Dish Suggestions

potato chips ✦ potato or pasta salad ✦ coleslaw ✦ baked beans ✦ braised garlicky greens ✦ grilled veggies

Shrimp and Sausage Jambalaya

SERVES 6

This festive dish is loaded with classic Cajun ingredients, beginning with what is called "the holy trinity": onion, celery, and green bell pepper. I think of it as the mirepoix of Cajun and Creole cuisine. Also included in this recipe is garlic (because garlic is essential), Cajun seasoning, green onion, and hot sauce.

Most restaurants and chefs blend their own Cajun spice mix, but to keep this recipe simple, use your favorite Cajun seasoning. Be sure to taste the seasoning before using. Some of them have a lot of heat. I've listed my favorite seasoning brands and where you can find them on page 316.

FIND YOUR FISH: This is a great recipe to use medium shrimp; however, large and jumbo work just as well here. Some recipes call for leaving the tails on, but I remove them, or purchase peeled and deveined shrimp for the recipe. Refer to the page 28 for thawing instructions.

3 tablespoons oil

8 ounces andouille sausage (or other smoked sausage, if desired), cut into ½-inch slices

1 onion, diced

1 green bell pepper, seeded and diced

3 celery stalks, diced

4 garlic cloves, minced

One 14-ounce can crushed tomatoes

1 to 2 tablespoons Cajun seasoning (check for heat)

1 teaspoon dried oregano

1 tablespoon chopped flat-leaf parsley, plus more for garnish

1 bay leaf

3 cups chicken stock

Salt and freshly ground black pepper

1½ cups uncooked white rice (I like long-grain with this recipe, but use whatever you prefer)

About 2 teaspoons Worcestershire sauce

Squeeze of lemon juice (about 1 tablespoon)

1 pound raw, thawed shrimp or prawns, peeled and deveined

⅓ cup sliced green onion

Tabasco or your favorite hot sauce for serving

CONTINUES ➡

1 Combine the oil, sausage, onion, bell pepper, and celery in a Dutch oven over medium heat and cook for 5 to 8 minutes, until the vegetables are wilted and soft.

2 Stir in the garlic and cook for 1 minute longer.

3 Stir in the crushed tomatoes, Cajun seasoning, oregano, parsley, bay leaf, and stock. Season to taste with salt and black pepper.

4 Bring to a boil and stir in the rice.

5 Cover and simmer over low heat for about 20 minutes.

6 Stir in the Worcestershire, lemon juice, shrimp, and half of the green onion, cover, and continue to cook over low heat for about 5 minutes longer, or until the shrimp are pink.

7 Remove from the heat and let sit, covered, for another 5 to 10 minutes.

8 Serve in bowls, with remaining green onion and chopped parsley for garnish.

Side Dish Suggestions

warm, sweet cornbread with butter ✦ a salad of fresh greens

Shrimp Étouffée

SERVES 4 TO 6

Étouffée is a classic Cajun and Creole dish and one that my family adores. Although many home cooks have their personal version, usually handed down from generation to generation, one of the tastiest recipes was prepared by a friend of mine while I was dining at her house one weekend. It was simple yet flavorful, and filled with the most plump and juicy shrimp and crawfish.

I find crawfish on occasion at local seafood markets, and though I like crawfish, I prefer this recipe with shrimp. So, if you happen to find crawfish, feel free to substitute.

¼ cup vegetable oil
¼ cup all-purpose flour
1 cup diced onion
½ cup diced celery
½ cup seeded and diced green bell pepper
3 garlic cloves, minced
1 jalapeño pepper, seeded and diced
¼ teaspoon cayenne pepper, or a dash of hot sauce
1 teaspoon Worcestershire sauce
1 tablespoon tomato paste
¼ cup dry white wine
1½ to 2 cups clam juice or seafood stock, or a mixture of both
1 bay leaf
½ teaspoon Cajun seasoning, or more to taste
1 pound shrimp (31/40 or 21/30 count; see Notes on page 123), peeled and deveined
¼ cup chopped green onion, plus more for garnish
2 teaspoons freshly squeezed lemon juice (from 1 large lemon)
Salt and freshly ground black pepper
4 to 6 cups cooked long-grain white rice
3 tablespoons chopped fresh flat-leaf parsley, plus more for garnish
Tabasco for serving

1 Heat the oil in a large pot over medium-low heat. Add the flour and cook, stirring to make a roux. Continue to stir the roux for to 20 to 25 minutes; you want it to develop slowly for the best flavor. When the roux is done, it will have the color of dark peanut butter.

2 Once the roux is ready, stir in the onion, celery, and bell pepper and cook until the vegetables are soft. This will take 5 to 8 minutes.

3 Then, stir in the garlic, jalapeño, cayenne or hot sauce, and Worcestershire. Cook for 1 minute more.

CONTINUES ➡

4 Add the tomato paste, white wine, 1½ cups of the clam juice, bay leaf, and Cajun seasoning, continuing to cook, stirring, until the ingredients are combined and the étouffée has come to a simmer. Let the stew simmer over low heat for 8 to 10 minutes. It will thicken slightly. If the étouffée feels too thick, add the additional ½ cup of clam juice or stock. The texture should feel a bit creamy, but not heavy.

5 Last, add the shrimp, green onion, and lemon juice. Bring the stew back to a very low simmer for 1 to 2 minutes and then remove from the heat. You want to gently poach the shrimp, which keeps them tender.

6 Remove the étouffée from the heat and season to taste with salt and black pepper.

7 Serve over rice and garnish with additional parsley or green onion and Tabasco.

Note

This dish is even better after it's rested for about 30 minutes before serving. This recipe can be prepared a day in advance with the étouffée refrigerated in a covered container. Reheat on the stovetop and then serve with the warm rice.

Side Dish Suggestions

a tossed green salad or coleslaw ✦ roasted or steamed vegetables

Panko-Fried Oysters with Remoulade Sauce

SERVES 4 TO 6

Panko-fried oysters with rémoulade sauce make our simple family gatherings taste like a celebration. This is a starter recipe that I make when all my kids are home and hanging out in the kitchen waiting for dinner to be ready.

I have everyone help me prep and assemble the oysters and sauce, and then I fry them. Rarely do these fried oysters make it to a platter, but rather get eaten right off the paper towel–lined plate.

FIND YOUR FISH: Most any shucked oyster will work here, but I think the small oysters are the sweetest. I find shucked oysters at my fish market and several local and national brands sell jarred shucked oysters in the refrigerated section of your local market seafood counter.

RÉMOULADE SAUCE

1 cup mayonnaise

⅓ cup chili sauce

1 garlic clove, minced

1 tablespoon capers, finely diced

1 to 2 teaspoons Cajun or Creole seasoning, to taste

1 tablespoon freshly squeezed lemon juice

¼ cup finely diced green onion

1 teaspoon Worcestershire sauce

1 tablespoon chopped fresh parsley

Dash of hot sauce or Tabasco (optional)

OYSTERS

10 to 12 ounces shucked oysters or oyster meat, drained of their liquor and patted dry

Salt and freshly ground black pepper

½ cup all-purpose flour

1 large egg, whisked with 1 teaspoon water

1 teaspoon Cajun or Creole seasoning

1 cup panko bread crumbs

High-heat oil for frying

1 Make the rémoulade sauce: Whisk together the mayonnaise, chili sauce, garlic, capers, Cajun or Creole seasoning, lemon juice, green onion, Worcestershire, parsley, and hot sauce (if using) in a small bowl. Set aside.

CONTINUES ➡

2 Prepare the oysters: Season the oysters with salt and pepper.

3 Whisk the egg and water with the Cajun or Creole seasoning.

4 Line up three bowls: one with flour, one with the whisked seasoned egg, and one with panko.

5 Dip the oysters in the flour and shake off any excess. Next, dip in the egg wash, and then in the panko. Place the panko-coated oysters on a parchment-lined baking sheet.

6 When all the oysters are coated, add high-heat oil to about 2 inches deep in a large skillet over medium or medium-high heat.

7 When the oil is hot and shimmering, add the oysters in batches and cook for 30 to 60 seconds on each side, until they are golden brown, adjusting the heat as needed.

8 Transfer the oysters to a paper towel–lined plate and serve immediately with the rémoulade sauce.

Baked Oysters Mornay

MAKES 8 TO 12 OYSTERS

Baked oysters Mornay is a bit like oysters Rockefeller meets a Gruyère white wine sauce. I admit, the ingredients in this recipe make my taste buds swoon. I love to serve these as starters or sometimes I make them for a Saturday night dinner paired with our favorite white wine.

I cook the oysters in real oyster shells that I got from my fishmonger, or in oyster tins that I purchased at a local kitchen store. You can also find the oyster tins online.

FIND YOUR FISH: I do prefer smaller oysters if I'm eating them raw. However, most any size oyster will work in this recipe. I use fresh shucked oysters when they're available or I'll buy them already shucked from my fish market.

8 to 12 shucked oysters or oyster meat, drained of their liquor
¼ cup panko bread crumbs
¼ cup Parmesan
1 tablespoon melted unsalted butter
1 tablespoon extra-virgin olive oil
1 tablespoon chopped shallot
1 garlic clove, minced
8 ounces cooked spinach, squeezed
Zest of 1 lemon
Salt and freshly ground black pepper
2 tablespoons unsalted butter
2 tablespoons all-purpose flour
½ cup white wine
1½ cups whole milk, warm
Pinch of freshly grated nutmeg
1 cup shredded Gruyère or aged Swiss cheese
Tabasco (optional) for serving

1 Preheat the oven to 400°F.

2 Place 8 to 12 oyster tins or oyster shells on a baking sheet and place one to two oysters (depending on size) in each tin or shell.

3 Mix together the bread crumbs, Parmesan, and melted butter in a small bowl. Set aside.

4 Heat 1 tablespoon of the oil in medium skillet over medium heat and add the shallot. Cook until soft and then stir in the garlic and cook for 30 seconds, just until fragrant.

CONTINUES ➡

5 Add the spinach and lemon zest. Heat through, season to taste with salt and pepper, then remove from the heat and set aside.

6 Melt the 2 tablespoons of butter in a saucepan over medium heat, then whisk in the flour. Let cook for about 30 seconds.

7 Slowly whisk in the white wine and then the warm milk, and continue to whisk until the sauce comes to a simmer. Continue to simmer until the sauce thickens.

8 Remove the pan from the heat and stir in the nutmeg and shredded cheese until smooth. Season to taste with salt and pepper.

9 Season the oysters with a little salt and pepper and divide the spinach mixture among the oysters, placing a tablespoon or two per tin or shell on top of the oysters.

10 Ladle the sauce over the spinach-topped oysters and then garnish with the bread crumbs. Reserve the remaining sauce for serving.

11 Place the baking sheet in the center of the oven and bake for 8 to 10 minutes. Then, turn on the broiler and broil just until the bread crumbs are golden brown.

12 Remove from the oven and serve with Tabasco (if using) and extra sauce.

Date Night Linguine with Pink Clam Sauce

SERVES 2 OR 3

A meal of pasta with red sauce and clams can feel extravagant. The tangy flavor of tomatoes along with aromatics, herbs, wine, lemon, and seasoning are the perfect backdrop for steamed clams.

In this sauce, I also add a splash of heavy cream and a smidgen of sugar, which bring together all those luscious flavors and makes the sauce slightly pink. After steaming the clams in white wine, I remove the clam meat from three-quarters of the clams, reserving the rest for garnish, and add them to the sauce at the end. I serve the sauce over linguine, but I think spaghetti, bucatini, or any long pasta would be delicious.

This is a dish I love to make for a date night in. I serve it with a warm toasted baguette, my best olive oil, a bottle of our favorite pinot noir, and a salad of baby greens.

2 tablespoons salt

10 to 12 ounces uncooked linguine

3 tablespoons extra-virgin olive oil

½ medium red onion, diced

3 garlic cloves, finely minced

1 tablespoon chopped fresh flat-leaf parsley

1 teaspoon chopped fresh oregano, or ½ teaspoon dried

Pinch of crushed red pepper flakes, or to taste

½ cup dry white wine

One 28-ounce can whole tomatoes with juice

1 tablespoon tomato paste

2 lemon slices, halved

Salt and freshly ground black pepper

½ teaspoon sugar

¼ to ½ cup heavy cream

Parmesan for serving

Chopped fresh basil or parsley for garnish

CLAMS

1 cup white wine

1 teaspoon salt

2 garlic cloves, smashed

1 to 1½ pounds fresh clams, cleaned and rinsed in cold water

1 Fill a large pot over high heat with water and add 2 tablespoons of salt. When the water comes to a boil, add the linguine and cook according to the package directions. Drain, then set aside.

2 While the pasta water is boiling, start the sauce: Heat the oil in a large skillet or Dutch oven over medium heat.

CONTINUES ➡

3 When the oil is hot, add the red onion and cook for 3 to 5 minutes, until soft and translucent. Then, stir in the garlic, parsley, oregano, and red pepper flakes and cook for 30 seconds more.

4 Stir in the white wine and let the mixture simmer until reduced by half.

5 Add the tomatoes and tomato paste and stir to combine. Bring the sauce to a gentle simmer and cook for 8 to 10 minutes.

6 Meanwhile, prepare the clams: Heat a medium pot over medium-high heat and add the wine, salt, and garlic.

7 As soon as the wine comes to a boil, add the clams and stir. Bring the wine back to a simmer, lower the heat to low, and cover the pot with a lid. Cook for about 5 minutes, or until all the clams have opened. Discard any clams that did not open.

8 While the clams are steaming, stir the lemon slices into the red sauce and season to taste with salt and black pepper.

9 Stir in the sugar, if needed, to balance flavors, and then stir in the heavy cream. Remove the sauce from the heat.

10 When the clams are done and cool enough to handle, drain and remove the clam meat from three-quarters of clam shells, reserving five or six clams per person for garnish.

11 Add the clam meat to the red sauce and stir gently. As always, check for seasoning.

12 To serve, toss a little red sauce with the linguine, just to coat. This loosens the pasta and helps it absorb the sauce flavors.

13 Then, plate the linguine and ladle the sauce over the top. Garnish with the steamed clams, grated Parmesan, and chopped basil or parsley. Serve immediately.

Pan-Seared Scallops with Tomato Ginger Jam

SERVES 6 AS AN APPETIZER OR 3 OR 4 AS AN ENTRÉE
MAKES TWO 8-OUNCE JARS OF JAM

Pan-seared scallops always taste like a special treat, but they're made even more special when served with this tomato ginger jam. The spice from the ginger and the sweetness from the tomatoes are a delicious complement to the briny and slightly rich flavors of scallops.

Summer tomato season is the perfect time to make this jam. I often make it over a weekend and then keep it in my refrigerator to serve with these scallops. This recipe makes a lovely starter or an entrée with an additional side dish.

TOMATO GINGER JAM

4 pounds Roma tomatoes

2 tablespoons extra-virgin olive oil

1 cup small diced sweet onion

One 2-inch knob ginger, peeled and finely minced

½ cup dark brown sugar

½ cup granulated sugar

1 teaspoon salt

1 tablespoon freshly squeezed lemon juice

SCALLOPS

1½ pounds fresh dry-packed sea scallops, patted dry and "foot" (adductor muscle) removed

Salt and freshly ground black pepper

2 tablespoons ghee

1 tablespoon chopped fresh chives or green onion for garnish

1 Make the jam: Lightly score an X in the bottom of each tomato.

2 Heat a large pot of water over high heat, and when it comes to a boil, add the tomatoes and blanch for 15 to 20 seconds.

3 When you see the skin begin to separate from the flesh, transfer the tomatoes to a baking dish and let them cool.

4 Peel the skin off the tomatoes and then seed, core, and chop them. You should end up with 5 to 6 cups of chopped tomatoes.

CONTINUES ➡

5 Next, heat the oil in a pot over medium heat. Then, add the sweet onion and cook just until soft and translucent.

6 Then, stir in the ginger and cook for 30 seconds more. Stir in the tomatoes, both sugars, salt, and lemon juice. Heat to a simmer.

7 Lower the heat to low and let the mixture simmer for 1½ to 2 hours, stirring occasionally, until jammy and sticky.

8 Transfer the jam to clean jars with lids. Cover tightly and refrigerate. The jam will keep for about 1 month refrigerated.

9 Make the scallops: Season the scallops with salt and pepper. Heat the ghee in a large, heavy-bottomed skillet over medium-high heat.

10 When the ghee is hot and frothy, add the scallops but don't overcrowd the pan. You may need to cook the scallops in batches.

11 Let the scallops brown, 1 to 2 minutes, and when they easily pull off the bottom of the pan, turn them over and brown the other side, adjusting the heat as necessary.

12 Transfer the scallops to plates or a platter laced with dollops of the tomato ginger jam. Garnish with chopped fresh chives or sliced green onion and serve immediately.

Note

This tomato ginger jam also pairs well with grilled fish, shrimp, or goat cheese on crostini.

Side Dish Suggestions

a crisp green garden salad or baby spinach salad with bacon ✦ French lentil salad or risotto ✦ roasted or grilled summer squash, zucchini, or asparagus

Crab and Spinach–Stuffed Shells with White Cheddar Béchamel

SERVES 6

This dish tastes like fancy comfort food. It's one of my family's favorite Sunday dinners and it usually happens shortly after crab season opens. It's the perfect recipe for leftover crab from a crab boil, and when I don't have leftover crab, I'll purchase shelled crab at my fish market.

FIND YOUR FISH: Fresh crab is delightful in this recipe; however, cooked lobster tail meat would also be an excellent substitution and pairs just as well with the white Cheddar béchamel.

STUFFED SHELLS

- 3 tablespoons salt
- One 12-ounce package jumbo pasta shells
- 8 ounces whole-milk ricotta cheese, drained
- One 16-ounce package frozen spinach, thawed and squeezed to remove excess liquid
- 2 to 3 garlic cloves
- 2 tablespoons freshly squeezed lemon juice
- 1 tablespoon chopped fresh parsley
- ¼ cup grated Parmesan
- 1 large egg
- ½ teaspoon salt, or more to taste
- ¼ teaspoon freshly ground black pepper
- 8 ounces lump crabmeat

BÉCHAMEL

- 3 tablespoons unsalted butter
- 3 tablespoons all-purpose flour
- 3 to 3½ cups whole milk, warm
- 1 teaspoon Dijon mustard
- ¼ cup grated Parmesan
- 4 ounces shredded white Cheddar
- Salt and freshly ground black pepper

TOPPING

- ¼ cup panko bread crumbs
- ¼ cup grated Parmesan
- 1 tablespoon extra-virgin olive oil

1 Preheat the oven to 400°F.

2 Place a large pot of water plus 3 tablespoons of salt over medium-high heat.

CONTINUES ➡

3 Bring to a boil and add the jumbo pasta shells. Stir, and let the shells gently cook for 9 minutes.

4 Drain the shells from the water, and when they're cool enough to handle, place them on a baking sheet until you need them.

5 Place the ricotta, spinach, garlic, lemon juice, parsley, Parmesan, egg, salt, and pepper in a food processor. Pulse the mixture until nicely combined. Then, stir in the crabmeat.

6 Make the béchamel: Heat the butter in a large saucepan or skillet over medium heat.

7 When the butter has melted, whisk in the flour.

8 Once the flour and butter are combined, slowly whisk in 3 cups of the warm milk. Bring the mixture to a simmer and let it thicken, lowering the heat to low, if needed.

9 Remove the pan from the heat and stir in the Dijon, grated Parmesan, and white Cheddar until thoroughly combined. The sauce should be slightly thickened but not too thick; stir in up to ½ cup of warm milk, if needed. Season to taste with salt and pepper.

10 Make the topping: Mix together the panko bread crumbs, Parmesan, and olive oil in a small bowl.

11 To assemble, place a bit of sauce in the bottom of a 9-by-13-inch baking dish.

12 Fill each shell with 1½ to 2 tablespoons of the crab and spinach filling. I use a mini muffin or small cookie scoop to fill the shells.

13 Next, set each filled shell in the baking dish. Continue, placing them in a single layer, until you've filled the baking dish or used all the filling. (You may have leftover shells; I like to toss them with my good-quality extra-virgin olive oil and grated Parmesan, a little salt and pepper. Sort of a little snack while I'm cooking.)

14 Then, ladle some of the white Cheddar béchamel over the shells. You can use all the sauce or use about three-quarters of it and serve the remaining sauce on the side. I like my shells lightly sauced. But it's up to you!

15 Sprinkle the topping over the shells and then place the baking dish in the oven and bake for about 20 minutes, or until the sides are bubbly and golden.

16 Remove the dish from the oven and let cool for about 5 minutes before serving.

Side Dish Suggestions

a fresh green salad or roasted vegetables ✦ a warm crusty baguette with extra-virgin olive oil

Note

This recipe is also delicious when served with the addition of warm marinara. I'll spread a little tomato sauce on the bottom of each plate and top with three stuffed shells. The combination of white sauce and tomato sauce is luscious. It makes this dish just a little more decadent.

Pappardelle Alfredo with Crab

SERVES 3 OR 4

Alfredo sauce is basically heavy cream, butter, and freshly grated Parmesan. But in this recipe, I fancy it up even more by adding flavors that complement the crabmeat. I also use pappardelle rather than fettuccine because the noodles hold up well to the sauce.

This dish is best when served as soon as it's done, while the sauce is warm and silky. As it cools, the sauce becomes firm. If you happen to have leftovers, reheat by adding a little water to the pasta and steam in a steamer or even a double boiler. A microwave-safe steam bowl also works.

This is also the kind of recipe you want to make when you have fresh lump crabmeat available. It's the star of the recipe and should be fresh and luscious.

- 4 tablespoons (½ stick) unsalted butter
- 2 garlic cloves, minced
- 2 cups heavy cream
- Zest of 1 lemon
- 3 tablespoons freshly squeezed lemon juice
- ¼ teaspoon freshly grated nutmeg
- 2 teaspoons chopped fresh flat-leaf parsley, plus more for garnish
- 2 teaspoons chopped fresh chives
- ¼ cup grated Parmesan (preferably freshly grated), plus more for serving
- Salt and freshly ground black pepper
- 8 to 10 ounces pappardelle, cooked according to package directions
- 8 to 10 ounces lump crabmeat

1. Heat the butter in a large skillet or saucepan over medium heat.
2. When the butter has melted, add the garlic and cook just until fragrant, about 30 seconds.
3. Stir in the heavy cream and bring to a gentle simmer. Lower the heat to low and continue to simmer for 5 to 8 minutes. Do not boil the sauce.
4. While whisking, add the lemon zest and juice, nutmeg, parsley, chives, and Parmesan. Season to taste with salt and pepper.
5. When the sauce is done, add the cooked pappardelle to the sauce and toss to coat.
6. Divide the pasta among plates and top with the crabmeat.
7. Garnish with chopped parsley and serve with grated Parmesan.

Side Dish Suggestions

Serve with a warm baguette and your best extra-virgin olive oil. For a complete meal, a crisp salad of baby greens with a French vinaigrette is lovely.

Broiled Lobster Tails with Cilantro-Lime Butter

SERVES 4

Broiled lobster tails feel fancy and indulgent. However, with a few easy steps, the recipe isn't too difficult and only requires a bit of patience while pulling the lobster meat from the shell.

First, be sure that the lobster tails have completely thawed in the refrigerator for 24 hours. This will make it so much easier to remove the lobster meat. However, if you need to quick thaw, refer to thawing methods for lobster on page 30. Just know the quick thaw for lobster isn't terribly quick; it'll take at least an hour or more, depending on the weight of the lobster tails.

Once the lobster has been prepped and butter has been melted, this recipe moves quickly, so be sure to have all your side dishes ready and waiting. These tails are best served hot right out of the oven.

4 lobster tails, thawed if previously frozen

8 tablespoons (1 stick) salted butter

3 garlic cloves, minced

¼ cup fresh cilantro leaves, chopped, plus 1 tablespoon for garnish (optional)

Zest of 1 lime

½ teaspoon salt

½ teaspoon freshly ground black pepper

½ teaspoon paprika

1 Place the four lobster tails, bottom (legs) side down, on a sturdy cutting board.

2 At the front of the tail where you can see the lobster meat, cut down the center of the upper shell with kitchen or seafood shears. Leave the tail fan intact and don't remove the underpart of the shell. That will be our cooking surface.

3 Rinse the tail and remove any vein or tomalley. Wedge your thumb or fingers between the meat and the shell to separate them, then lift the uncooked tail meat through the slit and rest it on top of the shell, leaving the very end of the lobster attached to the tail fan.

4 Place the prepped lobster tails on a baking sheet.

5 Next, heat the butter and garlic in a small pot over medium-low heat. When the garlic butter is just melted, add the cilantro and lime zest. Remove from the heat and let it sit for 3 to 5 minutes.

6 Reserving half of the butter, brush the remaining half over the lobster tails. Sprinkle the tails with a little salt, pepper, and paprika.

7 Preheat the broiler and then place the baking sheet in the center of the oven, on the center rack. Broil the lobster tails for 5 to 8 minutes, depending on the size of the tails.

8 Once the tails are done, place them on a platter, drizzle some of the reserved butter over them, and serve. Garnish with chopped cilantro, if desired.

Side Dish Suggestions

roasted new or fingerling potatoes ✦ potatoes gratin ✦ risotto ✦ creamed spinach ✦ roasted broccolini, asparagus, or a fresh salad of baby greens

Classic Lobster Rolls

MAKES 3 LOBSTER ROLLS

When I lived on the East Coast, we spent most weekends and vacations touring New England. While driving through Maine one summer, we stopped at almost every lobster shack we saw just so we could sample another lobster roll. Most of them consisted of succulent lobster in a savory dressing on a buttered roll, and a few included additional ingredients. All of them, however, were scrumptious.

I live on the West Coast now and I find myself missing those decadent lobster rolls. So, I make them at home. I love to bring them for lunch at the park or lazy weekends spent outside on the patio. And often I serve them on small slider buns as a starter.

FIND YOUR FISH: The recipe calls for uncooked lobster tails, but if you find cooked lobster meat, that'll work just as well. Just skip poaching and start the recipe at step 6.

1½ to 2 quarts seafood stock and/or water for poaching

2 garlic cloves, smashed

2 or 3 thyme sprigs

12 ounces uncooked lobster tails (I usually use 4-ounce tails), thawed

¼ cup mayonnaise, or to taste

¼ cup diced celery

Squeeze of lemon juice

1 tablespoon chopped fresh chives

Salt and freshly ground black pepper

Traditional lobster rolls, soft brioche, or Hawaiian bread hot dog buns

2 tablespoons melted salted butter

1 Poach the lobster tails: Add enough seafood stock or water (or a combination of both) to a medium or large pot to cover the tails.

2 Stir the garlic and thyme into the pot and bring to a boil over high heat.

3 Add the lobster tails, lower the heat to low, and simmer for about 4 minutes. Lobster meat will cook 1 minute for every ounce.

4 When the tails are done, remove from the pot and let them cool completely.

5 To remove the meat, use kitchen shears to cut down the back of the tails and split them open. The meat should come right out.

6 Chop the lobster into bite-size pieces and place in a bowl. Stir in the mayonnaise, celery, lemon juice, and chives and season to taste with salt and pepper. Place the bowl in the refrigerator to chill.

7 While the lobster is chilling, heat a skillet over medium heat and brush the outside of the lobster rolls or buns with melted butter. Grill the outside of the buns until golden.

8 Stuff the chilled lobster into each bun and serve.

Note

These are so fun to make, wrap, and take to the park for a lunch outdoors. I like to serve them with macaroni or potato salad and chips.

Summer Seafood Board with Dipping Sauces

SERVES 4 TO 6 AS A STARTER

This is such a fun and delicious way to serve seafood, especially as a starter for dinner guests or a weekend barbecue. Plan on 8 ounces of seafood per person along with three different dipping sauces. I make the sauces a day in advance and keep them in the refrigerator.

I also choose two or three fresh fruits, vegetables, and/or pickled vegetables for the board, along with fresh bread, crostini, or crackers. There is no right or wrong way to assemble this seafood board; just be creative and have fun.

BLENDER CHIMICHURRI SAUCE

- **½ cup packed fresh flat-leaf parsley leaves**
- **1 cup packed fresh cilantro**
- **3 green onions, root ends trimmed**
- **1 garlic clove**
- **1 tablespoon fresh oregano leaves**
- **Pinch of crushed red pepper flakes**
- **¾ cup extra-virgin olive oil**
- **1 tablespoon freshly squeezed lemon juice, plus more to taste (optional)**
- **2 tablespoons Champagne vinegar or white wine vinegar**
- **Salt and freshly ground black pepper**

GARLIC BUTTER

- **8 tablespoons (1 stick) salted butter**
- **1 to 2 garlic cloves, minced**
- **1 teaspoon lemon zest**

SEAFOOD RECOMMENDATIONS (CHOOSE 3 OR 4)

- **½ to 1 pound lobster tails, thawed, or already cooked and chilled**
- **½ to 1 pound cooked shrimp, chilled**
- **½ to 1 pound cooked crab claws, chilled**
- **6 to 12 raw oysters, shucked and placed back in shell, chilled**
- **6 ounces smoked fish, chilled**
- **4 to 6 ounces prepared seafood dip, chilled**
- **½ to 1 pound dry-packed sea scallops**
- **1 tablespoon high heat oil for scallops**
- **Salt and freshly ground black pepper**
- **8 ounces mussels**
- **8 ounces clams**

FRUIT RECOMMENDATIONS (CHOOSE 2 OR 3)

- **1 pint raspberries**
- **1 pint blackberries**
- **1 pint strawberries**
- **8 ounces grapes**
- **1 to 2 cups cubed pineapple**
- **1 to 2 mangoes, sliced**
- **1 papaya, peeled, seeded, and cubed**

CONTINUES ➡

VEGETABLES AND PICKLED VEGETABLES (CHOOSE 2 TO 3)

1 cucumber, sliced

1 pint cherry tomatoes

1 cup pickled cherry peppers

1 cup peppadew peppers

1 cup pepperoncini peppers

½ cup seaweed salad

SEAFOOD BOARD

Lemon wedges

Assorted crostini, fresh bread, and crackers

Classic cocktail sauce

Tartar sauce

Blender Chimichurri Sauce

Garlic Butter

1 Make the chimichurri: Combine all the chimichurri ingredients, except the salt and pepper, in a blender and puree until smooth. Season to taste with salt and pepper. Add additional lemon juice to taste.

2 Make the garlic butter: Heat the butter in a saucepan. When melted, add the garlic and lemon zest. Remove the butter from the heat and serve in a bowl with the seafood board.

3 To poach the lobster tails, use the poaching method described for the Classic Lobster Roll recipe (page 262). When the lobster is done, cool and cut into bite-size pieces.

4 To grill the scallops, pat dry with a paper towel and remove the "foot" (adductor muscle). Toss with oil, salt, and pepper. You can skewer the scallops on metal or wooden skewers, if desired. If using wooden, be sure to soak them in water for at least 20 minutes before using.

5 Preheat a grill to 400°F and make sure the grates are scraped clean. When the grill is at temperature, set the scallops on the grill and cook for 3 to 4 minutes. Then, flip and cook just until done, about 1 more minute. (For more detailed instructions on grilling, refer to the "Seafood 101" section, page 14.)

6 Remove the scallops from the grill and transfer to a plate or bowl and drizzle with a little of the blender chimichurri sauce. Keep in the refrigerator until you're ready to assemble the board.

7 To steam the mussels and clams, use the method described for Classic White Wine–Steamed Clams with Garlic and Herbs (page 124). Make these last just before you assemble the board, and toss in a little of the garlic butter.

8 To assemble the seafood board, spread a layer of crushed ice on a baking sheet. Then, set another baking sheet over the ice so that it's secure. This will keep the seafood cool.

9 Start by placing the sauces on the baking sheet. I like to place them near each end of the board.

10 Then, add small bowls or plates of clams, mussels, shrimp, lobster, scallops, smoked fish, or seafood dip throughout the baking sheet.

11 Fill in the spaces between the bowls and plates with crab claws or oysters. Then, tuck in lemon wedges, little dishes of fruit or small bunches of grapes, seaweed salad, vegetables, and pickled vegetables. Serve crackers, crostini, and fresh bread on the side along with the warm garlic butter.

12 Nestle as much on the tray as you can squeeze in. It'll be fun for your guests to browse through the board for their favorite seafood. Serve immediately.

Seafood Risotto

SERVES 4

I call this my special occasion risotto. It's topped with a variety of seafood, usually whatever is available locally or in season. Sometimes it's shrimp and crab or crab and lobster, or clams and shrimp, or simply scallops.

I prepare my seafood risotto a bit differently because I am a purist when it comes to risotto. I don't like much "in" the risotto, but I do like it adorned with delicious ingredients, such as seafood, vegetables, or mushrooms. This recipe calls for cooking the seafood first and then preparing the risotto. To serve, the risotto is plated, and the seafood is poured over the top for one gorgeous and tantalizing meal.

RISOTTO

2 tablespoons extra-virgin olive oil

1 shallot, finely chopped

1 cup uncooked Arborio rice

½ cup dry white wine

4 to 5 cups warm seafood stock

¼ cup grated Parmesan

Zest of 1 lemon

¼ cup heavy cream (optional)

Salt and freshly ground black pepper

2 tablespoons chopped fresh flat-leaf parsley for garnish

Lemon wedges for serving

SEAFOOD (ABOUT 1 POUND TOTAL, COOKED)

8 ounces shrimp, cooked using the Pan-Cooked Shrimp recipe (page 122)

8 ounces sea scallops, cooked using the Basic Pan-Cooked Sea Scallops recipe (page 117)

8 ounces clams, cooked using the Classic White Wine–Steamed Clams with Garlic and Herbs recipe (page 124)

6 to 8 ounces cooked lump crabmeat or crab claws

8 ounces cooked lobster tail or cooked claws

1 Prepare the risotto: Heat the olive oil in a large pot or Dutch oven over medium heat.

2 Stir in the shallot and cook until soft. Add the Arborio rice and cook for another 2 to 3 minutes.

3 Add the white wine and stir until most of the wine has been absorbed, then ladle in 1 cup of seafood stock and continue to stir until most of the stock has been absorbed.

4 Continue adding more stock ½ to 1 cup at a time, stirring often, and allowing each addition of stock to be absorbed before adding the next. This usually takes about 25 minutes. Cook until the rice is almost tender (al dente),

5 When the risotto is done, remove it from the heat and stir in the cheese, lemon zest, and heavy cream (if using). Season to taste with salt and pepper.

6 To serve, pour the risotto in a serving bowl or individual bowls and top with assorted cooked seafood. Garnish with the chopped parsley and serve with lemon wedges.

Side Dish Suggestions

roasted asparagus, broccolini, or braised greens ✦ a crisp green salad

Flatbread with Anchovies, Smoked Mozzarella, Olives, and Arugula

MAKES 4 FLATBREADS

This recipe makes an appetizing alternative for pizza night or Saturday afternoon lunch. I also slice them into small wedges and serve as a starter.

I've listed a smidge of pesto as the base, but feel free to skip the pesto and load on the anchovies and other ingredients. The lemon-dressed arugula completes the flavor profile and complements the anchovies, so don't skip this step.

2 cups all-purpose flour, plus more for dusting

½ teaspoon salt

1 teaspoon baking powder

¾ cup milk, at room temperature

3 tablespoons melted unsalted butter

1 tablespoon chopped fresh chives

Oil for skillet

4 ounces prepared pesto (check for salt; see Notes)

1 cup shredded smoked mozzarella

8 anchovies

½ cup sliced or halved pitted black or green olives

1 to 2 teaspoons freshly squeezed lemon juice

1 cup baby arugula

1 Whisk together the flour, salt, and baking powder in the bowl of a stand mixer fitted with the dough hook attachment.

2 On low to medium speed, mix in the milk, melted butter, and chives and continue to mix until the dough comes together and pulls off the side of the bowl, about 5 minutes.

3 Pour out the dough onto a lightly floured surface and form into a ball. Wrap in plastic wrap and chill in the refrigerator for 30 minutes.

4 Remove the dough from the refrigerator, unwrap, and place on a lightly floured surface. Cut the ball into four equal pieces.

5 Roll each piece into a ball. With a rolling pin, roll out each ball into a disk about ¼ inch thick.

6 Brush the surface of a skillet with a little oil and set over medium heat. When the skillet is hot, add a dough disk and cook until golden brown, then flip to the other side. The flatbread is done when it begins to form bubbles. Transfer the cooked flatbread to a plate.

CONTINUES ➡

7 Preheat the oven to 400°F.

8 To assemble the flatbreads, lay them out on one or two baking sheets. Lightly brush each flatbread with a little pesto or olive oil.

9 Sprinkle with mozzarella, then top with two anchovies per flatbread plus a sprinkle of olives.

10 Place the baking sheet(s) in the oven and bake for 8 to 10 minutes, until the cheese has melted and the edges of the flatbread are toasty.

11 Toss the arugula with 1 to 2 teaspoons of lemon juice and then sprinkle over the flatbread. Serve warm.

Notes

Be sure to taste the pesto before using. Some prepared pesto is very salty. If the pesto is salty, add a little lemon juice and reduce the amount used on the flatbread.

In a pinch, you can also make this recipe with prepared flatbread.

557405U
Rain

Avocado, Tomato, and Sardines Toast with Pickled Onions and Herb Dressing

MAKES 2 TOASTS

It's rare that I find fresh sardines in my local markets, so most of the time I use canned sardines. They make a delicious addition to salads, appetizers, and recipes like this avocado and tomato toast.

The avocado and tomato are subtle in flavor, so they make the most delicious backdrop for the sardines. The quick-pickled onions provide a little snap of tang, and the herby mayonnaise brings all the flavors together for one delectable—and a little fancy—toast.

½ red onion, thinly sliced

½ to ⅔ cup rice vinegar

1 teaspoon sugar

½ cup mayonnaise

1 tablespoon chopped fresh chives, plus more for garnish

1 tablespoon chopped fresh flat-leaf parsley

1 garlic clove, minced

1 teaspoon Dijon mustard

1 tablespoon freshly squeezed lemon juice, or to taste

2 slices Texas toast or thick-sliced bread

1 avocado, mashed

1 large ripe heirloom tomato (or whatever is in season)

2 to 4 canned sardines

Sea salt and freshly ground black pepper

1 Place the sliced onion in a nonreactive bowl or jar. Combine the rice vinegar and sugar in a small pot over medium heat. Heat to a simmer and then remove from the heat. Let cool slightly and pour over the slices. Let the slices sit while you prepare the toasts. Pickled onion can be stored in an airtight container in the refrigerator for 5 days.

2 Combine the mayonnaise, chives, parsley, garlic, Dijon, and lemon juice in a small bowl. Season to taste with salt and pepper.

3 Toast the bread in either a toaster or toaster oven. Spread with a dollop of the herb mayonnaise and then spread the mashed avocado over the mayonnaise.

4 Top with tomato slices and then one to two sardines.

5 Add a few of the pickled onion slices on top of the sardines and season with sea salt and pepper, if desired.

6 Mix a few tablespoons of the mayonnaise with a little water to thin. Drizzle over the toasts, garnish with chopped chives, and serve.

Asian Salmon Sliders with Quick-Pickled Cucumbers and Cilantro-Lime Aioli

MAKES TEN 3-INCH CAKES

Salmon is one of the most popular seafoods and for good reason. It's distinctive in taste and pairs well with so many fresh ingredients. I especially like salmon paired with ingredients like cucumber, arugula, green onion, and lemon. These sliders are bursting with luscious flavor and make a fun starter for a weekend gathering or outdoor barbecue.

The salmon cakes can be made a day in advance and panfried before serving. The pickled onions and aioli can be made two days in advance. This makes the perfect recipe for delicious entertaining.

ASIAN SALMON CAKES

1 pound salmon, skin on or skinless, pin bones removed

Extra-virgin olive oil, plus more for panfrying

Salt and freshly ground black pepper

⅓ cup sliced green onion

1 teaspoon grated fresh ginger

1 teaspoon Thai roasted red chili paste

2 tablespoons freshly squeezed lemon juice

1 large egg, slightly whisked

3 tablespoons mayonnaise

½ cup panko style bread crumbs, plus more if needed

AIOLI

½ to ¾ cup good-quality mayonnaise

1 small garlic clove, minced

Zest of 1 lime

¼ cup fresh cilantro leaves, finely chopped

¼ teaspoon wasabi paste (optional)

MARINATED CUCUMBERS

1 cucumber, thinly sliced

1 cup rice vinegar

TO SERVE

Slider buns

Fresh arugula leaves

1 Prepare the salmon cakes: Preheat the oven to 400°F.

2 Place the salmon on a baking sheet or in a baking pan and brush with a little olive oil. Season the salmon with salt and pepper. Place the pan in the oven and roast the salmon for about 10 minutes for every inch of thickness. When the salmon is done, remove from the oven and let cool.

3 While the salmon is cooking, make the aioli: Whisk together the mayonnaise, garlic, lime zest, cilantro, and wasabi paste (if using) in a small bowl. Set aside.

CONTINUES ➡

4 Make the marinated cucumbers: Combine the sliced cucumber and enough rice vinegar to cover in a nonreactive bowl. Let sit and marinate for about 15 minutes. Drain well and set aside.

5 Once the salmon has cooled, shred it, removing any bones and skin, and transfer it to a medium bowl. Add the green onion, ginger, Thai roasted red chili paste, lemon juice, and about ½ teaspoon each salt and pepper. Mix with a fork until nicely incorporated.

6 Next, gently mix in the egg, mayonnaise, and panko bread crumbs until all the ingredients are nicely incorporated. Don't overmix; mix just enough so the salmon will form into patties. If the salmon mix is too dry, add up to 1 additional tablespoon of mayonnaise. If it is too wet, add up to ¼ cup of panko bread crumbs.

7 Chill the salmon mixture in the refrigerator for 10 to 15 minutes. This will help you form the patties.

8 Scoop out the salmon mixture with a cookie scoop to form 2- to 3-inch patties. Place the salmon cakes in a single layer on a parchment lined–baking sheet.

9 Heat a large skillet over medium heat and add 2 to 3 tablespoons of olive oil—enough to cover the surface of the skillet.

10 When the oil is hot, but not smoking, add the patties to the skillet. You may need to do this in batches. Let the salmon cakes cook for 2 to 3 minutes on each side, until dark golden brown, almost toasted in color. Adjust the heat lower if the salmon cakes get too dark too quickly.

11 Once the salmon cakes are done, place each salmon cake on a slider bun and top with the aioli, marinated cucumber, and fresh arugula leaves. Secure the sliders with party picks and serve with additional aioli and cucumbers.

Salmon, Leek, and Potato Pie

MAKES 3 OR 4 INDIVIDUAL POTPIES OR ONE 9-INCH DEEP-DISH PIE

This is yet another delicious way to incorporate seafood into a recipe. This salmon, leek, and potato pie is flavorful, hearty, and the perfect dish for a cool fall, winter, or spring evening.

I like to make this recipe when I find spring leeks while also using my Homemade Seafood Stock (page 224). I've called for puff pastry instead of pie dough, but feel free to use your favorite pie dough recipe, if you like.

3 slices uncooked bacon, diced
3 tablespoons unsalted butter, plus more for the baking dish(es)
2 medium leeks, white and light green parts only, halved, rinsed, and chopped
1 medium shallot, diced
3 to 4 garlic cloves, minced
¼ cup all-purpose flour, plus more for dusting
½ cup white wine
2 cups Homemade Seafood Stock (page 224), or other prepared seafood stock
12 ounces Yukon Gold potatoes, cut into ½-inch cubes
2 teaspoons chopped fresh parsley
1 teaspoon chopped fresh thyme leaves
1 tablespoon chopped fresh chives
Salt and freshly ground black pepper
12 ounces raw salmon, skinned and cut into ½-inch cubes
1 tablespoon freshly squeezed lemon juice
½ cup heavy cream
1 package puff pastry (2 sheets), thawed according to package directions
1 large egg, whisked with 1 teaspoon water
Coarse salt (optional)

1. Preheat the oven to 400°F.
2. Cook the bacon in a soup pot or Dutch oven over medium heat. When the bacon is crispy and its fat is rendered, transfer the bacon to a paper towel–lined plate.
3. Remove all but 1 tablespoon of bacon fat from the pot.
4. With the soup pot or Dutch oven back over medium heat, add the 3 tablespoons of butter to the bacon fat.
5. When the butter is melted, stir in the leeks and shallot and cook for 5 to 8 minutes, until soft and slightly caramelized. Then, add the garlic and cook for 30 seconds more.

CONTINUES ➡

6 Stir in the flour and cook for about 30 seconds. While stirring constantly, add the white wine and seafood stock. Bring to a simmer.

7 Add the potatoes, parsley, thyme, and chives and bring back to a simmer. Lower the heat to low and simmer for about 10 minutes, or until the potatoes are mostly cooked.

8 Season to taste with salt and pepper.

9 Fold in the cubed salmon, lemon juice, and heavy cream. Bring back to a simmer, then remove the pot from the heat and stir in the chopped bacon.

10 Roll out the thawed puff pastry on a lightly floured surface to smooth out the creases and thin the pastry just a bit. Cut the pastry in 2- to 3-inch squares or rectangles.

11 Butter individual potpie baking dishes or one 9-inch deep-dish pie pan or baking dish.

12 Divide the salmon mixture equally among the prepared potpie dishes or pour it into the prepared pie pan.

13 Cover the salmon mixture with pieces of puff pastry, being as creative as you like. Then, brush the egg wash over the pastry. Sprinkle the egg wash with a little coarse salt, if desired.

14 Bake for 20 to 25 minutes, until the pastry is deep golden brown and the potpies are bubbly around the edges.

15 Let the potpies rest for 10 minutes before serving.

Side Dish Suggestions

a chilled green salad with a lemon vinaigrette

Spicy Ahi Tuna Sushi Stacks

MAKES FOUR 3-INCH STACKS

We eat a lot of sushi in my house. We've been known to have sushi-making nights for birthday celebrations or family dinners. So, it made sense to include a recipe for our sushi stacks in this book.

Truthfully, I'm not a wildly adventurous sushi connoisseur, but I do enjoy sushi-grade tuna and salmon. Most sushi grade-salmon and tuna are sold flash frozen, which is how I buy it. If properly thawed, it tastes just as good as fresh fish. (For more information on thawing fish, refer to page 28.)

I recommend finding quality 2-by-3-inch food molds for these sushi stacks. They can be purchased at most kitchen stores or online. When oiled, they make preparing these stacks easy. The food molds can also be used for many other savory and sweet recipes as well.

SPICY SAUCE

½ cup mayonnaise

1½ teaspoons sriracha

1 tablespoon soy sauce

1 teaspoon sugar

½ teaspoon toasted sesame oil

¼ cup minced green onion

1 teaspoon freshly squeezed lime juice

TUNA STACKS

1 pound sushi-grade ahi tuna, diced into small pieces

2 cups cooked sticky rice

1 teaspoon seasoned rice wine vinegar

1 teaspoon furikake seasoning or black or white sesame seeds

Oil for molds

1 cucumber peeled, thinly sliced, then quartered

1 cup grated or shredded carrot

1 to 2 avocados, thinly sliced

TO SERVE

Chopped fresh cilantro

Pickled ginger

Crumbled nori

1 Make the sauce: Combine the mayonnaise, sriracha, soy sauce, sugar, sesame oil, green onion, and lime juice in a small bowl.

2 Prepare the tuna stacks: Place the tuna in a medium bowl and stir in 1 to 2 tablespoons of the spicy sauce. Chill.

3 In a separate medium bowl, mix the rice with the seasoned rice wine vinegar and either the furikake seasoning or sesame seeds.

4 Brush the inside of four 2-by-3-inch food molds with oil. Place the molds on the plate or platter from which you'll be serving the sushi stacks.

5 Add rice to each food mold, pressing down firmly to pack down the rice. It should fill about one-third up the inside of each food mold.

6 Next, add the thin slices of cucumber in a single layer. Top with a layer of shredded carrot and press down firmly to secure the vegetables. Then, add a layer of thinly sliced avocado. You can mash the avocado a bit, if needed.

7 Top the avocado with a tablespoon or two of the spicy tuna and then gently, slowly pull the food mold up over the sushi stack.

8 Repeat until you've used all your tuna.

9 Garnish with fresh cilantro and serve with pickled ginger, crumbled nori, and spicy sauce.

Bacon-Wrapped Stuffed Trout with Lemon White Wine Pan Sauce

SERVES 2 OR 3

This is my go-to recipe after family fishing trips. Each trout is stuffed and then wrapped in bacon and roasted to sumptuous perfection. Trout is a delicious whole fish to roast, and I find that stuffing it with assorted aromatics, fresh herbs, and citrus infuses the delicate flesh with loads of flavor.

I've kept the aromatics in this recipe traditional—shallot and garlic—because I'm using bacon. But you can use a variation of them, such as thinly sliced fennel, sliced leek, or sweet onion. I've also used orange slices and rosemary, and a mix of citrus with cilantro and chile peppers.

Have fun, play with flavors, and create your favorite version.

2 pounds trout, cleaned, fins removed

1 to 2 tablespoons extra-virgin olive oil

Salt and freshly ground black pepper

1 small shallot, thinly sliced

1 to 2 garlic cloves, thinly sliced

1 to 2 lemons, sliced

Handful of assorted fresh herbs, such as thyme, parsley, chives, savory, and oregano

8 ounces uncooked bacon

Lemon wedges for serving

1. Preheat the oven to 450°F.
2. Place the trout on a baking sheet and make three or four diagonal slices in the body of the fish, just enough that the seasoning, bacon flavors, and lemon will get into the flesh.
3. Drizzle the inside of the fish with a little olive oil and sprinkle with salt and pepper.
4. Stuff the cavity with the shallot, garlic, a few lemon slices, and assorted fresh herbs.
5. Sprinkle the outside of the fish with salt and pepper. Then, beginning at the collar/neck area, wrap a slice of bacon around the fish, making sure the seam is under the fish. Continue to wrap with bacon until you reach the tail area.
6. Place three or four lemon slices on top of the fish, drizzle with a little olive oil, and place the baking sheet in the oven.

CONTINUES ➡

7 Roast the fish for 20 to 25minutes. Then, turn on the broiler and broil for a few minutes to crisp the bacon and finish cooking the fish.

8 Remove from the oven and transfer to a platter. I like to set the fish on the table, remove the bacon and skin from the top of the fish, and let everyone dig in. Serve with lemon wedges.

Note

When I find small trout (1 to 1½ pounds) I'll purchase one per person and serve on individual plates with lemon wedges.

Side Dish Recommendations

roasted or mashed potatoes ✦ rice or couscous ✦ roasted vegetables ✦ a fresh green salad with buttermilk dressing

West African–Inspired Fish Stew

SERVES 8

I adore the combination of spinach and sweet potatoes, and I have an affinity for sunflower seed butter. This gorgeous stew uses all three ingredients and, as a bonus, incorporates white fish for a luscious one-pot meal.

This is similar to a West African fish stew; using that as a guide, I have created a recipe similar in flavor profile but with ingredients found close to home and that taste brilliant together. For example, although peanut butter is traditional, I use my favorite brand of sunflower seed butter that is lightly sweetened with honey. But if you have peanut butter on hand, that will work just as well. I've also used my favorite fish base bouillon here, mixed with hot water, but you can also use a traditional seafood or vegetable stock.

2 tablespoons extra-virgin olive oil or coconut oil

1 medium sweet onion, small-diced

1 red bell pepper, small-diced

1 jalapeño pepper, seeded and diced

1 teaspoon grated fresh ginger

3 garlic cloves, finely chopped

1 teaspoon ground coriander

1 teaspoon mild curry powder

2 cups hot water plus 2 teaspoons Better Than Bouillon Fish Base (see Notes), OR 2 cups Homemade Seafood Stock (page 224)

One 14-ounce can diced tomatoes

1 tablespoon tomato paste

One 14-ounce can full-fat coconut milk (not light)

1 pound sweet potato (about 1 large or 2 small) peeled and ½-inch cubed (bite-size)

Pinch of cayenne pepper (optional and if curry powder is mild)

5 ounces baby spinach

¼ cup sunflower seed butter

1 to 1½ pounds white fish, cut into 1-inch cubes and checked for bones

½ cup chopped fresh cilantro

1 tablespoon freshly squeezed lime juice

Salt and freshly ground black pepper

1 Heat the oil in a Dutch oven or large soup pot over medium heat. When the oil is hot, stir in the onion, bell pepper, and jalapeño. Cook for about 5 minutes, or until the vegetables are soft and wilted.

2 Stir in the ginger, garlic, coriander, and curry powder. Cook for 1 minute.

CONTINUES ➡

3 Add the water, prepared fish bouillon, diced tomatoes, tomato paste, and coconut milk. Stir to combine. Bring the liquid to a boil over high heat and then add the sweet potato.

4 Lower the heat to low and simmer for about 15 minutes, or until the sweet potatoes are soft.

5 When the sweet potato is soft, stir in the cayenne (if using) and baby spinach. Once the spinach is incorporated and wilted into the stew, stir in the sunflower seed butter and additional hot water, if needed, ½ cup at a time. This is a stew, so it will be thick and hearty.

6 Taste for salt and black pepper and then gently add the fish and toss to combine. Partially cover the pot and let the fish cook in the simmering stew for about 5 minutes. When the fish is opaque, it will be done. It doesn't take long for the fish to cook as it's cut into such small pieces.

7 Gently stir in the cilantro and lime juice. Check for salt and black pepper and adjust as needed.

8 Remove the stew from the heat and let sit for about 5 minutes prior to serving.

9 I serve this stew à la carte as it's an entire meal in one pot. It is lovely served as is, or garnished with additional chopped cilantro and toasted sunflower seeds.

Notes

My go-to fish stock is the Better Than Bouillon brand Fish Base. For more information this product and where to purchase, refer to the Resources (page 315).

Be sure to let the stew sit for a few minutes before serving. This helps all the flavors meld deliciously together.

Bourride

(FRENCH-STYLE FISH STEW WITH AIOLI)

SERVES 6

French cuisine and seafood have always been two of my favorite pairings. So, as I'm sure you've guessed, this recipe is at the top of my menu for soups and stews.

This French-style fish stew is traditional in preparation but made all the more flavorful and creamy with a swirl of homemade lemon garlic aioli. I seriously can't get enough of this stew.

FIND YOUR FISH: I use whatever mild white fish I have on hand, which is usually rockfish, cod, or halibut. But any white fish that is medium-firm and flaky will work. For a list of mild white fish, refer to the Seafood Chart on page 22.

AIOLI

2 large egg yolks

2 garlic cloves, minced

1 teaspoon Dijon mustard

1 tablespoon freshly squeezed lemon juice, or more to taste

½ teaspoon salt

Pinch of cayenne pepper

1 cup extra-virgin olive oil

FISH STEW

2 tablespoons extra-virgin olive oil

2 medium leeks, sliced lengthwise in half and then cut into half-moons

1 fennel bulb, diced

1 tablespoon chopped fresh flat-leaf parsley

2 thyme sprigs

½ cup dry white wine

1 pound fingerling potatoes, cut into bite-size pieces (½- to 1-inch pieces)

Pinch of crushed red pepper flakes (optional)

1 dried bay leaf

3 to 4 cups water plus 3 to 4 teaspoons Better Than Bouillon Fish Base (see Note), OR 3 to 4 cups Homemade Seafood Stock (page 224)

Salt and freshly ground black pepper

1 pound mild white fish with a medium firm texture, cut into 1½-inch cubes or bite-size pieces

1 tablespoon chopped fresh dill

1 teaspoon white wine vinegar

Chopped fresh dill or parsley for garnish

Warm, crusty bread for serving

CONTINUES ➡

1 Make the aioli: Combine the egg yolks, garlic, Dijon, lemon juice, salt, and cayenne in a medium bowl. While whisking, slowly drizzle the olive oil into the mixture until it's smooth, creamy, and glossy. Alternatively, place all the aioli ingredients, except the olive oil, in a food processor and then, while the food processor is running, drizzle in the oil slowly until smooth, creamy, and glossy. Taste for salt, cayenne, and lemon.

2 Make the fish stew: Heat the olive oil in a Dutch oven or soup pot over medium heat. When the oil is hot, add the leeks and fennel and cook over medium or medium-low heat for 8 to 10 minutes, until they are soft and slightly golden.

3 Stir in the parsley, thyme sprigs, and white wine and bring to a simmer. Reduce the wine by half.

4 Then, add the potatoes, red pepper flakes (if using), bay leaf, and enough of the prepared fish bouillon to cover the potatoes.

5 Bring the liquid to a boil, then lower the heat to low and simmer for 8 to 12 minutes, until the potatoes are soft. Season to taste with salt and black pepper. Remove the thyme sprigs, if needed.

6 Add the fish to gently simmering broth and cook for about 5 minutes, or until the fish is just done.

7 Put ½ cup of the aioli into a bowl and slowly whisk in ¼ cup of the fish stew liquid. This is to temper the aioli. Once the mixture is smooth, stir it into the fish stew.

8 Stir in the dill and white wine vinegar and taste to adjust the salt and black pepper.

9 I like to place a piece of warm, crusty bread in the bottom of a bowl, ladle soup over the top, and garnish with a dollop of remaining aioli plus chopped dill or parsley.

Note

My go-to fish stock is the Better Than Bouillon brand Fish Base. For more information about these products and where to purchase, refer to the Resources (page 315).

Side Dish Suggestions

a salad of mixed greens or butter lettuce and cucumbers with a French vinaigrette

Irish-Style Fish Chowder

SERVES 4 TO 6

Irish fish chowder uses many of the same ingredients as a traditional chowder; however, along with white fish, smoked fish is also included. This gives the chowder an entirely new flavor profile and makes a delightful change.

This chowder varies from chef to chef and home cook to home cook, using a variety of fish, shellfish, and fresh ingredients. So, there is a lot of room here for your own interpretation. I've written this recipe with a little wiggle room. This chowder isn't quite as heavy as a traditional chowder, so I've called for a cornstarch slurry if you like a heavier chowder. As well, the chowder needs at least ½ cup of heavy cream, but 1 cup will make it even creamier. The goal here is to have fun and create your favorite version.

FIND YOUR FISH: I use locally smoked sablefish, but any smoked fish will work. I've even substituted smoked salmon for a delicious result. I've also made the recipe with only white fish and smoked fish, but on occasion, I'll reduce the white fish to 8 ounces and add 8 ounces of clam meat, shrimp, or mussels.

3 slices uncooked bacon, diced

1 tablespoon extra-virgin olive oil

1 onion, diced

1 carrot, diced

1 celery stalk, diced

3 garlic cloves, minced

2 tablespoons all-purpose flour

3 to 4 cups Homemade Seafood Stock (page 224), OR 3 to 4 cups water plus 3 to 4 teaspoons Better Than Bouillon Fish Base (see Note)

1 pound potatoes, cut into ½-inch cubes

1 tablespoon chopped fresh chives

1 tablespoon chopped fresh parsley, plus 1 tablespoon for garnish (optional)

2 thyme sprigs

Salt and freshly ground black pepper

1 pound cod or rockfish, or other mild-flavored, medium-firm-textured white fish, cut into 1-inch cubes

4 ounces smoked fish, chopped

½ to 1 cup heavy cream

1 teaspoon white wine vinegar

1 teaspoon cornstarch plus 1 teaspoon cold water (optional)

CONTINUES ➡

1 Heat a soup pot or Dutch oven over medium to medium-low heat and cook the bacon slowly to render the fat. Once the bacon is done, transfer to a paper towel–lined plate.

2 Keep 1 tablespoon of bacon fat in the pot and add the olive oil over medium heat.

3 Add the onion, carrot, and celery and cook until soft, about 8 minutes.

4 Add the garlic and cook for 30 seconds more. Then, stir in the flour and cook for another 30 seconds.

5 Stir in 3 cups of the seafood stock and bring it to a simmer.

6 Then, add the potatoes, chives, parsley, and thyme sprigs and stir to combine. Add additional stock, if needed to cover the potatoes.

7 Bring the chowder to a simmer and then lower the heat to low. Simmer for 10 to 12 minutes, until the potatoes are soft. The chowder should begin to thicken. Season to taste with salt and pepper.

8 Stir in the raw fish and let the chowder gently simmer for about 5 minutes. Then, stir in the smoked fish and ½ to 1 cup of heavy cream.

9 Bring the chowder back to a gentle simmer, then add the white wine vinegar and taste to adjust the seasoning. Remove the chowder from the heat.

10 If the chowder feels too thin, you can make the cornstarch slurry and add it to the simmering chowder. This will slightly thicken the chowder.

11 Ladle into bowls and garnish with chopped bacon and chopped fresh parsley, if desired.

Note

My go-to fish stock is the Better Than Bouillon brand Fish Base. For more information on this product and where to purchase, refer to the Resources (page 315).

Side Dish Suggestions

warm soda bread or sweet cornbread ✦ salad of mixed greens with lemon balsamic vinaigrette

Salsa Verde Fish Enchiladas

MAKES 9 TO 10 ENCHILADAS

My family adores Mexican and Latin American cuisine and all the amazing flavors, such as chiles, lime, smoky spices, and fresh cilantro, which accompany these types of recipes. Luckily, they blend beautifully with most seafood and especially with white fish. On occasions when I've served up way too many taco nights and I need more of a family-style meal, this is the perfect way to switch things up.

These enchiladas tick all the boxes for taste, texture, and seafood. If I'm running short on time or I can't find fresh or canned tomatillos, I'll substitute with my favorite brand of prepared salsa verde or Mexican green sauce.

Don't skip frying the tortillas. I know this is one extra step; however, frying the tortillas keeps them from getting soggy and breaking. I never sauce the bottom of the baking dish as this, too, will cause soggy enchiladas. The sauce is best when used in small amounts inside the enchilada and a drizzle down the center of the enchiladas once they're all in the baking dish. The remaining sauce can be served on the side.

SALSA VERDE

1 pound fresh tomatillos, husks removed, washed, or one 16-ounce can tomatillos (If you cannot find fresh or canned tomatillos, use your favorite jar or can of mild green enchilada sauce or salsa verde.)

3 garlic cloves, smashed

1 jalapeño pepper, halved, stemmed, and deveined

½ white onion, halved or quartered

½ cup chopped fresh cilantro

¼ cup chicken stock

Juice of 1 lime

Salt and freshly ground black pepper

2 tablespoons oil (corn oil is traditional)

ENCHILADAS

2 teaspoons chili powder

1 teaspoon smoked paprika

½ teaspoon ground cumin

½ teaspoon ground coriander

Salt and freshly ground pepper

1½ pounds skinless white fish fillet (rockfish, halibut, or cod), deboned

1 to 2 tablespoons oil for brushing

½ cup sour cream

½ cup heavy cream

Freshly squeezed lime juice

High-heat oil for frying tortillas

8 to 10 large corn tortillas (from one 16-ounce package of 12)

Salt

½ cup thinly sliced white onion

½ cup chopped fresh cilantro

¾ cup crumbled Cotija

Avocado slices for serving

Lime wedges for serving

1 Make the salsa verde: If using fresh tomatillos, preheat the oven to 425°F. Place the tomatillos, garlic, jalapeño, and white onion on a baking sheet and place in the oven. Let them roast for about 10 minutes, or until the tomatillos are soft.

2 Remove from the oven, let them cool, and then combine the tomatillos, garlic, jalapeño, white onion, cilantro, chicken stock, and lime juice in a blender or food processor. Blend until smooth. Season to taste with salt and black pepper.

3 Heat the oil in a saucepan over medium heat and stir in the salsa verde. Let it come to a simmer and then remove from the heat. Set aside.

4 Prepare the enchiladas: Preheat the oven to 400°F.

CONTINUES ➡

5 Combine the chili powder, smoked paprika, cumin, and coriander in a small bowl.

6 Place the fish on a baking dish and brush with the olive oil. Season with a sprinkle of salt and black pepper. Then, sprinkle all but ½ teaspoon of the spice mixture evenly over fish.

7 Place the baking dish in the oven and bake for 8 to 10 minutes, until the fish is just flaky.

8 While the fish is baking, combine the sour cream, heavy cream, and lime juice in a bowl. Stir in the reserved ½ teaspoon of the spice mixture. Set aside; this is your crema.

9 Pour enough high-heat oil into a large skillet to reach a depth of ¼ inch and heat over medium heat. When the oil is hot, fry the tortillas, one at a time, just until the edges are golden brown. The tortillas should be firm, slightly golden, but not crispy. We want them flexible enough to roll our enchiladas. Place them on a paper towel-lined baking sheet or large plate. Season with salt.

10 When the fish is done, flake it in bite-size pieces with a fork. Keep the oven temperature at 400°F.

11 Assemble the enchiladas: Add a few tablespoons of flaked fish at one end of the tortilla. Top with some sliced white onion, chopped cilantro, crumbled Cotija, and a teaspoon or two of the salsa verde. Roll up and place, seam side down, in a baking dish. Repeat until all the fish has been used, making 9 to 10 enchiladas.

12 Pour the salsa verde over the center of the enchiladas, reserving any remaining sauce, and then sprinkle with the remaining Cotija, white onion, and cilantro.

13 Place the baking dish in the oven to bake for about 10 minutes, or until the cheese is melted and the salsa verde is slightly bubbly.

14 Remove from the oven, drizzle a little of the crema over the top of the enchiladas, and serve with remaining salsa verde, avocado slices, lime wedges, and extra crema.

Note

Cotija is found in most markets these days; however, if you can't find it, substitute pepper Jack, Monterey Jack, or your favorite Mexican cheese

Side Dish Suggestions

Spanish rice ✦ refried black beans ✦ tossed green salad with an avocado vinaigrette

Cornmeal-Crusted Fish Tacos with Mandarin-Radish Slaw

SERVES 4

I spent many Friday nights as a teenager at our local Friday night fish fry where an abundance of cornmeal-coated fried fish was served. This traditional fish coating is complementary in taste as well as texture. For this recipe, I've used the cornmeal-coated fish fillets and made them into tacos.

The slaw includes mandarin oranges and watermelon radish, two opposing flavors that complement not only each other, but also seafood. When combined with the green onion and cilantro, it makes for a mouthful of delicious flavors.

Every taco needs a sauce, but I kept this one simple. I want the cornmeal-crusted fish to shine as well as the tasty slaw. I've given instructions for assembling the tacos; however, I like to set out all the taco fillings and make a taco bar.

FISH

1 cup buttermilk

1 pound mild flavored, medium-firm, white fish, patted dry with a paper towel and cut into 2-inch pieces

1 cup cornmeal

½ cup all-purpose flour

¼ teaspoon cayenne pepper

1 teaspoon salt

½ teaspoon freshly ground black pepper

High-heat oil for frying

CREMA

½ cup sour cream

½ cup mayonnaise

1 teaspoon sugar

Juice of 1 lime

Dash of hot sauce

Salt and freshly ground pepper

SLAW

2 to 3 cups shredded napa cabbage

1 cup mandarin oranges

½ cup shredded watermelon radish

½ cup sliced green onion

¼ cup chopped fresh cilantro

FOR SERVING

8 to 10 corn tortillas

Thinly sliced red onion (optional)

Avocado and lime wedges (optional)

CONTINUES ➡

1 Soak the fish: Pour the buttermilk into a medium bowl and add the fish pieces to the buttermilk. Set aside.

2 Make the crema: Combine the sour cream, mayonnaise, sugar, lime juice, and hot sauce. Season to taste with salt and pepper. Set aside.

3 Make the slaw: Gently combine the cabbage, oranges, watermelon radish, green onion, and cilantro in a separate medium bowl. Set aside.

4 To fry the tortillas, line a plate or platter with paper towels and set it to one side on the counter. Add enough high-heat oil to cover the surface of a skillet. Place the skillet over medium heat. You may have to adjust heat consistently while frying the tortillas.

5 When the oil is hot and slightly smoking, add one tortilla, using tongs. Let it brown just a bit and then flip to the other side to brown just a bit, adjusting the heat lower or higher as needed. Transfer the tortilla to the paper towel–lined plate and fold it in half like a taco. Do this with as many tortillas as you like.

6 Now, it's time to make the fish: Combine the cornmeal, flour, cayenne, salt, and pepper in another medium bowl. Line a baking sheet with parchment.

7 Take each piece of fish out of the buttermilk, shake off any excess, and dredge through the cornmeal mixture until coated. Place the breaded fish on the prepared baking sheet.

8 When all the fish are coated, add high-heat oil to a large skillet to a depth of 1 inch.

9 Heat the pan over medium heat, and when the oil is hot and shimmering, add the fish. You may need to do this in batches.

10 Cook the fish until the bottom is golden brown and then gently flip to the other side. This should take 2 to 3 minutes on each side, depending on the thickness of the fish. If the fish brown too quickly, adjust the heat.

11 Transfer the cooked fish to a paper towel-lined plate.

12 To assemble the tacos, add the slaw to the bottom half of each tortilla, top with fish, drizzle with crema, and then garnish with sliced red onion and avocado, if using. Serve immediately with lime wedges, if using, and extra crema.

Side Dish Suggestions

chili beans, black beans, refried beans ✦ Mexican rice ✦ chips and salsa

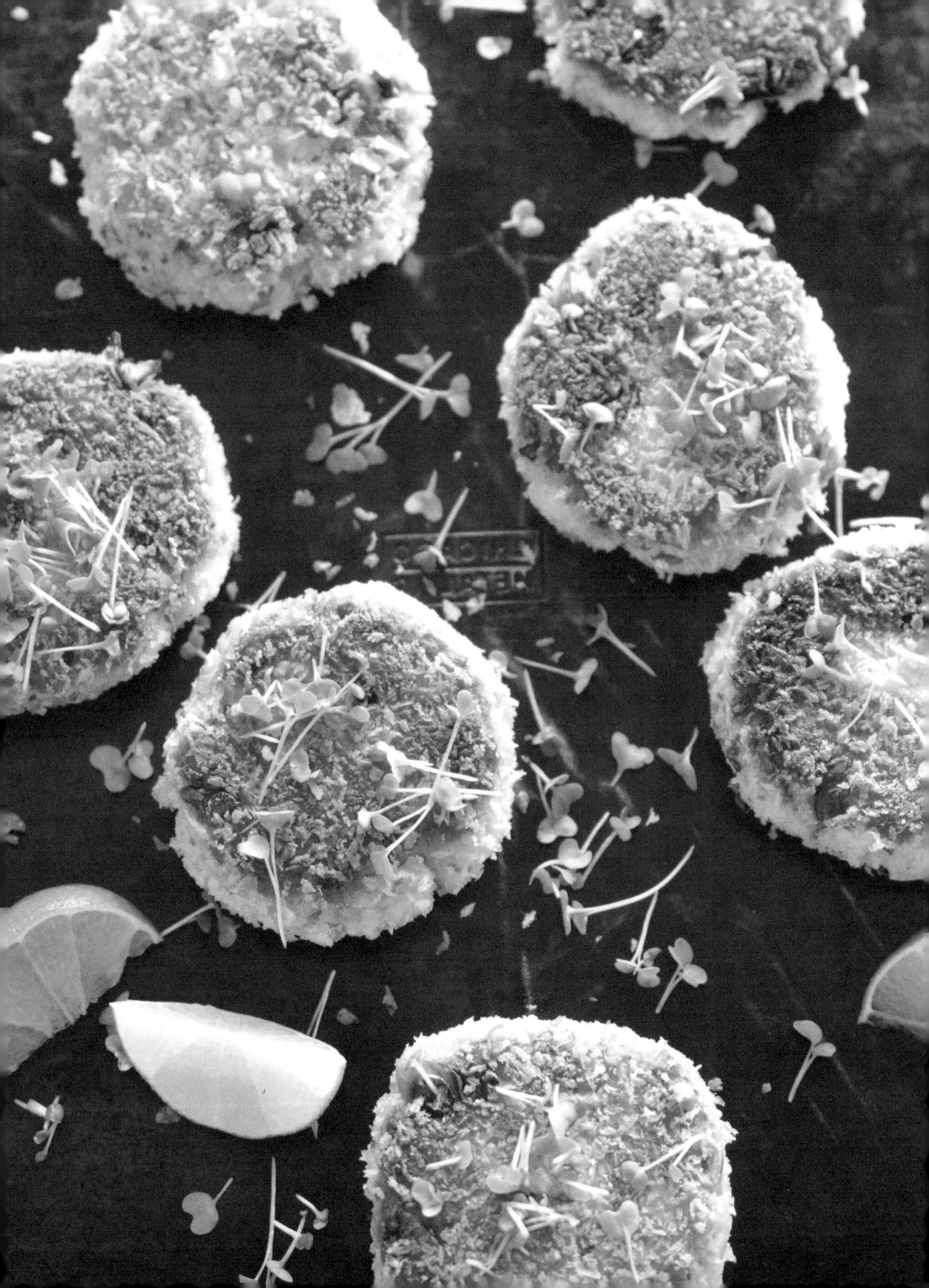

Curried Fish Cakes with Lime and Mint Yogurt Sauce

MAKES TEN TO TWELVE 3-INCH CAKES

When I was working as a private chef, one of my client families liked fish but it wasn't their favorite ingredient. They would ask me to make it for dinner, and then I'd come in the next day and find half of it still in the refrigerator.

I didn't want the fish to go to waste, so I used the leftovers to make these fish cakes, which my clients loved. They especially enjoyed them with the sauce and, luckily, they liked them so much that the family started requesting them. And then there were never any leftovers.

You don't have to reserve this recipe for leftover fish; it's equally delicious with freshly roasted fish. Just let the fish cool before forming the patties and be sure to check for bones that may have been missed.

This sauce is so tasty with the flavor profile of this fish cake, but I also think a mango chutney would be fabulous as well.

SAUCE

1 cup plain yogurt

1 tablespoon chopped fresh mint

1 tablespoon chopped fresh cilantro

Zest and juice of 1 lime

1 garlic clove, minced

1 tablespoon grated cucumber

½ teaspoon ground cumin

Salt and freshly ground black pepper

FISH CAKES

1 pound white fish (cod, rockfish, flounder, or halibut), skinned and boned, patted dry with paper towels

1 tablespoon extra-virgin olive oil

Salt and freshly ground black pepper

1 tablespoon curry powder

¼ cup sliced green onion

3 tablespoons mayonnaise

1 garlic clove, minced

1½ teaspoons grated fresh ginger

1 large egg, whisked

Zest of 1 lemon

1 cup panko bread crumbs, or more as needed

High heat oil for frying

1 Make the sauce: Combine the yogurt, mint, cilantro, lime zest and juice, garlic, cucumber, and cumin in a small bowl. Season to taste with salt and pepper. Set aside.

CONTINUES ➡

2 Make the fish cakes: Preheat the oven to 400°F. Place the fish on a baking sheet or in a baking pan. Brush the fish with the oil and season with salt and pepper.

3 Place the baking pan in the oven and cook the fish for 8 to 10 minutes, or until it slightly flakes and is opaque. Remove from the oven and let the fish cool. Once the fish is cool, flake with a fork, removing any bones, and transfer the flaked fish to a medium bowl.

4 Add the curry powder, ½ teaspoon of salt, ½ teaspoon of pepper, green onion, mayonnaise, garlic, and ginger to the fish and gently toss to combine.

5 Gently mix in the whisked egg, lemon zest, and ½ cup of the panko bread crumbs, using additional panko, if needed to help the fish mixture bind together.

6 Place the remaining ½ cup of the panko bread crumbs in a shallow bowl. Using a cookie scoop, form 3-inch patties, lightly dredge each patty in the panko, and place in a single layer on a parchment lined-baking sheet.

7 Let them rest in the refrigerator for about 15 minutes.

8 When ready to panfry, add enough high-heat oil to cover the surface of a large skillet and place over medium heat.

9 Panfry the fish cakes until golden brown on each side, adjusting the heat as needed. You may need to do this in two batches.

10 Transfer the fish cakes to a paper towel-lined cooling rack or plate.

11 Serve the fish cakes with the sauce.

Note

The patties can be prepared a day in advance, kept in the refrigerator, and then panfried just before serving.

Side Dish Suggestions

coconut rice ✦ a tossed green salad

Sablefish with Creamy Piquillo Pepper Sauce and Lemon Cream

SERVES 4

Sablefish, or what is often called black cod or butterfish, is actually quite buttery in texture, hence the nickname, and distinctive in taste due to its higher fat content. It's most commonly found in the north Pacific, but many online seafood markets and community-supported fisheries make it available for shipping.

Due to the richness of the meat, this fish holds up well to the bold Spanish flavors in this recipe. The peppers lend a smidgen of sweetness, with a hint of spice from the smoked paprika, while the lemon cream brings everything together.

FIND YOUR FISH: If you can't find sablefish, blue fish, Chilean sea bass, or even salmon will work well in this recipe

CREAMY PIQUILLO PEPPER SAUCE

3 tablespoons extra-virgin olive oil

⅔ cup small-diced sweet onion (about ½ onion)

1 tablespoon chopped fresh flat-leaf parsley

1 teaspoon minced garlic (about 2 medium cloves)

¼ cup white wine

One 9.5- to 10-ounce jar piquillo peppers, drained

¾ teaspoon smoked paprika

¼ cup heavy cream

Salt and freshly ground black pepper

LEMON CREAM

½ cup heavy cream

2 tablespoons freshly squeezed lemon juice

Salt

1 teaspoon cornstarch plus 1 teaspoon cold water

FISH

1½ pounds sablefish (also called black cod), cut into 4 pieces, removed from refrigerator 15 minutes prior to cooking and pin bones removed

Salt and freshly ground black pepper

2 tablespoons ghee

CONTINUES ➡

1 Make the creamy piquillo pepper sauce: Heat the olive oil in a saucepan over medium heat. When the oil is hot, stir in the onion and cook until soft, wilted, and slightly golden.

2 Stir in the parsley and garlic and cook for 30 seconds more. Add the white wine and bring to a simmer.

3 Then, remove pan from the heat and add the peppers, smoked paprika, and onion mixture to a blender or food processor. Puree until smooth.

4 Add the sauce back to the pan over low heat, just to warm. Once it begins to simmer, remove it from the heat and stir in the heavy cream. Season to taste with salt and black pepper.

5 Make the lemon cream: Heat the heavy cream in a small saucepan over medium heat. When it comes to a simmer, stir in the lemon juice and let the cream reduce by half. Season to taste with salt and pepper.

6 To make a thicker lemon cream, add half of the cornstarch slurry to the cream while it's simmering. Let it simmer for 15 seconds or more to thicken. Remove from the heat and set aside.

7 Make the fish: Season the fish with salt and black pepper. Heat a large skillet over medium-high heat and add the ghee.

8 When the ghee is hot and shimmering, add the fillets to the skillet and cook for 3 to 5 minutes, until a golden-brown crust forms around the edges.

9 With a fish spatula, gently lift one corner of the fish. If it doesn't lift, leave it for another 30 seconds to 1 minute to cook. Once the fish lifts off the pan, flip it to the other side.

10 Let the fish continue to cook over medium to medium-high heat for another 3 to 5 minutes, until opaque and just beginning to flake with a fork. Fish typically cook through in 8 to 10 minutes for every inch of thickness.

11 Transfer the fish to a plate or platter and drizzle with the creamy piquillo pepper sauce and then add a little drizzle of the lemon cream. Serve immediately.

Side Dish Suggestions

whole wheat orzo with extra-virgin olive oil and Parmesan, pasta, rice, quinoa, farro, pearled barley, or couscous ✦ roasted or grilled vegetables ✦ tossed green salad

Pan-Cooked Fish with Honey-Poached Kumquats, Fennel, and Olives

SERVES 4

Kumquats are tangy, intensely citrusy, and somewhat sour. I love to snack on these little orange jewels, but they also make a delicious complement to seafood, especially when poached in honey. There are a few steps in this recipe, but I promise, the result is completely worth the effort!

FIND YOUR FISH: I've used rockfish, but any mild-flavored white fish will work. Choose a fish that is medium firm and not too delicate, so it will hold up to the bold flavors in this recipe. Refer to page 18 for more information about medium-firm, mild-flavored fish.

1 pint kumquats, sliced

1 to 2 cups water

1 cup honey

4 tablespoons extra-virgin olive oil

2 fennel bulbs, trimmed and thinly sliced

1 tablespoon chopped fresh parsley, plus more for garnish

2 teaspoons finely chopped garlic

½ to ¾ cup thick sliced or halved Kalamata olives, pitted and drained

Salt and freshly ground black pepper

1 tablespoon unsalted butter or ghee

1½ pounds rockfish, patted dry with paper towels and removed from refrigerator 15 minutes prior to cooking

1 Combine the kumquats, water, and honey in a saucepan over medium heat, adding additional water as needed to just cover the kumquats.

2 Heat just until the liquid comes to a simmer and then lower the heat to low. Simmer over low heat for about 10 minutes, or until the kumquats have softened but are not falling apart.

3 Remove the pan from the heat. Drain the kumquats and set aside, reserving at least ½ cup of the cooking liquid.

CONTINUES ➡

4 Add the liquid back to the pot and simmer over low heat until it has reduced by half. The liquid should have a syrupy texture.

5 Heat 2 tablespoons of the olive oil in a skillet over medium heat. When the oil is hot but not smoking, add the fennel. Cook the fennel until slightly tender and it starts to caramelize, 5 to 8 minutes, adding a tablespoon or two of water to the pan for some steam.

6 Then, stir in the parsley and garlic and cook for 1 minute longer.

7 Remove the fennel from the heat and toss in the olives, then season to taste with salt and pepper. Toss in ½ cup of the honeyed kumquats and then transfer the mixture to a platter or divide among four plates.

8 Combine the remaining 2 tablespoons of oil and the butter in a large cast-iron fish pan or skillet over medium-high heat. Season the fish with salt and pepper, and when the oil is hot, add the fish to the skillet.

9 When the fish is lightly browned on the bottom, flip to the other side.

10 Place the cooked fish on top of the fennel, kumquat, and olive mixture. Garnish with extra chopped parsley, a few more kumquats, and a drizzle of the kumquat reduction. Serve immediately.

Notes

For a little more crust on the fish, after seasoning the fish with salt and pepper, dust it with a little cornstarch or flour, then shake and pan cook according to the directions.

You can make the kumquats a day in advance and store in a lidded jar in the fridge until needed.

Side Dish Suggestions

couscous, rice, pearled barley, or risotto ✦ roasted potatoes

Halibut and Leek au Gratin

SERVES 4

When I'm planning a special family celebration or maybe just a date night in, this is one of the dishes I prepare. What could be more elegant than pieces of flaky white fish bathed in a creamy leek and white wine sauce and then garnished with a crispy topping?

This recipe calls for lightly poaching the fish prior to adding it to the baking dish. It might seem fussy, but this prevents the fish from weeping extra liquid into the sauce and keeps the sauce texture luxurious.

I've lightened the sauce just a bit, using seafood stock along with white wine and heavy cream. The sauce is silky but not quite as heavy as a traditional gratin. It is then garnished with garlic bread crumbs and baked to a dreamy perfection.

FIND YOUR FISH: This recipe is prepared with halibut, but flounder, haddock, fluke, cod, or another mild-flavored, medium-texture fish would also be a good substitute.

BREAD CRUMBS

- **¾ cup panko bread crumbs**
- **1 garlic clove, minced**
- **¼ cup grated Parmesan**
- **1 teaspoon chopped fresh parsley**
- **2 tablespoons melted unsalted butter**

FISH

- **4 tablespoons (½ stick) unsalted butter**
- **2 medium leeks, white to light green part only, halved, washed, and sliced into half-moons**
- **2 cups Homemade Seafood Stock (page 224), OR 2 cups water plus 2 teaspoons Better Than Bouillon Fish Base**
- **1½ pounds halibut fillet, cut into 1½-inch cubes (bite-size pieces), any bones removed**
- **Salt and freshly ground black pepper**
- **1 garlic clove, finely chopped**
- **3 tablespoons all-purpose flour**
- **½ cup white wine**
- **½ to ¾ cup warm heavy cream**
- **1 teaspoon chopped fresh thyme**
- **1 tablespoon chopped fresh parsley, plus more for garnish**
- **1 tablespoon freshly squeezed lemon juice**

CONTINUES ➡

1 Preheat the oven to 400°F. Butter a baking dish or individual gratin dishes with 1 tablespoon of the butter.

2 Make the bread crumbs: Combine the panko, garlic, Parmesan, parsley, and butter in a small bowl. Set aside.

3 Prepare the fish: Heat 3 tablespoons of the butter in a medium saucepan or skillet over medium or medium-low heat. When the butter is melted, stir in the leeks. Cook the leeks slowly, lowering the heat if needed, for 5 to 8 minutes, until they are soft, wilted, and slightly golden.

4 While the leeks cook (but keep an eye on them), heat the seafood stock in a medium pot over medium heat. When it comes to a gentle boil, lower the heat to low and add the cubed fish. Season with salt and pepper. Just when the liquid comes back to a simmer, 1 to 2 minutes, using a slotted spoon or mesh strainer, transfer the fish cubes to a plate. Don't cook the fish through, as it'll finish cooking in the oven. Do not discard the broth and keep it warm.

5 When the leeks are golden, stir in the garlic and cook for about 30 seconds.

6 Stir in the flour and continue to stir for about 30 seconds. While stirring, add the wine, 1½ cups of the reserved seafood broth, ½ cup of the heavy cream, and the thyme, parsley, and lemon juice.

7 Continuing to stir, bring the sauce to a gentle simmer and allow it to thicken slightly, 1 to 3 minutes. This sauce shouldn't be too thick or too thin. If the sauce feels too thick, stir in the remaining ¼ cup of heavy cream or additional seafood stock. Season to taste with salt and pepper.

8 Transfer the fish to the prepared buttered baking dish or individual gratin dishes. Pour the sauce over the fish and sprinkle with the bread crumbs. Place the baking dish in the oven. If using individual gratin dishes, place them on a baking sheet and then place the baking sheet in the oven.

9 Bake for 7 to 10 minutes, until the gratin is bubbly around the edges and the fish is cooked through. For additional browning of the bread crumbs, place the gratin under the broiler for 10 to 15 seconds.

10 Let the gratin cool for a few minutes before serving. The sauce will be hot.

Side Dish Suggestions

steamed or roasted asparagus, broccolini, Brussels sprouts, carrots, haricots verts or zucchini ✦ roasted new or fingerling potatoes

Resources

Here, I've compiled a short list of resources that either I mention in this book, or I find helpful to me and to the home cook. The list includes links to seafood watch organizations that I frequent, various seafood education that I have found helpful, finding locally sourced seafood, and a few pantry staples that I keep stocked in my kitchen.

Seafood Watch Resources

Monterey Bay Aquarium Seafood Watch (www.seafoodwatch.org)
Ocean Wise Seafood (seafood.ocean.org)
EDF Seafood Selector (seafood.edf.org)
Oceana (oceana.org/living-blue-sustainable-seafood-guide)
Audubon G.U.L.F. (www.audubongulf.org)

Seafood Education

The Fish Talk Podcast (thefishtalkpodcast.com)
Paul Greenberg, author of *American Catch* and *Four Fish* (www.paulgreenberg.org/books)
FoodPrint (foodprint.org/issues/sustainable-seafood)
Sustainable Fisheries (sustainablefisheries-uw.org)
Last Man Fishing (lastmanfishing.com)

Community-Supported Fisheries

Local Catch Network (localcatch.org)
This is one of the best tools to find a CSF in your region. If there are no community-supported fisheries in your area, there are online direct-to-consumer sustainable seafood delivery options available, such as Sitka Salmon Shares, Salmon Sisters, Wild Alaskan Company, PureFish, Pure Food Fish Market, Fulton Fish Market, Lummi Island Wild, Sizzlefish, Honolulu Fish Company, and more. I highly recommend researching which option is best for you. Some of the online fish markets specialize in Pacific, Atlantic, or Gulf seafood, delivering nationwide or regionally, and sometimes specialize in finfish, shellfish, or other seafood related items.

Pantry Items

I cook with a lot of fresh ingredients; however, a few ingredient brands are always stocked in my pantry.

Spices and Salts

Spiceology (spiceology.com)
Jacobsen Salt Co. (jacobsensalt.com)
Barnacle Foods (www.barnaclefoods.com)
New York Shuk (harissa; www.nyshuk.com/harissa101)
Mina (harissa; mina.co/collections/harissa)

Broths and Stocks

Better Than Bouillon (www.betterthanbouillon.com)
Bar Harbor Foods (barharborfoods.com)

General Seafood Provisions

Patagonia Provisions (www.patagoniaprovisions.com)
Salmon Sisters (aksalmonsisters.com)

Rice, Grains, and Pasta

Bob's Red Mill Natural Foods (www.bobsredmill.com)
Bluebird Grain Farms (bluebirdgrainfarms.com)
Lundberg Family Farms (www.lundberg.com)
Ralston Family Farms (www.ralstonfamilyfarms.com)
Jovial Foods (jovialfoods.com)

Acknowledgments

I have to begin by thanking my amazing husband, Craig Bennett, for sharing with me your love of the ocean and seafood all those years ago. You continue to be my biggest supporter and have been an important part of completing this book. From listening to, and joining in, my perpetual conversation about seafood education, our beloved oceans and more, to washing mountains of test recipe dishes, taste testing, and never complaining when dinner was put on hold for a photo shoot. Thank you for enjoying every bite of this delicious life with me, I love you!

My sincerest thanks to my incredibly talented editor, Isabel McCarthy at Countryman Press, for making my work shine, and to my fantastic agent, Jessica Alvarez with Bookends Literary Agency, for believing in my ideas and my work. I am so grateful for you both!

Huge thanks to recipe tester extraordinaire, Judy Niver, whose valuable input exceeded my expectations and helped me finish this book. You are a superstar!

Many thanks to the talented Betty Boyce with Betty Boyce Photography, for capturing the essence of the fishing community with your gorgeous landscape photos and for so beautifully portraying my love of cooking seafood.

Thank you to Mike Baran, CSF manager at Port Orford Sustainable Seafood, for answering my endless questions and for giving me a plethora of valuable seafood education.

And many thanks to David Hands, for lending your palate to taste almost every recipe in this book, for your support, the excellent bottle of Scotch and creative feedback that kept me laughing.

My deepest thanks to my siblings, Kristin Bryan and Cameron Taylor. I am so grateful to meander this wild and adventurous life with you. You have been a constant source of inspiration, support, advice, and humor when I needed it most. Even though the miles keep us apart, our constant communication never fails to bring my heart so much joy, laughter, and peace.

My love and thanks to my beautiful family: Kevin, Paula, Alan, Sharon, Aubrey, Sebastian, Carolina, Taylor, Alex, Theo, Brianna, Ben, Max, Ellen, Don, and the entire Taylor family. You are bright, shining lights of love and support, and I am so grateful to call you family.

All my love and gratitude to my amazing daughters, Alexandria Bennett and Amelia Bennett, and to Maxwell Husbands. You are my greatest joy in life and I'm so proud to be your mom!

Index

A

anchovies
- flatbread with, smoked mozzarella, olives, and arugula, 271
- lemon herb ricotta toasts with, 47
- spaghetti with, and olives, 184

B

black cod. *See* sablefish (black cod)
butter fish
- spiced, 191
- *See also* sablefish (black cod)

C

clams
- classic white wine-steamed, with garlic and herbs, 124
- date night linguine with pink clam sauce, 249
- New England-style clam chowder, 137
- Spanish-style steamed, 140

cod
- citrus-roasted, with honey-tarragon brown butter, 71
- Irish-style fish chowder, 293
- weeknight lemon-baked, with pesto yogurt dressing, 61

cooking methods, basic, 32
- baking, 32
- broiling, 32
- deep-frying, 32–33
- grilling, 33
- pan cooking, 33
- pan searing, 33–34
- poaching, 34
- roasting, 34
- steaming, 34

cooking terms and definitions, basic, 34–36
cookware and utensils, 39
crab
- and Boursin cheese quiche, 135
- cakes with tangy dipping sauce, classic, 128
- imperial-style crab dip, 130
- Louis-style salad, 132
- pappardelle alfredo with, 258
- and spinach-stuffed shells with white cheddar béchamel, 255

F

finfish. *See specific finfish*
fish
- fillets
  - easy acqua pazza (fish in crazy water), 188
  - fish amandine, 210
  - Mediterranean roasted, with Parmesan polenta, 76
  - orange, fennel, and avocado salsa with pan-cooked fish, 213
- steaks
  - grilled, with blueberry ginger butter, 175
- whole
  - simple oven-roasted whole fish, 205
- *See also* seafood

H

halibut
- butter-poached, with roasted cherry tomatoes, leeks, and potatoes, 219
- grilled fish steaks with blueberry ginger butter, 175
- and leek au gratin, 311

I

ingredients, pairing with seafood, 36–38

L

lobster
- rolls, classic, 262
- tails, broiled, with cilantro-lime butter, 260

M
mussels
sake-steamed, with lemongrass and lime, 143

O
oysters
baked oysters mornay, 247
panko-fried, with remoulade sauce, 243

P
pantry items, basic, 38
prawns
English prawn cocktail, 148

R
rockfish
chile-spiced, with summer peach and jalapeño quinoa salad, 85
crispy white fish burgers with smoked provolone and special sauce, 196
Irish-style fish chowder, 293
pan-cooked fish with honey poached kumquats, fennel, and olives, 309
tacos, cornmeal-crusted, with mandarin-radish slaw, 299

S
sablefish (black cod)
with creamy piquillo pepper sauce and lemon cream, 305
salmon
basic pan-cooked, with lemon dill crème fraîche and Persian cucumber, 90
Dijon and Parmesan-crusted, baked spicy, 66
en papillote with easy lemon aioli (salmon baked in parchment), 57
grilled, with pistachio lemon pesto, 172
grilled fish steaks with blueberry ginger butter, 175
grilled salmon Caesar salad with Parmesan garlic bread crumbs, 101
lox, smoked, with crème fraîche on mini corncakes, 44
lox and three-cheese puff pastry pinwheels, 164
pasta with brown butter, peas, mint, and, 166
poke bowl, spicy, 161
roasted, with savory strawberry sauce, 169
roasted furikake salmon, 79
salmon, leek, and potato pie, 279
salmon fried rice, 120
sliders, Asian, with quick-pickled cucumbers and cilantro-lime aioli, 276
spicy orange marmalade–roasted, 68
sardines
avocado, tomato, and sardines toast with pickled onions and herb mayonnaise, 275
scallops
pan-cooked sea scallops with miso ginger butter, basic, 117
pan-seared, with tomato ginger jam, 253
seafood
risotto, 268
stock, homemade, 224
summer seafood board with dipping sauces, 265
See also fish; *specific types of seafood*
seafood basics, 14
complementary ingredients, 36–38
cooking methods, 32–34
cooking terms and definitions, 34–36
cookware and utensils, 39
frequently asked questions, 18–22
fresh *vs.* frozen, 17
pantry items, 38
preparation tips, 28, 30–32
purchasing seafood, 14–16
seafood chart, 22–28
sustainability, 16–17
thawing seafood, 28, 30
shellfish
boil, my favorite, 158
See also clams; crab; lobster; mussels; oysters; prawns; shrimp
shrimp
bay shrimp and pepper Jack-stuffed roasted mini peppers, 51
bay shrimp salad melts on thick toast, open-face, 48
coconut, with sweet and spicy apricot glaze, 225

shrimp (*continued*)
deveining, 31–32
enchilada soup with lime crema, 150
English prawn cocktail, 148
étouffée, 240
grilled shrimp, avocado, bacon, and creamy herb dressing, butter lettuce with, 229
pan-cooked, with lemon, garlic, and fresh herbs, 122
panzanella salad with basil vinaigrette, 231
po'boy with spicy Cajun dressing, 235
salad, vintage macaroni and, 52
and sausage jambalaya, 237
shrimp, black bean, and corn chilaquiles, 156
Southern-style, and cheesy grits, 145
tacos, grilled, 153
sole
roasted teriyaki, with shelled edamame and cilantro-lime rice, 73
swordfish
grilled, with elote-style corn and roasted poblanos, 181

T

trout
bacon-wrapped stuffed, 285
tuna
cakes, wild albacore, with chipotle lime dipping sauce, 55
and potato stew, Basque-style (marmitako), 115
salsa, wild albacore, 42
seared ahi tuna wonton tacos with mango pico de gallo, 178
sushi stacks, spicy ahi, 282

W

white fish
baked
fish with ramen noodles and broccolini, hoisin five-spice sauce, 88
salsa verde fish enchiladas, 296
za'atar-spiced fish with orange cumin vinaigrette and fresh greens, 83
marinated
white fish ceviche, basic, 187
pan-cooked
fish, easy whipped pimiento sauce with, 106
fish with herbed gremolata and white beans, 216
fish with summer blackberry orange relish, 104
white fish with papaya red pepper salsa, 95
panfried
cornmeal-crusted rockfish tacos with mandarin-radish slaw, 299
curried fish cakes with lime and mint yogurt sauce, 303
fish meunière, simple, 93
panko panfried fish with Japanese-style tartar sauce and kimchi slaw, 202
salt and vinegar potato chip-crusted fish fingers with dipping sauces, 199
pan-seared
white fish with sauce verte, 99
poached
bourride (French-style fish stew with aioli), 291
Brazilian fish stew, simple (moqueca), 111
curry poached fish with mango ginger pearled couscous, easy, 109
Irish-style fish chowder, 293
spiced butter fish, 191
West African-inspired fish stew, 287
roasted
fish, Moroccan-style, 208
fish fillets with Parmesan polenta, Mediterranean, 76
fish taco Buddha bowls with creamy blender chimichurri, 193
five-spice white fish tacos with apple cabbage slaw, 63
See also specific white fish